AMERICAN INCARNATION

American Incarnation

THE INDIVIDUAL, THE NATION,
AND THE CONTINENT

Myra Jehlen

HARVARD UNIVERSITY PRESS
Cambridge, Massachusetts
and London, England
1986

90-1156

Copyright © 1986 by
the President and Fellows of Harvard College
All rights reserved
Printed in the United States of America
10 9 8 7 6 5 4 3 2 1

Publication of this book has been aided
by a grant from the
Andrew W. Mellon Foundation.

This book is printed on acid-free paper, and
its binding materials have been chosen
for strength and durability.

Library of Congress Cataloging-in-Publication Data

Jehlen, Myra.
    American incarnation.

    Bibliography: p.
    Includes index.
    1. National characteristics, American.
2. Individualism.   3. United States—Intellectual life—
1783–1865.   4. United States—Intellectual life—
1865–1918.   5. United States—Territorial expansion.
I. Title.
E169.1.J435 1986   973   86-4628
ISBN 0-674-02426-5 (alk. paper)

For Jessica

✳ Acknowledgments

$\mathcal{A}$lthough this book is about the culminating evolution of individualism, in writing it I have not been at all self-sufficient. I have no regrets about this; on the contrary I want to celebrate interdependence as a great principle of intellectual ethics. For one moral clearly pointed by the writings surveyed here is that self-sufficiency is a dubious virtue; doubly dubious, since it is not certain even to exist. And the argument encapsulated in the book's title, *American Incarnation*, makes it doubly fitting that I represent my indebtedness embodied in real persons.

There are many pleasures then in thanking these friends and colleagues for their very material help: Sacvan Bercovitch, Joe Cady, Charles Feidelson, Martin Golding, Carolyn Heilbrun, Evelyn Keller, Amy Lang, Frank Lentricchia, Leo Marx, Helene Moglen, Donald Pease, Richard Poirier, John Richetti, Jessica Riskin, Donald Scott, Michael Seidel, Camille Smith, Henry Nash Smith, Patricia Spacks, Catharine Stimpson, Eric Sundquist, Cecelia Tichi, Jane Tompkins, Alan Trachtenberg, Lindsay Waters, Marilyn Young. I am, as always, grateful to Sonia Jehlen and Albert Jehlen for teaching a daughter the joy of thinking. John Simon's support and intelligence have been essential.

A Fellowship from the National Endowment for the Humanities permitted me to begin; I finished the last revisions while a Fellow at the National Humanities Center in Research Triangle Park, North Carolina.

✳ Contents

AMERICAN INCARNATION

Give me the map there.

King Lear

O my America! my new-found-land,
My kingdom, safeliest when with
    one man manned,
My mine of precious stones, my empery,
How blest am I in this discovering thee!
To enter in these bonds is to be free;
Then where my hand is set, my seal shall be.

John Donne

When the bark of Columbus nears the shore of
America;—before it, the beach lined with savages, fleeing out of all their huts of cane; the
sea behind; and the purple mountains of the
Indian archipelago around, can we separate the
man from the living picture? Does not the New
World clothe his form with her palm-groves and
savannahs as fit drapery?

Emerson

The New World, existing in those times beyond
the sphere of all things known to history, lay
in the fifteenth century as the middle of the
desert or the sea lies now and must lie forever,
marked with its own dark life which goes on to
an immaculate fulfillment in which we have no
part. But now, with the maritime successes of
that period, the western land could not guard
its seclusion longer; a predestined and bitter
fruit existing, perversely, before the white flower
of its birth, it was laid bare by the miraculous
first voyage . . .

William Carlos Williams

No ideas but in things . . .

William Carlos Williams

INTRODUCTION

✳ *One Man, One World*

*W*hen the country was "coming of age," early in this century, William James urged Americans to adopt the philosophy of Pragmatism, which like the nation had only just "become conscious of a universal mission . . . [and] a conquering destiny" (*Pragmatism*, 45). Aptly, the anecdote he used to illustrate the benefits of a mature Pragmatism drew the lesson of America's infancy.

"Some years ago," the anecdote begins, "being with a camping party in the mountains, I returned from a solitary ramble to find every one engaged in a ferocious metaphysical dispute" (41). In "the unlimited leisure of the wilderness," esoteric discussion has been "worn threadbare" and James's companions are at an impasse. They cannot resolve the following problem: supposing a squirrel circles a tree so as to stay out of sight of a man circling in pursuit, *"Does the man go round the squirrel or not?"* James's answer is, he does and he doesn't.* For "which party is

---

*By "a man" James means the generic human being, and I take this as an opportunity to stipulate that throughout this essay the generic person will indeed be male. This is because the writers whose ideas I analyze assume that men, and not women, represent the species. "Man" sometimes subsumes "woman" and at other times excludes her, but in the writings treated here, "man" is never interchangeable with "woman." To say "he or she" in such a case would be to obscure or even to deny the feminist argument intended by the double pronoun.

1

right . . . depends on what you *practically mean* by going round the squirrel" (42). If you mean circling the squirrel's location, then going around the tree takes you around the squirrel as well, but if you mean surveying the squirrel on all its sides, then since it remains constantly opposite, you do not go around it just by circling the tree. James's point is that the meaning of going round is not a universal abstraction but defines itself practically, through its embodiment in this or that concrete situation. In the parable of the squirrel and the tree, the detachment of the campers from the surrounding reality renders their argument not only unresolvable but ultimately senseless. James, in contrast, makes sense by making connections: he connects the men with their actual location and the location with an actual nature. And, unlike his lounging companions, James himself has been out exploring. His very entrance into the campsite brings a sense of purpose and "Pragmatic" direction, "towards concreteness and adequacy, towards facts, towards action and towards power" (45).

The embrace of the factual by which James located himself in the wilderness was an impulse from the heart of his American identity. For that mountain debate can be read as one of innumerable versions of America's primal scene, Columbus arriving on an unknown shore.[1] Puzzled as to whether he had come to the other side of the world, Columbus reasoned much like James's fellow campers, and he too was unable to arrive at an answer because he posed the question abstractly. To determine where he was, instead of consulting the beach on which he stood, he pondered theoretical globes. So long as by sailing around the world he meant an abstract and absolute circumnavigation, his Caribbean landings were inexplicable failures. Had he defined his position in its own actual terms, that astounding beach would have revealed itself the threshold to a whole new world.

Thus because he failed to take the "concreteness and . . . facts" of the unknown islands as the ground of his deliberations, Columbus could not realize his discovery. Then, as the story goes, Amerigo Vespucci achieved the power to project his own name upon two continents simply by recognizing their existence. The drama of America's discovery describes an archetypal conjunction of personal identity and national identification coming together in the very earth of the New World. In that drama, the first act in knowing "America" is acknowledging it as a concrete fact. What James recalled to his fellow campers as the essential reference point of effective thought was the solid reality, the *terra firma* on which Columbus disembarked—and which certainly, from an American perspective, made all the pragmatic difference in the world. This then is my opening proposition: that the decisive factor shaping the founding conceptions of "America" and of "the American" was material rather than conceptual; rather than a set of abstract ideas, the physical fact of the continent.

In themselves, this country's originating ideas were neither original nor exceptional; they derived from the essential principles of the European Reformation and Enlightenment. These principles—notions of individual autonomy defended by natural inalienable rights, of the sanctity of private property as it fulfills individual self-possession, and of representative government as an ideal social order implied by such self-possessive individualism—bespoke another liberal nation, not a new world. But when the democratic Enlightenment became associated with the North American continent, something new did emerge, for with this added dimension the theory of liberal individualism entered a culminating stage that was substantially different from its intermediate European form. Grounded, literally, in American soil, liberalism's hitherto arguable theses metamorphosed into nature's material necessities. Thus European reformers had argued in accord with Natural Law philosophy that their societies should parallel and complement nature. But the forming of American society was a still more ambitious enterprise. Americans saw themselves as building their civilization out of nature itself, as neither the analogue nor the translation of Natural Law but its direct expression. Fusing the political with the natural, human volition with its object, and hope with destiny, they imagined an all-encompassing universe that in effect healed the lapsarian parting of man and his natural kingdom.

The modern revision of identity in the seventeenth and eighteenth centuries had begun by projecting a new division. Countering the inequalities of societal origin, it deeded each man with a natal estate in nature and pictured him then entering into political relations voluntarily and freely. This ontological separation and abstraction liberated the individual from a net of social and political interdependencies and, by rendering him inherently whole and self-sufficient, empowered him to act upon the world on his own (and on his own behalf). No longer defined primarily by family or class, a man molded himself, then the world in his image. Such quasi-blasphemous potency, however, also projected a new limitation. In the guise of Capitalist and of Poet, the self-reliant individualist may perpetually remake the world, but since he himself is disembodied, he can never finally incorporate it—as on the contrary Oedipus did embody his kingdom and Lear, even divested of his deed, still embodied his. One source of the sense of personal alienation that characterizes modern life lies in the contradiction between this idealist self-definition, which means that one's possession of the material world must remain figurative, and the general belief that a man's value manifests itself in material possession. For while the material world became the property of the insurgent middle classes, in another sense they never possessed it—it was theirs but not *them*.

In America it was both. The entrepreneurial pioneers owned the land and also identified with it. After all, had it not first appeared, first *been* in their name? This "primordial wilderness" was also "vacant": when the European settlers saw themselves as quickening a virgin land, the modern spirit completed its genesis by becoming flesh in the body of the American continent. The ideology of this incarnation as it fulfilled Europe's ideal liberalism, and as it is represented, appropriately incarnate, in the form and matter of American writing, is my central concern in this book.

In Europe, when Natural Law theorists such as Locke and Rousseau contended that the natural sanctity of the individual and the equally natural equipoise of the market dictated a democratic system of government based on contracts and laws, they were inevitably conscious, even as they appealed to nature, of the historical context of preexisting alternative forms. In order to refute feudalism's appeal to divine authority, the proponents of any willed change needed to demonstrate that political systems in general were historically contingent (that the current political order did not reflect cosmic necessity); so while they might claim that their proposed system was more harmonious with nature, they could not ascribe it directly *to* nature. How faith in the world's timeless and unchanging order failed before the refutation of recurrent revolution is well known, but I want to stress that this fall into history was self-perpetuating. The case for liberal democracy in Europe rests at least in part on the notion that it is men who make society, not any transcendent necessity. Thus the better the liberal case is made, the more it exposes its lack of natural sanction, just as when theater is at its best its very persuasiveness serves to heighten the audience's appreciation of artifice.

To its European settlers, however, America did not connote society, or history, but indeed in its natural parameters, geography. America was an avatar of the world prior to feudalism and, in the sense that it still awaited its primal molding, it was anterior to the old world's divisions. Responding only to nature (as it had no history), American civilization remained at one with it and embodied nature's laws organically, as the adult embodies the child rather than as a painting represents the landscape. The European immigrant who became an American saw himself not as entering a better society but as leaving society altogether. And in the reconciled natural civilization that once and for all transcended the old world's successive dialectical compromises, he assumed a natural, therefore absolute and not politically disputable, dominion. As insurgencies are successful when, after having displaced the established group, they finally replace it, this new natural ruler completed the liberal revolution by succeeding to, precisely, the landed status of his aristocratic forebears.

Thus, incarnate in the continent, the elsewhere embattled ideal of liberal individualism established itself in America as simply a description of things not only as they are but as they manifestly need to be. The most interesting aspect of the general belief in a national destiny to expand ever westward is one we tend to overlook, perhaps because we take it for granted: the American teleology cites the will of heaven and the human spirit, but it rests its case on the integrity of the continent.[2]

Were only heaven and the human spirit invoked, there would be little to comment upon. For American history was from the start an inspirational story whose fairytale beginning, once upon a time, promised a transcendent resolution. By comparison with this intentional plot, the histories of most other nations seem to have just grown, first prehistorically over indistinct and indefinite lapses of time before time, then through multiple incomplete versions whose coherence and meaning are produced afterward, by retrospective interpretations. But in this country the beginning of things, which had been announced almost before the fact in numerous filed agreements and covenants, was at once a matter of dates, surveys, measurements, and identifications—a matter of language.

But this experience of conscious self-construction, which might have inspired a particularly acute sense of history, seems to have had something like the opposite result. The Europeans who became Americans conquered and developed in their own image a territory of whose very existence their forebears had been ignorant. In that way they were quintessential aliens—yet they described their national origin and growth as an impulse of the land itself. And, as the land's basic dimension is not time but space, the United States was defined primarily as a place. Indeed, the chroniclers of the early history viewed the possibility of change over time, as opposed to expansion through space, as inimical, possibly regressively entropic, or at any rate a sign that the growth was *not* going well. The first overall history published in this country to instruct the newly fledged citizens of the just-founded nation about the world they had made themselves was entitled *The American Universal Geography* (1797). Its author, Jedediah Morse, boasted that, thanks to the excellent administrations of presidents Washington and (in the second edition) Jefferson, "the United States were happily distinguished by affording few materials for history" (1805 ed., 308–309). Reversing the old Chinese curse that one's enemies might "live in interesting times," Morse expressed a pious hope that the future would continue thus, still and uneventful.

From such indications, it has become a truism that Americans lack a sense of history. The most common explanation for this lapse is that, in their energetic impatience to get to their futures, Americans have no interest in how they arrived at the present, for, optimistic and sure of their ground, they want only to go forth each generation and each day anew. Of course some accounts are

6

more critical, and it has not been uncommon in recent times to blame both offensive foreign policies and short-sighted domestic programs on our "historical amnesia." What the differing analyses agree on is the notion of absence: something is missing in the national philosophy, and its lack results in an inadequate account of the past.

This consensus, however, fails to account for the fact that Americans are in another way highly conscious of their national heritage and, as much as any people, celebrate a gallery of monumental heroes and events; it might be argued, on the contrary, that they are *too* faithful to founding principles that, after two centuries, remain axiomatic. In not considering this cluster of images, exempla, and principles a "sense of history," the critics reveal a European orientation whose bias is more evident today because the European historical model is itself in question. For the modern notion that "history" means a dialectical process by which the past and the present are continuously transformed and the future forever uncertain has, in the last two decades especially, come to seem less self-evident. As other definitions of history—structuralist, ecological, cyclical—have gained recognition, the solved problem of America's "ahistoricity" has become newly problematical. Indeed, in the context of rethinking the definition of "history," the original question becomes reversible: rather than ask why Americans lack a "sense of history," we can now as well ask why Europeans have the particular sense of it that they do.

And thus reversed, the question has at least one very good answer: the seventeenth- and eighteenth-century redefinition of history as an unending dialectical process served insurgents interested in demonstrating the contingency of the old feudal order. Better than previous notions of cyclical or providential history, or myths of past golden ages, this new definition, by proposing the continual progressive mutability of the social process, implies both the feasibility and the righteousness of radical political transformations. As the doctrine of the divine right of kings prohibited their overthrow as a violation of the cosmic scheme, "historicizing" feudal and royal regimes permitted it by making an alternative system thinkable. What since that period of insurgency Westerners have commonly called a sense of history is largely a vision of the past as the stuff from which to make a different future.

Once a new order has taken the ideological keep, it generally pulls up the drawbridge and asserts *its* global, natural right, and in fact Hobbes, Locke, and Rousseau themselves, in their anthropologies and natural sciences, laid the ground for this next stage. For the theorists of the new competitive individualist system presented this social mode as not less but *more* harmonious with natural law than the one that had preceded it. Yet, for reasons that probably implicate the whole of Western civilization and are certainly beyond the scope of this discussion, history, and not nature, remained the context of politics and society, and the European social contract remained subject not only to abrogation, which Jefferson also envisaged in the form of a counterrevolution, but more significantly, to redrafting.

It is characteristic of Romantic and Victorian European culture that many of its major figures opposed, beyond the distortions, the very ideals and values of the dominant class (to which they almost all belonged). Dickens and Flaubert were "antibourgeois" as Marlowe and Shakespeare were never antiaristocratic or Chrétien de Troyes and Chaucer antifeudal, though the last four could be highly disapproving of the way the aristocracy or the feudal nobility conducted their inevitable rule. This alienated culture represents the uncertain position of the European middle class, trapped in a contingent historicity as in an antechamber and unable to move through it into the throne room of nature. This concept of a man-made history has rendered even basic principles of the bourgeois ideology debatable. Balzac, chronicler par excellence of the French bourgeoisie, mourned the monarchy; the plays of George Bernard Shaw polished the intellectual manners off Britain's elite, but the playwright was a socialist. Throughout the period the middle class has ruled Europe, a surprising number of those who are precisely the creators of its culture have been able and prone to imagine a different social model altogether, adding insult to injury by arguing on the ground of nature.

If the European middle class never passed beyond history, however, its American counterpart, and successor, did. The process interrupted in Europe was completed in America, where the ideology of liberal, democratic individualism reached maturity as

8

no longer the historical dispossessor of past rulers but the natural possessor of its own world. Jedediah Morse's recasting of history as geography, his sense that what there was to tell of American progress was geographical, celebrated the incarnation of the spirit of liberal idealism and of the individualist self in the North American continent. When the liberal ideal fused with the material landscape, it produced an "America" that was not allegory, for its meaning was not detachable, but symbol, its meaning inherent in its matter.

The very notion of an American "discovery" had already forecast this incarnation. By translating infinite time into universal space, the conception of a New World permitted principles that in the old world were rendered relative by their connection to process and growth to become absolute, timeless natural laws in the new. Reconceived as a spatial concept, process did not mean transformation but expansion. In disputing the previously occupied territory of Europe, the bourgeoisie could only claim to rule it *better*—and thus already in laying its claim conceded its relativity. But the coincidence of America's discovery and settlement by Europeans with the decisive political rise of a new class identified the very land with the ascendants: beyond any political or economic superiority, the material fact of the North American continent itself enabled insurgent merchants, artisans, and adventurers to declare themselves *incomparable* and the universal representatives of mankind. Their personal and political ways thus became, indistinguishably, the ways in and, more important, *of* America. The prior vacancy of the continent was their crucial founding fiction, both asserted directly and implicit in the self-conscious narrativity with which the story of America "began." To be born an American is simultaneously to be born again. Americans assume their national identity as the fulfillment of selfhood rather than as its point of origin, so that they travel their lives in a state of perpetual landing.

I want to stress the land, the continent's physical reality, or more basically, its physicality. For it is precisely because the concept of America is rooted in the physical finite that it can be infinitely metaphysical. The concept of the New World could not come to everyday life as a pure abstraction; it had to interpret

9

some actual territory, a real place. Lately, in order to refute the identification of the United States with the whole continent, historical revisionists have worked to separate the idea and myth of America from its material reality. The dichotomy that is thus established very usefully counters a prior tendency among even historians and critics to assume that "America" is a reality as such, so that we have only to examine its historical implementation. But through such demystifications, the connection of mystique to reality can be lost to analysis, and it is particularly this connection that interests me. For the myth of America has been *both* ideal and material (idealist and materialist): if it is transcendent, it is *immanently* transcendent.

The theme of the following familiar passage from Thoreau's *Walden* is precisely the substantial corporeality of the American and the American's ideal:

> Time is but the stream I go a-fishin in. I drink at it; but while I drink I see the sandy bottom and detect how shallow it is. Its thin current slides away, but eternity remains. I would drink deeper; fish in the sky, whose bottom is pebbly with stars. I cannot count one. I know not the first letter of the alphabet. I have always been regretting that I was not as wise as the day I was born. The intellect is a cleaver; it discerns and rifts its way into the secret of things. I do not wish to be any more busy with my hands than is necessary. My head is hands and feet. I feel all my best faculties concentrated in it. My instinct tells me that my head is an organ for burrowing, as some creatures use their snout and forepaws, and with it I would mine and burrow my way through these hills. I think the richest vein is somewhere hereabouts; so by the divining rod and thin rising vapors I judge; and here I will begin to mine.   (400–401)

Transforming time into space (the flowing current of the stream slides away to reveal an eternal bottom, which extends without movement or change) enables Thoreau to aspire and to grow without becoming different (which would render relative both his former and his present selves); instead he develops by unfolding his permanent inherent nature. On the one hand, then, the fusion of idea and matter permits growth with total stability. On the other,

10

it is even more powerful in allowing him (potentially) to know and possess the entire world, to penetrate to outermost limits because they are at the same time innermost, as the water reflects the sky and, beneath the water, the pebbles are identical with the stars deepest within (also farthest out in) the sky. This collapsing of in and out enables Thoreau to say his "head is hands and feet," so that, by burrowing (probing mole-like, blind and mute) head-down, he mines an ideal transcendent truth. The final pun proclaims the triumphant fusion of self and universe by means of (mediated by) the land.

I would suggest that this passage is not essentially different from the apparently opposite revelation Emerson reports at the beginning of his essay *Nature*, and that the similarities are characteristic of American thought: "Standing on bare ground,—my head bathed by the blithe air, and uplifted into infinite space,— all mean egotism vanishes. I become a transparent eye-ball; I am nothing; I see all; the currents of the Universal Being circulate through me; I am part or particle of God"(10). Not blind like a mole but become "a transparent eye-ball," not pressed about by actual soil but abstracted into the most insubstantial spirituality, a "nothing" through which "the currents of the Universal Being circulate" freely, Emerson is nonetheless located in a nature that he explicitly possesses as (spiritual) property. Incarnation (the assumption of the continental body) is for him also the basic condition for transcendence and is, in fact, what ensures arriving at the *right* spiritual principle. A more free-form transcendence, guided only by one's own imagination, can readily go astray. (We will see this possibility represented in the inventions of fiction in later chapters.) But like the fixed foot of Donne's compass, the material landscape makes the ideal circle just.

Donne is a useful reference here, for the ideal-material fusion in America also rises to the metaphysical through paradox. What in the context of a European definition of history emerges as contradiction—the limits of the self in relation to others, or individual freedom versus social cohesion, or infinite ambition stymied in a finite world, or simply the private and the public—America's spatial idiom transforms into paradox. The dialectic is a function of time, and not all oppositions are dialectical. Only those made by

11

their environment to interact and ultimately to exclude one another are thereby forced into the reconstitutions of synthesis. The passing of time is a medium of change precisely because each present moment is inelastic. In that the next moment is not simply more of this one (as a larger space may be just more of a smaller) but minimally another version, stasis itself is in part a new development whereby opposition has been not-resolved. But one way or the other, yes or no, something happens, which, entering organically into the definition of both dialectical terms, confirms their engagement with time and with each other. On the other hand (as I will try to show more fully in Chapter 3 through the example of Emerson's complementary dualities), outside of time, opposites can cohabit indefinitely, unchanged and independent, if only their common space can be made large enough. Conversely, resolution through encompassment need not mean something different but only a wider circle. For Emerson it is always possible to broaden the horizon so as to embrace ostensible oppositions, which in the new context become complementary and that way even promote universal unity. Tocqueville's observation that despite the remarkable diversity (ethnic, racial, religious) of American society, Americans seemed peculiarly intolerant of nonconformity, documents the process of encompassment as a broad ideological phenomenon. For in the context of Emersonian pluralism, diversity connotes not difference but instead avatars of the universal. Such a concept of diversity tends in fact to deny difference precisely by expressing it, as yet another facet of the enlarged whole.

In general the concept of nonantagonistic opposition implies the possibility of an energy untaxed by dialectical friction and, indeed, multiplied by the broadening sphere of its exercise. If in a dialectical setting contradiction signifies either-or, as paradox it ultimately means both-and. Its productivity is an endless reproduction, a multiplication, an increase essentially without costs. In this way, the paradoxical nature of American ideology—its celebration of the single self and simultaneous apotheosis of an all-encompassing "America," its secularism and religiosity, its commitment to nature as well as to the machine—has functioned as a dynamo. Paradox generates not only good poetry but also goods. Again, the crux of the matter is the identification of certain abstract

ideals with the physical American landscape. For when that identification is made, the setting of self-realization and of action becomes a permanent and all-encompassing nature, in which the
limits of each person are not others (as in society) but, at one end
of the natural continuum, the universe itself, and at the other, the
individual self. But as these are in the largest sense the same, their
transitory difference amounts to a stage in the reproduction of
both, or makes of each a catalyst for the other. Thus in the American incarnation the Protestant soul acquired a newly powerful
body.

To establish the ground for personal autonomy, seventeenth-
century political philosophy redefined the dichotomy between body
and soul as essentially a property relation whereby the latter literally owned the former. But in basing the autonomy of the self
on inalienable self-possession, the individualist argument laid the
ground for a debilitating existential alienation. Able now to call
both body and soul his own, a man was however newly unable
to integrate them. Subject implies object, so that in returning a
man's hands to him as his inalienable possessions, self-possessive
individualism implied that the self and the body were ontologically
separate. More simply, the empowerment of self-consciousness is a
function of the division of the self. The sense of being cut off from
the natural and corporeal that seems to have plagued the modern
psyche represents another and disabling aspect of this division,
however. In this aspect, existential self-consciousness amounts to
the self's exile from the body it propels. Seeking to end that exile
by returning mind to body, Freud's "discovery" that sex is at the
crux of personal identity might be seen as paralleling the "discovery" of America. In these two "discoveries"—of his body and his
world—the self-possessive ideal individual repossesses the material universe; he appropriates them as not only his but him. It
is suggestive of such a notion of parallel discoveries that Freud's
theories were received earlier and more readily here than in Europe. Indeed, in a country whose historical identity is seen as
inherent in its land, theories that locate the roots of personal identity in bodily attributes clearly make pragmatic sense.

Thus, by assuming the American land (not the landscape but
the land), the American man acquired an individualist substance.

13

His self-consciousness rendered cosmic by comparison to the unconscious earth, he was nonetheless reintegrated—his body and soul, himself and the world, made one—through his identification with the physical universe, an identification whose natural priority, moreover, ensured his transcendent primacy. It made him both ideally self-reliant and self-sufficient. For to realize himself in this world he did not have to bring about anything new, or to deal with others. In contrast to self-realization through financial success or political power—in contrast, in other words, to a historical self-realization—one becomes oneself in nature simply by being in it. Such being is really the apotheosis of becoming (amounting to the fulfillment of history in History). It co-opts the dynamic of process and masses time (which each person experiences as subjective duration rather than objective chronometry) into an endless landscape in which the self travels at will. Emerson envisioned this ultimate intensification of self-consciousness dissolving all external domains into itself but not thereby losing its connection with a real nature. For it is only through possession of a physical universe that self-possessive individualism fulfilled itself as individualist universalism.

Identity with the natural universe generalized the individual into Man: it did the work of history and society at no cost to him, nationalizing and even moralizing him without (apparently) limiting him. Thus the totally separate individual of American mythology, the Adamic man alone in a vacant wilderness, builds his own world (according to the myth), without having to expend himself in the construction of society. It is another truism, therefore, that Americans lack a sense of community. But again, the submerged, or perhaps subterranean, term of American identity, the physical place as such, embodies an ideological corrective (and connective). While society, defined as the collected competitive needs of others, figures in American culture only as a scorned opponent, at the same time, *civilization* is fully affirmed as a kind of natural impulse or, more materially, as what Crèvecoeur called "the salubrious effluvia of the soil" (*Letters from an American Farmer*, 22). Literally inspired by the land's physical emanations, the abstract individual becomes an American, and it is as an American that he becomes not only singular but representative. The representativeness of the autonomous individual in turn provides a basis for community that comes from within, rather than as an external and limiting obligation. Since it is by being autonomous that each man thus connects to others, he remains free, in fact becomes free in the connection. But the connection is not therefore less adhesive. Where others have found an absence, I see on the contrary the powerful presence of a civilization conceived to be inherent in nature, springing forth coeval with each American as an organic part of his very individuality.

Envisioning such reconciliation, "America" in the United States, and also abroad, connotes not only the strenuous spirit of individualism but also—and perhaps more—its material effectiveness in the real world. The American Dream, whose rhetoric most often invokes family and home, is a dream of the Pilgrim's homecoming—a vision, finally, not of voyages and breached frontiers, but of safe arrivals. Huck Finn escapes from a society that *claims* to be civilized into a nature that really is: both ethically and aesthetically, the raft and presumably the West are not just nicer places but specifically more civilized. They are never jungle-like, but are pastoral very much in the style of the Forest of Arden. As in Thoreau's cabin with its view of Walden Pond, the aesthetic qualities of life on the Mississippi raft are absolutely superior to, and more civilized than, the Grangerford parlor. And like the beanfield at Walden, the raft recovers a true political economy the shore has long abandoned: to start with, its civilized inhabitants do not trade in human beings. At the same time, like Thoreau, Huck understands exchange value as well as any merchant.

In fact, he understands it better, or more profoundly, for it comes to him naturally. In comparison with such fictional counterparts as Robinson Crusoe, who serves an apprenticeship by reinventing mercantile England on a desert isle and then in its name and to its ends capturing the island's natural resources, Huck finds full blown in his heart and in his instincts the blueprint for a way of life whose true civilization is proven by its accord with nature. As Thoreau reaps an abundant crop by following the lead of his beans themselves, and forbearing to weed them too much, the raft is buoyed by a confluence of nature and a natural civilization, whose practical invisibility in accounts of American thought

15

is a function of its absolute sway, or more precisely, of its internalization into an aspect of personal (inherent, natural) identity.

In other words, contrary to the conventional wisdom, the relationship of the individual to his world may be *closer* in America than in Europe. Consider the essentially opposite principles that advance the quests of Crusoe and Huck Finn. Crusoe's voyage away from England and his reconstruction of the island into another England progress through separation: of the restless sailor from his family and friends, of London civilization from a desert nature, and perhaps most basically of the hero's adventurous, transcendent spirit from his limited and mortal body. Huck, on the other hand, leaves Hannibal, Missouri, because it is *not* home and, as did Thoreau in the passage cited earlier, he always moves toward reconciliation. First on the island, then on the raft, in the end putatively in the West, his progress unites: himself with Jim in a real home, their restored community with nature, and again most basically, the hero's adventurous transcendent spirit with his liberated (barefoot) body. But of course incarnation *means* reconciliation, and most literally, of mind and body. Like monarchs or lords who identified (named) themselves through their lands, the American identifies himself through his.

The power of that annexation, of the repossession of body and land such that vision and ambition have hands and feet, was definitively claimed by Emerson. Urging each man to build his own world—not only to imagine it but to realize it, to have its value in goods and cash—he could guarantee success because the world already belonged to, in fact *was*, each man. The extraordinary ideological potency of the concept of the American incarnation lies in this guarantee, which is also the crux of the translation of contradiction into paradox. In the light of contemporary definitions of ideology that stress what ideology enables over what it prohibits (its consciousness rather than its false consciousness), the final version of liberal individualism appears a remarkable creed. For Emerson's vision amounts to an apotheosis of productivity that, by collapsing the distance between intent and achievement, transcends work or at least effort, so that one has the sense of being able to do anything. One builds one's world, Emerson explains, simply by conforming one's "acts" to "the pure idea" in one's mind. Since "what we are, that only can we see," to see is to realize, and the word "realize" achieves all its etymological potency. So when a man sees that his spirit is everywhere incarnate in American nature, when, in Emerson's very precise terms, he aligns his "axis of vision" with the "axis of things," "the kingdom of man over nature, which cometh not with observation,—a dominion such as now is beyond his dream of God,—he shall enter without more wonder than the blind man feels who is gradually restored to perfect sight" (*Nature*, 48–49).

The Emersonian mode of production is not that of Milton's Adam, but of his God. God envisioned the world into real being by simply projecting outside what was already there within. Adam's "observations" were sterile because, while his fall had fortunately gained him self-consciousness, it also dispossessed him; until, that is, he landed in America, just in time to inherit his dead Father's world.

He also inherited its headaches. The powerful accord achieved in the American incarnation generated newly powerful disharmonies. I proposed earlier that an incomplete ideological hegemony inspired Europe's alienated culture. American culture has not been alienated in that sense, but its participation in the dominant ideology, which it therefore assumes as inevitable, has produced problems of another sort. To project a later argument (see especially Chapter 6), let me just suggest here that the darkness of American fiction, sometimes explained as a reaction to the glare of American reality, more profoundly expresses a tragic vision inspired precisely by the fulfillment of the ideology of liberal individualism.

For since tragedy results from rebellion against the impassable limits of an absolute situation, it cannot be imagined in the relativist context projected by the modern sense of history in Europe. Indefinitely and ongoingly mutable, a progressively evolutionary world must always contain hope in the form of further possibilities. In such a world, even death, as Emma Bovary's suicide grimly demonstrates, is only an abandonment of the confrontation: it "calls" a game in which there is no final score and, with melodramatic but not tragic irony, no fatal move. The next instant something else has happened that retrospectively reinterprets a

17

past that can never take conclusive form. America's translation of time into space, however, reintroduces the category of finality; and a distant finality intensifies the final conflict. This is a characteristically paradoxical situation. Since the New World encompasses all possibilities, and in that way is "infinite," it also definitively precludes *more* new worlds, and in that way is absolutely prohibitive. Thus tragedy became possible and, given the exceptional ambition of the self-made man, likely, when the liberal individualist universe co-opted the universe of possibilities.

Deriving the basic form of their work from the European novel, American novelists developed that middle-class historicist genre into a form of tragedy. The other side of the benevolent recreation that Emerson envisioned as the consummation of the marriage of self and world was the power for a commensurately cosmic destruction. No wonder Nietzsche, who mourned the loss of a tragic sensibility as a radical diminution of the human spirit, so greatly admired Emerson. What Nietzsche may or may not have seen is that Emerson's cosmic self was made so by having a real world he could call his own; and that possessing this world in turn lent a definitive substantiality to the worlds he and his literary compatriots imagined. In America, the literary culmination of the modern middle-class ideology also projected a real embodiment. The act of writing, which in the European novel remains historically contingent and thus creative only of itself, becomes in the novels of Hawthorne and Melville an act of incarnation, an authentic and therefore *blasphemous* creation. In *The Marble Faun*, Hawthorne drew back at the last minute from just such an explicitly blasphemous act (see Chapter 5). In *Pierre*, Melville "crossed the Rubicon" and plunged to infernal extinction (see Chapter 6). The tragic fiction of the doctrinally optimistic American Renaissance amounts to a kind of Black Mass, and is cataclysmically destructive in proportion to its belief in transcendent creativity.

American ideology and culture, then, represent the transforming completion of both the possibilities and the problems of political and cultural liberal individualism. In the discussion of completion, possibilities, and problems in subsequent chapters I begin with the idea of "discovery" as already containing the crux of the concept of incarnation, then go on to sketch its basic codification in a distinctive view of the physical environment. Three of the four remaining chapters are close readings of texts in which the American incarnation is itself incarnate: Emerson's *Nature*, Hawthorne's *The Marble Faun*, and Melville's *Pierre*. In the first of these three infinite power emerges as the reward of the American's oneness with America; in the other two, after a theoretical examination of the relation of the form of the novel to the concept of modern individualism, it becomes evident that incarnation also created some newly stringent limits. Hawthorne's *Marble Faun* and Melville's *Pierre* are arguably their authors' most troubled works. I focus on them for just that reason, because as I understand the novels, their troubles arise from pushing the enterprise of novel-writing in America to the edge. *Nature* unfolds all incarnation's potential for expansion. *The Marble Faun* and *Pierre* discover its outer limits. Indeed, in the early and Renaissance American fiction, finding the limits of the New World is often an explicit theme, a theme represented most intimately as a search for the limits of language. The continent that was the modern spirit's flesh was also its word.

I have set out this argument in some detail at the start because, as my subject is the ground itself, lying below the cited grounds of thought, it is sometimes difficult to see in the course of travel. Constituting what one thinks and talks *with* rather than *about*, it poses problems of articulation. Reaching down to levels of consciousness that are themselves mute—never told but retold inside consciously constructed arguments—sometimes seems to render the observer precursive as well. In fact, trying to read a text beneath the text is a paradoxical enterprise. On the one hand, it could amount to little more than reading it "once more with emphasis." On the other, in trying actually to see the limits of a language, and therefore to see what it denies as well as what it asserts, what it suppresses as well as what it expresses, one reads in opposition to the text or, less anthropomorphically, to the author. An exposition of the limits of thought involves saying what the writer has *not* said, and the not-said can become an antitext. The process thus threatens to slide the critic on one side into the obvious and on the other into the disputatious. This Introduction is intended as a sort of handrail. By stating directly what I will be after in the explications that follow, I hope both to alert readers to the point of some apparently self-explanatory paraphrases and to warn them of my ulterior meaning.

On the other hand, it is not easy to define, or to claim, the status of the ideas I describe. Clearly, to describe such large structuring ideas is not to define anyone's thinking. Rather, one thinks in relation to such ideas, or in their context—so that they define not the content of thought but its conditions. I would suggest, then, that the ideas sketched here functioned both at the highest and at the lowest level of thought, but probably not very much in between. That is, they constituted the givens of the universe of American thought, the subterranean foundation upon which statement, argument, decision, consciousness arose; and they were also the ultimate points to which these reached.

In other words, when Americans said "America" they meant something they took to be fact: that their country, whose foundation defined and identified a previously vacant continent, represented a new and culminating development in world history and thus the fulfillment of progress. They could also, perhaps in smaller numbers, mean an idea as such, an idea not necessarily enacted in the real country: a vision, even self-consciously a myth, of individual transcendence and democratic equality, of spiritual redemption and ultimate technological competence; or, for that matter, a travesty in both fact and idea, the doom of real and ideal hopes.

At one end of the spectrum, where the idea of America is taken as more or less factual, idea functions as ideology; at the other, where it is understood as a vision, idea functions as ideal. To be sure, it is in between that we really think, reexamining our axioms insofar as we can identify them as such, and questioning our myths to the extent that we can deconstruct them. This book is an attempt to analyze not our thinking itself but its limits, to pursue it to the point where it disappears into the opaque ground under our feet or dissolves on the horizon into an all-encompassing blur.

Therefore I do not mean that Americans explicitly thought the continent incarnated the spirit of individualism. That would have made incarnation the content of their thinking. I mean rather that an idea of incarnation can be seen to organize American self-consciousness as grammar organizes speech, without specifying its content. In that sense, this book might be best taken, in contrast to, say, a dictionary or a reader, as an ideological grammar.

But considering the idea of incarnation as a principle of linguistic organization immediately raises the equally basic question of who spoke this language: in America? in Europe? For it is no longer possible, if it ever was, to assume any constituency for sovereign ideas, let alone one so grandly titled "Americans." I do not assume such a constituency; in any case, probably no one and certainly no group of people ever thinks either so explicitly or so encompassingly as the system outlined here. My concern has not been to ascribe but, on the contrary, to abstract, both in the sense of getting at a model and in the sense of extracting it. In this endeavor, I am aware of going counter to the major tendency in current cultural and social historiography to particularize and con-textualize. But I would only suggest that this avenue too leads somewhere interesting; and that to locate even the particular one needs points on two axes: on the horizontal axis drawn by pluralistic social history, and also on the model-reconstructing vertical axis. In short, while perhaps no one, not even those whose actual words I cite, thought entirely or explicitly or exclusively in the terms I set out in this book, most people, and not least those who rejected these terms, thought in relation to them. The issue here is not who answered maybe or no, but what one was led to ask, what one asked naturally. Nature is as far as thought goes, for once thought enters nature, idea becomes fact. In this book I examine as a point of such entrance what the dominant American ideology has cast as its point of departure: the meeting point of the modern spirit and the continent.

1 * Starting with Columbus

*W*e know now that it did not start with Columbus, that Viking ships reached the American continents long before the *Nina*, the *Pinta*, and the *Santa Maria*, and that even they may not have been the first. Columbus's discovery was really only the last and at that no epiphany but a protracted and uncertain process lasting almost a decade. The legend is misleading, moreover, not only about when and who but about what, for on coming ashore, rather than a few scattered savages whose nakedness classed them with the local fauna, the disoriented explorer found vigorous civilizations it would take all the savagery of Europe to conquer. The story of how Columbus convinced King Ferdinand and Queen Isabella that the earth was round has been reclassified as a variety of Creationism. Most of the new history textbooks explain that the discovery of America evolved through the explorations of many, and that indeed its traditional assignment to Columbus illustrates the vagaries of historical selection.

Columbus himself makes an ambiguous discoverer, denying strenuously to the end that he had found a New World. From his accounts of his four voyages, the Mexican historian Edmundo O'Gorman has reconstructed the series of hypotheses that Columbus proposed instead, beginning with the reasonable supposition that he had first disembarked on islands off easternmost Asia and ending in some disarray with the claim that he had found the old biblical Eden. The later recognition that this was a continent hitherto unknown to Europeans was forced upon Amerigo Vespucci as a last possible explanation and, from the contemporary perspective, the least likely. The notion of discovery was, then, hardly contemporary with the event; O'Gorman and others have seen it rather as a later development having to do not with the actual finding of the new continents but with their settling. In that context the discovery of America is entirely associated with the United States, which emerges as a or rather *the* New World, not, like Europe or Asia, defined by its ongoing history, but a new entity with an inherent primordial destiny. Ironically, the initial vestment of "America" in the United States antedates the Revolution and reflects not this country's power but that of the British Empire. Ratified by independence, however, the identification has never wavered: the reference to America is always clear and never signifies Canada or Mexico, let alone any country in South America. As a way of divesting the United States of this continental and indeed global aura, by invalidating all such transcendent auras, O'Gorman sought in his book *The Invention of America* to show that the "discovery" was instead an "invention," a construction of and by history, not a serendipitous revelation.

In recent years, historians in the United States have had similar goals. Recently, for instance, writing about Jefferson's assembly of the Declaration of Independence from several European political philosophies, Garry Wills used almost the same title, *Inventing America* (1978), to make, among others, the same point, that America was not a divine gift or mandate, but the product of human acts and deliberations. By tracing Jefferson's arguments to their sources, Wills intended to dispel the notion that the United States began history anew, whether in 1492 or in 1776, and the "belief in our extraordinary birth, outside the processes of time, [that] has led us to think of ourselves as a nation apart, with a special destiny, the hope of all those outside America's shores" (xix).

Teleology is everyone's first historical mode, and it always makes personal sense. One reason the Columbus story is so memorable is that it ends happily with *us*. Like the child who culminates his mother's story of her life before his birth with "and then you had me!" we listen to the tale of Columbus, his small ships and his fearsome faith, in the pleasant anticipation of being its punch line. It is difficult to view the events that usher one into the world as less than intentional. Still, despite such notorious throwbacks as Ronald Reagan's "City on a Hill" speech, the conviction that America has a special divine destiny seems to have receded. It has, at any rate, become more widely recognized as conviction rather than fact, and that recognition has permitted some skepticism. Wills's mocking tone has had echoes; and by thus rising into fuller consciousness, the American telos has lost an important part of its ideological force. Though it can still move people and even cause them to act, they now retain the existential control of self-consciousness over what they feel and do. Ideas are more powerful at a lower level of consciousness where we do not think to ask why we think them. Ascending into recognized rhetoric, the myth of destiny has left some such ideas behind as axiomatic reality. It was these that all along constituted the core of the discovery myth, a belief not so much in a special national mission as in a special national character.

The year after Wills published *Inventing America*, a book called *Discovering America* came out, with a preface by Henry Steele Commager and Richard Morris explaining its title. The question of exactly who got there first, whether Columbus or Norse adventurers or Prince Madoc of Wales, did not interest these historians, for these first sightings amounted at most to a kind of "aerial reconnaissance." The real discoveries, Commager and Morris explained, were made by "ten generations" of people who lived on the new land, explored it, and experienced it. The authors of *Discovering America* thus would define discovery as life not legend, history not myth: "The whole process of discovery was a kind of anticipatory vindication of Robert Frost's insight, that 'the land was ours before we were the land's.' The land was indeed ours, by conquest or, as many Americans believed, by Manifest Destiny: Americans fell upon it, cultivated it, exploited it, ravaged it" (xiii).

Incorporating more than a decade of revisionist histories, this passage is a remarkable example of how traditional models can embrace revisionism and yet remain essentially intact. The authors begin by replacing the old hero- and event-centered narrative with the social history of exploration and settlement. Then, agnostically ascribing a belief in Manifest Destiny to "many Americans" while in their own voice only claiming "conquest," they acknowledge the mixed character of the ways of settling, which both improved the land and despoiled it. In this account, discovery is the continent's historical development and that development is open to criticism. O'Gorman's and Wills's objections would seem to have been met. But they have not been; or rather, in appearing to meet them, the Commager-Morris accommodation points deeper, to a more essential aspect of the discovery myth that survives unscathed the quasi-abandonment of the notion of a special destiny. I will suggest here and seek to demonstrate further in Chapter 2 that the essence of the myth, which Commager and Morris do not question, lies in its welding of the meaning of America and the continent. This fusion is what is almost universally taken to characterize America. To whatever end the land is used, for God's work or the devil's or man's, America remains a matter, as Commager and Morris say clearly because they too assume it, of our being the land's.

In other words, at the heart of the American teleology was an entelechy (a perfect and complete potentiality moving of itself to its realization) that continues to animate the new discovery story, making it retrospectively evident that it was also the crux of the old. We can now see that in the concept of Manifest Destiny the emphasis was on Manifest; and that when the Puritans represented themselves as the Chosen People entering the Promised Land, the emphasis was on the Promised Land. What makes the discovery work as a classic myth of origin is its projection of a new and unique, living entity, an "America" not, as O'Gorman depicted it, ready-made and complete since the creation, but completely ready-to-be-made. The concept of America is thus better described as an entelechy than as a teleology. A telos is a once and future thing. But as the course of history inevitably diverges from the founding vision, a potential not for this or that achievement but for achievement as such—for potential as such—has maintained "America" invulnerably present-tense not only for Commager and Morris but even for critics who decry the American telos.

Thus Richard Slotkin's *Regeneration through Violence* (1973), a work that undoubtedly helped to inspire Commager and Morris's references to exploitation and ravage, ends on a passionate denunciation of the American myth from a standpoint that seems to me to be still inside that myth's bounding assumptions. It is so powerful an assault on those boundaries that its failure to break through can only be proof of their extraordinary resilience. In the last three paragraphs of the book, Slotkin writes angrily:

> the cycle of the myth never really ends. The animal skins on the wall, the tree stumps in the yard, the scalp bounty money in the bank, and the pervasive smell of burning are proofs of what we have been; and they suggest that we still will play, in concept or action, the same role in dialectical opposition to a new Indian, a new social or political antithesis . . . Our heroes and their narratives are an index to our character and conception of our role in the universe . . . Under the aspect of mythology and historical distance, the acts and motives of the woodchopper, the whale and bear hunter, the Indian fighter, and the deerslayer have an air of simplicity and purity that makes them seem finely heroic expressions of an admirable quality of the human spirit. They seem to stand on a commanding ridge, while we are still tangled in the complexities of the world and the wilderness. But their apparent independence of time and consequence is an illusion; a closely woven chain of time and consequence binds their world to ours. Set the statuesque figures and their piled trophies in motion through space and time, and a more familiar landscape emerges— the whale, buffalo, and bear hunted to the verge of extinction for pleasure in killing and "scalped" for fame and the profit in hides by men like Buffalo Bill; the buffalo meat left to rot, till acres of prairie were covered with heaps of whitening bones, and the bones then ground for fertilizer; the Indian debased, impoverished, and killed in return for his gifts; the land and its people, its "dark" people especially, economically exploited and wasted; the warfare between man and nature, between race and race, exalted as a kind of heroic ideal; the piles of wrecked and rusted cars, heaped like Tartar pyramids of death-cracked, weatherbrowned, rain-rotted skulls, to signify our passage through the land. (564–565)

To the mythology of a redemptive mission to reclaim the earth for nature and nature's God, Slotkin here counterposes a history of exploitation and killing. He thus demystifies on the levels of both form and content, exposing myth with history and the claim of benevolence with proof of malignancy. But his own account is also mythical, projecting the converse, the antimyth of Manifest Destiny, which continues to assume crucially that the meaning and the morality of American life are defined by the use of the continent itself. The "woodchopper, the whale and bear hunter, the Indian fighter, and the deerslayer" are antiheroes for having abused a relation that is defined not first among them, but with the land. The connections between men come indirectly through their common connection to the land; their macabre "trophies" desolate a landscape that is common ground rather than community. Significantly, the single reference to modern devastations is "the piles of wrecked and rusted cars," again evaluating a human enterprise, and in this case one not directly related to nature, in terms of its effect on the land. When Slotkin thinks of the automobile industry's assaults on life, it is not the ruin of men on assembly lines that first comes to his mind but the ruin of the landscape; not, therefore, the building of cars as it contributes to an unhappy reconstruction of society, but the pollution of the earth by the bodies of cars when they leave the social world—their afterlife in a transcendent realm that is the real and ultimate America.

In this sense, although he denies the purported purity of America's heroes as an ahistorical illusion, Slotkin himself seems to envision a true heroism also defined in relation to the land. The animus of the passage bespeaks a sense of betrayal that presupposes possibility. We *should have* signified our passage through the land with better trophies. The great moral force of *Regeneration through Violence* depends at least in part on the conviction that we could have.

This vision—meaning here a way of seeing rather than a conscious fantasy—organized, indeed inspired, the work of many of Slotkin's historical and critical predecessors as well, so that even as they dismantled the American teleology they confirmed the entelechy at its core. The study of America as such, of the American character and ethos, of its culture and characteristic aesthetic, has been overwhelmingly a study of origins. Deliberately so: the scholars set out to examine the conviction that there was something special about the origin of America. And the examination did set this conviction in a historical context that demystified it. But though they pulled it up to examine its roots, somehow the myth went on flowering.

Consider Perry Miller, who originated the origin studies, explaining the origin of his own work. The vision came to him, he recalled later, not at his desk but when he was thousands of miles away, posted during World War I "on the edge of a jungle of central Africa," and "in that barbaric tropic . . . unloading . . . drums of case oil flowing out of the inexhaustible wilderness of America." Comparing himself to Gibbon called to tell the story of the Roman Empire, Miller felt that he had had his life's work "thrust" upon him. He had been given "the mission of expounding what I took to be the innermost propulsion of the United States." Unlike Gibbon's, however, the story Miller was to tell was not that of a rise and fall but only of a rise—witness the drums of oil. So he would begin "at the beginning of a beginning" to recount "the massive narrative of the movement of European culture into the vacant wilderness of America" (*Errand into the Wilderness*, vii–viii).

That narrative, starting with the Puritan migration, focused on ideas and language, precisely because Miller was acutely aware of American myth making. The titles of two of his books, *Nature's Nation* (1967) and *Errand into the Wilderness* (1956), explicitly identify the national self-image as myth. There is no question of catching him in naive fantasies of divine election. His subject, after all, is the projection of such fantasies onto a "vacant wilderness." This last phrase poses a problem, for of course the wilderness was not vacant; its vacancy was itself a fantasy, as Slotkin and others have shown so starkly. It is not this misperception, however, that mythicizes Miller's account (though it badly biases it), but rather the way he situates the problem in space and not in time, the way he tacitly assumes that the basic organization of the narrative of American history is geographical, that it begins at Plymouth and ends at the Pacific, and that it develops, propelled from within, by unfolding across the intervening space. Miller saw with definitive clarity that the terms by which Americans interpreted the continent were invented. But he took it for granted that, one way or another, as England and Rome were historical, America was objectively continental.

So did Henry Nash Smith, when he introduced *Virgin Land* (1950) as a study that "traces the impact of the West, the vacant continent beyond the frontier, on the consciousness of Americans and follows the principal consequences of this impact in literature and social thought down to [Frederick Jackson] Turner's formulation of it" (4). The way this project can be seen to participate in American mythology, despite the fact that *Virgin Land* is at once a founding and a definitive analysis of that mythology, is, again, not primarily through its assumption of a vacant continent. Smith has long since recanted that assumption. But it is significant that he was able to do so without basically altering his analysis—just as finding that Columbus was not the first European to see America does not basically alter the discovery myth. This is because, in *Virgin Land* as in that myth, the crux is not who was there or who came there, but the "there" itself, the primacy of the place over time and actors, who are all mutable while it remains permanent.

The difficulty American critics have had in penetrating to the bottom assumptions of the national mythology may have come in part from a tendency to methodological insularity. When the object of analysis is global, or claims to be, the analyst needs an external perspective, somewhere off the globe. The image of an America that grew from the American soil is all-pervasive in the national culture, even among those who recognize its mythic quality; it may be impossible to see it as fully contingent except by comparing it to equally contingent alternative Americas. One such alternative is the description of the "Physical Aspect of the Argentine Republic, and the Forms of Character, Habits, and Ideas Induced by It," that opens Domingo Sarmiento's *Civilization and Barbarism* (1845).

Sarmiento was an Argentinian educator, writer, and political figure. When he wrote this book he was in exile in Chile for his opposition to the dictatorship of Juan Manuel Rosas; he would return to become president of Argentina. A member of the European-oriented intellectual and professional community that aspired to an enlightened, liberal Latin America, Sarmiento admired the United States and was well liked and well connected there. Emerson praised his writings warmly, and Mary Mann, the wife of Sarmiento's close friend Horace Mann, translated *Civilization and Barbarism* into English. Thus the idea that America might provide a particularly congenial home for democracy was entirely familiar to Sarmiento—but he clearly did not consider the continent itself the source of that congeniality. On the contrary. *Civilization and Barbarism* is about the conflict between European civilization and the barbarism of the Argentine wilderness, the Pampas, where violent gauchos drown in blood all attempts at cultural and moral improvement. Not one to sing the romance of the cowboy, Sarmiento lays much of the blame for the failure of Argentine civilization on a too widely ranging landscape that all but precludes the growth of civilization.

> The vast tract which occupies [the extremities of Argentina] is altogether uninhabited, and possesses navigable rivers as yet unfurrowed even by a frail canoe. Its own extent is the evil from which the Argentine Republic suffers; the desert encompasses it on every side and penetrates its very heart; wastes containing no human dwelling, are, generally speaking, the unmistakable boundaries between its several provinces. Immensity is the universal characteristic of the country: the plains, the woods, the rivers, are all immense; and the horizon is always undefined, always lost in haze and delicate vapors which forbid the eye to mark the point in the distant perspective, where the land ends and the sky begins. (1–2)

Compare this to a passage from Thomas Jefferson's *Notes on the State of Virginia*. Separated by about a generation, Jefferson and Sarmiento had much in common both philosophically and politically. When he wrote the *Notes,* in 1781–1783, Jefferson too was a future president of the country he surveyed; also, as the governor of Virginia, he was a man who thought of limits as well as of possibilities. But Jefferson and Sarmiento looked at the land's apparently infinite and unexplored expanse altogether differently. For Jefferson, its wildness makes the passage of the Potomac through the Blue Ridge "one of the most stupendous scenes in nature" and "worth a voyage across the Atlantic." He exults in the elemental wars that must have attended its genesis:[1]

> On your right comes up the Shenandoah, having ranged along the foot of the mountain an hundred miles to seek a vent. On your left approaches the Patowmac, in quest of a passage also. In the moment of their junction they rush together against the mountain, rend it asunder, and pass off to the sea. The first glance of this scene hurries our senses into the opinion, that this earth has been created in time, that the mountains were formed first, that the rivers began to flow afterwards, that in this place particularly they have been dammed up by the Blue Ridge of mountains, and have formed an ocean which filled the whole valley; that continuing to rise they have at length broken over at this spot, and have torn the mountain down from its summit to its base. The piles of rock on each hand, but particularly on the Shenandoah, the evident marks of their disrupture and avulsion from their beds by the most powerful agents of nature, corroborate the impression. (*Notes*, 143)

Rocky wastes and "tremendous" vistas do not discourage Jefferson, they inspire him. The scene's more than human scale does not make him feel excluded; his pleasure in it is deeply personal, the stupendous view is *his* view. "You stand on a very high point of land," he begins the description, and thereafter he is a constant presence who reacts to the scenery less than he actively interprets it. The story told by this prehistoric landscape concludes in the present, with Jefferson himself. Its violent genesis in time has delivered the land into a peaceful infinity. In contrast to its tumultuous foreground,

> the distant finishing which nature has given to the picture is of a very different character. It is a true contrast to the fore-ground. It is as placid and delightful, as that is wild and tremendous. For the mountain being cloven asunder, she presents to your eye, through the cleft, a small catch of smooth blue horizon, at an infinite distance in the plain country, inviting you, as it were, from the riot and tumult roaring around, to pass through the breach and partici-

pate of the calm below. Here the eye ultimately composes itself . . . (143)

Note the sense of a direct connection between the landscape and
the observer in the phrases "she presents to your eye" and "in-
viting you." Recalling now Sarmiento's definition of the Argentine
horizon, "always undefined, always lost in haze and delicate va-
pors which forbid the eye to mark the point in the distant perspective," shows the difference one's perspective makes. It also
reveals how deeply embedded in the physical landscape Jefferson
felt the national identity to be, even in the middle of the Revolution, when, peculiarly, historical process might have appeared
to be the more important factor. The passage continues: "and that
way, too, the road happens actually to lead." "Happens to lead,"
as if by a wonderful coincidence the road had naturally appeared
as just another aspect of the landscape, expressing a cosmic purpose that included, along with rivers reaching the ocean, men
reaching their towns: "You cross the Patowmac above the junction,
pass along its side through the base of the mountain for three
miles, its terrible precipices hanging in fragments over you, and
within about twenty miles reach Fredericktown, and the fine country round that" (143). Nature seems not to have built roads in
Argentina, however, and travel across that country's wild landscape has little forward momentum. If Jefferson's line of sight is
infinitely horizontal, Sarmiento's describes a tight circle:

> When the solitary caravan of wagons, as it sluggishly tra-
> verses the pampas, halts for a short period of rest, the men
> in charge of it, grouped around their scanty fire, turn their
> eyes mechanically . . . upon the faintest whisper of the wind
> among the dry grass, and gaze into the deep darkness of
> the night, in search of the sinister visages of the savage
> horde, which, at any moment, approaching unperceived,
> may surprise them. (*Civilization and Barbarism*, 2)

Far from embodying the national promise, this countryside is its
major opponent. Gazing into the deep dark night of a barbaric
wilderness drains the life-force of civilization. The would-be settlers
look mechanically at an impenetrable Argentine horizon that inspires only a nihilistic pessimism; the "constant insecurity of life

outside the towns stamps upon the Argentine character a certain stoical resignation to death by violence, which is regarded as one of the inevitable probabilities of existence"(3).

Sarmiento does have better things to say about the settled parts of the country, which are, indeed, "unusually favored by nature." But not favored to the extent of roadbuilding. The terrain goes its own way, and men follow as best they can. The three kinds of inhabited landscapes in Argentina possess "distinct characteristics, which cause differences of character among the inhabitants, growing out of the necessity of their adapting themselves to the physical conditions which surround them" (3). Thus if the country is favored by nature, this does not necessarily favor the settlers. The northern forests evoke superlatives but no personal enthusiasm; covering "a space whose extent would seem incredible if there could be any marvel too great for the colossal types of Nature in America," it is from the human perspective "an impenetrable mass of boughs" (3).

It may appear from all this that Sarmiento was but a reluctant inhabitant of the New World, yearning for the civilization of European cities. But while he does generally identify civilization with Europe and sees no need for the cultural independence Emerson declared in "The American Scholar," Sarmiento complicates the simple contrast we are accustomed to drawing between the Americanism of the United States and the European orientation of Latin America and Canada. He would like to share Jefferson's vision of an American new day. He too sees its genesis still freshly imprinted on the New World landscape, and the potential for new beginnings. The southern plain is a "smooth, velvet-like surface unbounded and unbroken . . . It is the image of the sea upon the land; the earth as it appears upon the map—the earth yet waiting for the command to bring forth every herb yielding seed after its kind" (3–4). But the command is always problematical, and thus far in Argentine history it has been the wrong command, bringing forth the dragon's seed.

The unhappy state of Argentina is certainly not all to be blamed on the land. If in some parts of the country nature defeats men's best efforts, in other parts it is men who use nature badly. Sarmiento points for instance to the neglect of a major natural resource, the navigable rivers; "these immense canals excavated by the careful hand of Nature" are treated only as obstacles to be forded by "the sons of the Spanish adventurers" who think themselves unmanned when unhorsed (4). So while he takes a dim view of the recalcitrant Argentine landscape, he is as critical of Argentinians who have failed to make the best—or even some good—of it. The fault, in the case of the rivers, is not only theirs but in them: "The instinct of the sailor, which the Saxon colonists of the north possess in so high a degree, was not bestowed upon the Spaniard. Another spirit is needed to stir these arteries in which a nation's life-blood now lies stagnant" (5). Sarmiento is saying here explicitly, and his own sense of the country as a physical entity expresses implicitly, that his America has not achieved the fusion of the American incarnation. Although he is incapable of the fused vision reflected in Jefferson's description of the Blue Ridge, he still regrets the lack of fusion. And what he misses is not the promise of safe arrival in an ultimate harbor, but the inborn tendency to sail that would pump the national life-blood through the continental rivers and bring life at once to nation and continent.

The Argentine Sarmiento associated this tendency with Saxon blood. But there were Saxons, too, who apparently lacked it. In the Introduction I identified the spirit incarnate in America as the Protestant soul, but America and the Protestant ideology did not fuse automatically: Canadians, equally as Saxon as the citizens of the United States, seem nonetheless to have viewed their landscape much as the Catholic Argentinians did theirs. Margaret Atwood, in *Survival*, summarizes an extensive criticism of Canadian literature and culture as shaped above all by terror of the vast wilderness, toward which the stance of explorer, settler, and poet alike was to try to survive. Northrop Frye, in his "Conclusion" to the *Literary History of Canada*, observes in the Canadian literary tradition "a tone of deep terror in regard to nature . . . not a terror of the dangers or discomforts or even the mysteries of nature, but a terror of the soul." He explains this terror as the expression of a "garrison mentality" reflecting the harsh conditions of Canadian settlement—the isolation of small communities "confronted with a huge, unthinking, menacing, and formidable physical setting"

(830). In that setting, what Frye has called "the famous Canadian problem of identity" (*The Bush Garden*, i) emerged as a profound sense of inadequacy in the face of an overwhelming nature. D. G. Jones, invoking Frye's metaphor to describe Canada as "a garrison culture confronting a hostile wilderness" (*Butterfly on Rock*, 5), finds the central theme of Canadian writing to be "a sense of exile, of being estranged from the land and divided within oneself" (*Butterfly on Rock*, 5). Atwood, Frye, and Jones celebrate the hard-won insights of an "imaginative legacy of dignity and of high courage" (*Literary History of Canada*, 849). Jones, indeed, absolves Canadians of any special timidity, claiming that their anxiety about the wilderness reflects the pervasive attitude of western culture generally. Still, the consensus among Canadian historians and critics seems to be that the representation of nature in nineteenth- and twentieth-century writings, as something to be overcome lest it destroy a mostly terrified trespasser, bespeaks a failure to rise to the American occasion, a failure, in a word, to Americanize— as did the Americans just to the south.

This consensus is unremittingly self-accusatory. Atwood shrugs that Canada is simply not "a self-respecting nation" (*Survival*, 14), and in this too she represents the majority. Indeed the self-reproach in Canadian scholarship is astonishing, especially to an American critic; and it all seems to come to the same conclusion: that for not having identified with its land, Canada has no identity at all; it remains a colony of England and to a lesser degree of France, a stunted child thrust unwillingly from its home and aghast at the amplitude and potency of the New World. Marcia Kline, in a comparative study of Canada and the United States, hardly exaggerates the general condemnation of the former (and the way it tends to imply a surprising acceptance of the myth of the latter) when she sums things up this way:

> Thus the Canadians, rejecting the New World environment, opted for an instrumentality that fostered their dependence on the parent civilization—thereby opening the floodgates to terror when they did have to meet the wild and the natural. But the Americans, cutting themselves loose from civilization so that they could be "born free" as de Tocqueville said it, went happily into their New World, defending them-

35

selves from the terror with the construct of Nature's Nation. (*Beyond the Land Itself*, 59)

When one turns to the writings that have inspired such opprobrium, the situation is not as extreme as reported, but what the critics object to becomes clearer. Susanna Moodie's *Roughing It in the Bush* (1852) was one of the first full-length accounts of English settlement in Canada. In the end, it is true, Moodie counsels against coming, so that a comparison of her book with a work like Caroline Kirkland's description of frontier Michigan, *A New Home—Who'll Follow?* (1839), would bear out the contrast between Canadian and American attitudes. But *Roughing It in the Bush* also opens with a description of the landscape of the St. Lawrence River valley that is fully as optimistic as Jefferson's of his Appalachian pass (and uses much the same language). Moodie is here still aboard the ship that has brought her to Canada, and sees the New World essentially for the first time:

> The previous day had been dark and stormy; and a heavy fog had concealed the mountain chain, which forms the stupendous background to this sublime view, entirely from our sight. As the clouds rolled away from their gray, bald brows, and cast into denser shadow the vast forest belt that girdled them round, they loomed out like mighty giants—Titans of the earth, in all their rugged and awful beauty—a thrill of wonder and delight pervaded my mind. The spectacle floated dimly on my sight—my eyes were blinded with tears—blinded with the excess of beauty. I turned to the right and to the left, I looked up and down the glorious river; never had I beheld so many striking objects blended into one mighty whole! Nature had lavished all her noblest features in producing that enchanting scene. (6)

Like Jefferson, Moodie insists on the uniqueness of the landscape: "it was a scene unlike any I had ever beheld, and to which Britain contains no parallel" (7); the view down the St. Lawrence is "scarcely surpassed by anything in the world" (7). And she too chides the local inhabitants for having become jaded to the "astonishing beauty" of their surroundings. Nor does she omit the obligatory gazing at the horizon: "Your eye follows the long range of lofty mountains until their blue summits are blended and lost in the blue of the sky" (8). She is in every way buoyed by her first vision of America and by the encouraging sight of neat cottages, orchards, and farmhouses scattered on the slopes of the mountains. Struck by a fellow passenger's whimsical comparison of the white houses on the hillside to clothes hung out to dry, she says, "I could scarcely convince myself that the white patches scattered so thickly over the opposite shore could be the dwellings of a busy, lively population" (9).

After Moodie lands and travels inland into the bush, things change drastically, and she is beset almost beyond endurance by both natural and human enemies. But rather than any unwillingness to engage these or any failure of nerve, what defeats her ultimately, I think, is something already latent in the logic of her initial enthusiasm. This logic differs in important ways from Jefferson's. For all its "stupendous" sublimity, the Blue Ridge view could never blind Jefferson. His sight seems rather (paradoxically) to illuminate the view, to bring it into visible focus. He chooses the best position from which to see it, scans it, reflects upon it, boasts of it, and interprets it into a story that ends with him, drawing a circle of which he is at once center and encompassing circumference. The signs of "a war between rivers and mountains, which must have shaken the earth itself to its center" (*Notes*, 143), as his eye gathers them, thereby center on him, so that he becomes not only an observer but an observation point, a place of mutuality between the eye and the object of sight. The "I" in the scene is enormously impressed but not overwhelmed, rather enlarged by the largeness of the vista. Moodie is precisely overwhelmed by the power of the scenery, which almost renders her its object or even its captive, pervading her mind, enchanting her, astonishing her, and in its culminating effect, blinding her.

Moodie's language is highly derivative, and being "blinded with the excess of beauty" is a Romantic cliché. Still, she might as conventionally have been transported out of herself and thus, like Jefferson, entered the scene she now only witnesses. We need to take into account also, in making the comparison, the real differences between their two positions: Jefferson's as an established man, a landowner and powerful political figure, and Moodie's as an arriving immigrant woman who is in fact the outsider she sees herself to be.[2] But if Jefferson's objective position is the reverse of Moodie's, his stance implies a different organization altogether, not the other term of her dichotomy but its resolution. In brief, for Moodie vision is dialectic and thus at best it reconciles, while for Jefferson it unites by revealing a prior unity. The observer calling up the view and then projecting himself into it on the road to Fredericktown, as a "you" universalizing Jefferson's presumed "I," the rivers that rush together and split the mountain only to pass into the plain (whose "true contrast" to the mountainous landscape, instead of separating them, invites the observer to pass from one to the other), the precipices overhanging the road that follows the natural terrain to town, these are the components of a resolution that has turned every opposition into a complement.

Moodie's "I" is only personal, and defines itself, at its limits, through its engagement of others: other people, the landscape, the unknown. Both writers describe views, but only Moodie raises the problem of sight. The St. Lawrence landscape, like that of the Blue Ridge Mountains, may seem to extend into infinity, but Moodie sees it only to the extent of her capacity to see. The scene is first concealed by fog, then blurred by her tears, and finally, in the far distance, "lost in the blue of the sky." For Jefferson, the horizon is where the eye composes itself, his vision being coterminal with the view, and coinfinite.

To see oneself in categorical opposition to the world does not automatically imply one will suffer at the world's hands. But as an ideology, Susanna Moodie's understanding of her relation to the St. Lawrence valley is at least open to the contemplation of defeat. Indeed, her ideology lends defeat a poetic rightness, renders it *aesthetically* likely. The reader is not surprised when her reveries on the sublime landscape are suddenly interrupted by the appearance of her husband and the boat's captain, who announce "No bread . . . you must be content to starve a little longer. Provision ship not in till four o'clock" (9). She greets "these unwelcome tidings" with a "look of blank disappointment" that prefigures coming hard times. But in formal terms, as figures in the narrative, lack of bread and blankness juxtaposed to spiritual elation not only point a moral but organize the story. In a story structured by a dichotomy of self and world, they provide an expected, or at least a satisfying, symmetry. Thus the formal logic of the scene not only permits disappointment but, having permitted it, almost suggests it. A few moments later, Moodie is asked if she wants to go ashore. When she answers enthusiastically, "Oh, by all means, I long to see the lovely island. It looks a perfect paradise at this distance," we have the sense that, as a writer, she may even welcome (that in the act of writing it, she does welcome) the retort that foretells the hardship of her real-life enterprise. "Don't be too sanguine, Mrs. Moodie," the captain says, "many things look well at a distance which are bad enough when near" (9). And so they would prove to be, very bad indeed.

Susanna Moodie's problems, then, begin not in the bush but when she lands in Canada. They arise at the point of origin, in the formulation of the origin, which is for her not a discovery (or for that matter an invention) but a stage in an ongoing battle that no one finally wins. Margaret Atwood cites a short story that she says gives "a very Canadian version of the discovery of America." In this story,

> Columbus is hardly a triumphant discoverer of a new continent. Because he has somehow got his times mixed up and has arrived too late, he is forced to work as a sideshow freak, giving a recital each night of the horrors of the voyage and collapsing each time in a cold sweat of terror. His memories of his life in Spain are of tortures and dearths, his life in the present is haunted (understandably) by a feeling of utter placelessness; he has discovered nothing and understands nothing except that it has all somehow gone hideously wrong. (*Survival*, 117–118)

This account of the discovery as if according to Beckett makes the central point I would derive from both the Argentinian and the Canadian comparisons. What modern Canadians feel ashamed of in their past and what Sarmiento earlier castigated in his countrymen is at bottom the same thing: their refusal to enter into their situation and be at one with it, their sense instead of wandering a meaningless but deadly landscape, their nostalgia for past connections while they lament their present alienation—their failure to identify themselves not only with, but through America.

My interest here is not in this judgment itself but in its cat-

39

egories, which apply specifically to life on these continents, and not elsewhere. I suspect that if Canadians compared themselves to the French or the English, they would appear (to themselves) much less lacking and possibly even sophisticated about the ambiguities and contradictions of nationality and of nationalism. The American way of being an American, however, persuasive if only because it has produced so powerful a country, implies the inadequacy of other ways, or more precisely, in the terms I set forth in the Introduction, their incompleteness. Terrifying or terrified, the Argentine and the Canadian are homeless, placeless, bodyless individualists who, by comparison with individualists who have assumed each one the whole of his world, do indeed appear fragmented and lost.

The American incarnation was an international event. "America" completed the bourgeois revolution in the eyes of Europeans as well, and came to mean essentially the same thing everywhere (though hardly anywhere valued the same). In other words, Columbus discovered a new world for the inhabitants of the old as well as for immigrants to the new. Tocqueville viewed the American continent in Jefferson's terms, not in Sarmiento's. *Democracy in America* (1835) opens with an account of the Exterior Form of North America, which, like Jefferson's description of the Blue Ridge genesis, projects an inherently meaningful landscape. Over all North America, "A sort of methodical order seems to have regulated the separation of land and water, mountains and valleys. A simple but grand arrangement is discoverable amid the confusion of objects and the prodigious variety of scenes" (18). Bearing this out, the book's geographical first chapter, for all its mappings and measurements, is really a story, the story of God's creation of "a magnificent dwelling-place," a home fit for gods, or for Americans: "those coasts, so admirably adapted for commerce and industry; those wide and deep rivers; that inexhaustible valley of the Mississippi; the whole continent, in short, seemed prepared to be the abode of a great nation yet unborn" (26).

Taking geography as the point of departure for his work, Tocqueville emphasizes his sense that it is America's point of departure as well. Only the last paragraph of his first chapter names the book's subject, which was not nameable as an abstraction. (Continental precedence is the first American symbol: leaving the anxiety of allegorical interpretation behind with the historical dialectic, it derives the meaning of the American nation directly from God's earth.) Place is not everything, perhaps, but before it, there was nothing: "In that land the great experiment of the attempt to construct society upon a new basis was to be made by civilized man; and it was there, for the first time, that theories hitherto unknown, or deemed impracticable, were to exhibit a spectacle for which the world had not been prepared by the history of the past" (26). The spectacle envisaged here is of a kind with the view from the Blue Ridge Mountains; the road to Fredericktown "happened" also to lead to the new society.

The idea of the American incarnation seems to resolve prior conceptual problems so well, to be such a happy ideological discovery, that I should perhaps say at once that it also presents difficulties. I indicated something of this earlier in speaking of the development in America of a new kind of literary tragedy that explored incarnation's dark and blasphemous underside. The concept of discovery is at the origin of this development too. As if, when Columbus tried to sail around the earth, his prow had caught the edge of a sheet shrouding a great work of art and he had pulled the sheet off unaware, the discovery myth projects an America that is already art—the art of nature and nature's God, but only the more artlike for its all-creative authors, indeed in that way the apotheosis of art. In the twentieth century William Carlos Williams described "The Discovery of the Indies" in just these terms, as an uncovering of preexisting meaning and form:

> The New World, existing in those times beyond the sphere of all things known to history, lay in the fifteenth century as the middle of the desert or the sea lies now and must lie forever, marked with its own dark life which goes on to an immaculate fulfillment in which we have no part. But now, with the maritime successes of that period, the western land could not guard its seclusion longer; a predestined and bitter

fruit existing, perversely, before the white flower of its birth, it was laid bare by the miraculous first voyage . . .   (*In the American Grain*, 7)

The land that bears fruit before flowers has its story complete before it is written, and its writers have only to give that story voice. Rhetorically the image of America as a work of art is familiar: Whitman said it directly, the United States are the poem; and for him the idea both inspired and enabled the writing of poems that took the national Poem as their theme. But for writing fiction, as we will see, that conception was deeply problematical, and ultimately seemed to forbid narratives that would reinterpret the ur-narrative, casting them as blasphemy. And by the same logic as alternative fictions, real-life political alternatives were also rendered either unimaginable or catastrophically subversive.

2 ✳ The Mammoth Land

Some ideas work only as assumptions—that is, once made explicit or identified as ideas, they lose their potency. They may remain interesting, and even attractive, but with the possibility of choosing whether or not to think them, we become fatally skeptical. Doubt may well confirm faith, but analysis transforms it into a conception that even ultimate persuasion cannot change back into the simple truth; and the ideas I refer to define truths, such as the truth that God made the world or that life has a purpose. Immersed in these truths like Prufrock among the mermaids, we drown when voices wake us—or the truths evaporate.

"America" is such an idea. Denunciations of the reality of life in America as a travesty of the idea, or even the idea itself as a travesty, need not impair the idea's capacity to organize the world for those who continue to believe. Indeed, the idea can even continue, as the converse of belief, to organize the thinking of those who abjure it. But just agreeing to consider the definition of America as wholly a matter of interpretation would invalidate that definition for the patriot as for the critic. In the syllogisms of American life, America is the universal axiom.

It seems appropriate, therefore, to demonstrate the existence of the idea of incarnation—the idea that the ethos of liberal individualism inheres in the American continent—first in a set

43

of texts in which it is only implicit, and not, as it might be in philosophical or imaginative writings, also consciously debated. These are texts whose stance is objective, texts that purport to tell the truth, to report facts, to describe.[1] Even the most objective description, of course, is informed by its writer's outlook, but that is just the point. The outlook one gleans from writing that intends only to report is the ground of perception. If the idea of America involves the sense that the continent, the American place, is specially constituted, this will be expressed in accounts of it as a place. A classic example of such accounts is Jefferson's *Notes on the State of Virginia*, from which I have already discussed the description of the Blue Ridge mountain pass.

Jefferson began with almost aggressive objectivity. Writing in response to a questionnaire submitted to the Continental Congress by the French legation late in 1780, he set to work at once to answer the first Query for "An exact description of the limits and boundaries of the State of Virginia." The *Notes* begin, "Virginia is bounded on the East by the Atlantic; on the North by . . ." The French clearly had requested the information as a basis for reevaluating their support for the then flailing Revolution. The factual opening implicitly acknowledges the problem and inspires trust by its thorough responsiveness. At the same time, one would expect Jefferson to show Virginia in the best possible light, by stressing the qualities that make her viable and a valuable ally.

He marshals abundant proof of exceptionally rich agricultural and extractive resources, of a stable political system, and generally of a yet untapped potential. At first coolly reasonable, his statistical rigor grows impassioned—but not because he has risen from fact gathering to political pleading. On the contrary, he has sunk below facts, to the contemplation of a deeper level of what he takes to be America's nature—the level at which America is precisely *not* in the process of becoming viable or valuable because it has been what it is, as a natural given, all along.

The change occurs in the response to Query VI, "A Notice of the mines and other subterraneous riches; its trees, plants, fruits, etc." Up to now and again later, most of the responses, including the description of "the present state of manufactures, commerce, interior and exterior trade," take, in the published version, only two to three pages of straightforward exposition. The account of the state constitution runs to twenty only because it reproduces the text. The answer to Query VI is fifty pages long. This imbalance can be explained partly by the great interest of the question, natural resources being still the main attraction of the colonies, and the more so in the South where they were particularly abundant and the colonial population itself, unlike that of the Northeast, more interested in extraction than in subsistence farming.[2] But, in fact, few of the fifty pages are given over to either mining or agriculture; most of the section celebrates a nature that is pre-Columbian and in places even primeval.

Jefferson begins soberly enough with ores and minerals. Fourteen pages take him through gold, lead, iron, various kinds of stones, a catalog of trees and plants, and a summary of common crops and average yields, all of which evoke remarkably little enthusiasm. Much of this information he simply lists. Neither lead nor copper mines occupy him long, though he reports casually having heard of several that are unusually rich. Nor does he stress the abundance of coal in west Virginia, merely mentioning in passing that it is sufficient "to have induced an opinion that the whole tract between the Laurel mountain, Mississippi, and Ohio, yields coal" (152). He is matter-of-fact about cornucopia gardens of "muskmelons, water melons, tomatas, okra, pomegranates, figs, and the esculent plants of Europe," and abundant orchards of "apples, pears, cherries, quinces, peaches, nectarines, apricots, almonds, and plums" (165). He casts a sidelong glance on the careful cultivation of "potatoes, both the long and the round, turnips, carrots, parsneps, pumpkins, and ground nuts" (164). Farming generally receives only perfunctory treatment from the man who lent his name to the belief that laboring in the soil is the most valuable way of life. The physiocrat François Quesnay, reputed author of the French questionnaire, must have been disappointed by Jefferson's attitude if not by his brevity.

Suddenly, however, in the next paragraph, the subject comes up of "our quadrupeds" as they have been described by Linnaeus and Buffon, and the *Notes* come to life. The account of the quadrupeds, which in this context might have been expected to mean primarily cows, horses, mules, and pigs, begins instead, in an

45

unperceived shift of organizational principles from use to inherent character, with "the largest." And in a second more important alteration, the scene changes from the colonizing present to the prehistoric past. Jefferson has discovered, he says, that the large four-legged animal the Indians call the "big buffalo" is actually the primeval mammoth. Extinct everywhere else in the world, the mammoth is alive and well in America. Offering detailed evidence to refute the belittling claim of some European naturalists that the extant remains are those of large elephants, he rebukes those who persist in confusing mammoths and elephants despite the Creator's pains to differentiate them. But if the skeptical refuse to be persuaded that the mammoth still roams the New World, "it is certain such a one has existed in America, and that it has been the largest of all terrestrial beings" (169). Anxiously calculating the military odds, the French legation in Philadelphia probably awaited other reassurance.

But Jefferson's defense of the continent's aboriginal fauna did find an interested French audience: chiefly a man with whom Jefferson had earlier debated American nature, Georges-Louis Leclerc de Buffon, the author of the first systematic natural history in the West, which began appearing in 1749 and became the central text of Enlightenment naturalism. It was to Buffon specifically that Jefferson referred in the *Notes* when he complained that the indubitable fact that the great mammoth had roamed the Americas

> should have sufficed to have rescued the earth it inhabited, and the atmosphere it breathed, from the imputation of impotence in the conception and nourishment of animal life on a large scale; to have stifled, in its birth, the opinion of a writer, the most learned, too, of all others in the science of animal history, that in the new world, "la nature vivante est beaucoup moins agissante, beaucoup moins forte": that nature is less active, less energetic on one side of the globe than she is on the other. (169)

For this was the insulting conclusion to which Buffon claimed his scientific researches led. On the basis of eyewitness reports and numerous samples, he had found that nature in the Americas was, to put it bluntly, degenerate. Under "a niggardly sky," an "un-prolific land" could sustain only a stunted natural life, inferior to the European in size, variety, and fecundity. This condition of diminished capacity, "the general contraction of animated Nature throughout the whole continent," prevailed all the way to the top of the natural order and was expressed in the primitive state of the native people, in their failure to establish a civilization at all comparable to the European or even to reproduce in adequate numbers. The latter failure, in fact, pointed to the root defect. Buffon had discovered that "in the savage, the organs of generation are small and feeble. He has no hair, no beard, no ardour for the female." Indifferent to procreation, the Indians were not much interested in other forms of creation either. "They have been refused the most precious spark of Nature's fire," and their culture is therefore cold and sterile (quoted in Chinard, "Human Habitat," 31).

Offended in his American pride, Jefferson took the occasion of the *Notes* to pen a polite but firm rebuttal. His research showed that the New World was, if anything, more fertile than the old. To be precise, it had spawned 100 species of animals to the old world's 126. And, he calculated, "the residue of the earth being double the extent of America, the exact proportion would have been but as 4 to 8" (182), which amounts to a fertility ratio of eight to five in America's favor. Moreover, the size and vigor of the native animal life had been misreported to Buffon by observers careless in their measurements and sloppy in their comparisons. Having arranged for the delivery of an elk—skin, skeleton, and antlers—to Paris, Jefferson tried to correct his colleague's errors. Drawing up three tables—one of aboriginals of both continents; the second of aboriginals of one only, of which there were more than three times as many American as European; and a third of animals that had been domesticated in both (eight in all compared to over a hundred of the wild)—Jefferson compared weights and sizes to justify, modestly, only "a suspension of opinion until we are better informed, and a suspicion in the mean time that there is no uniform difference in favor of either; which is all I pretend" (172).

Actually, he pretended more, especially about native fertility.

Buffon had argued that, because of the debilitating climate, not only the indigenous fauna but imported domestic animals were subject to degeneration. On this question Jefferson was relatively open-minded, trying to rebut but also sometimes conceding, and only suggesting that other nonnatural factors, like careless or inexperienced husbandry, were also present. But his defense of the native wildlife is unequivocal, most strikingly in exonerating the vigor and potency of the Indians, whose low birthrate he asserted was voluntary, whose hairlessness he attributed to assiduous plucking, and whose manly courage and sensitivity, "vivacity and activity of mind," he declared "equal to ours in the same situation" (185).

Not only were Indians the physical equals of whites but, it seems, their mental equals as well. Sexually as potent as any European, the Indians were verbally more potent than most. Jefferson went on to make an extraordinary statement: "I may challenge the whole orations of Demosthenes and Cicero, and of any more eminent orator, if Europe has furnished more eminent, to produce a single passage, superior to the speech of Logan, a Mingo chief, to Lord Dunmore, when governor of this state" (188). He could not have claimed more. Eloquence, the *locus classicus* for the expression of intellectual power, is here granted to an Indian in the same measure as the greatest ever possessed by white men in the highest moments of the golden age of their culture. It is difficult to see how Jefferson might reconcile this with colonizing an Indian America, let alone offer it as a vindication of white America.

Indeed, Buffon's denigration of the Indians, and of the wilderness, might seem a more useful premise for arguing the rectitude and likely success of the Revolutionary cause. Why was Jefferson so quick to take offense? Buffon had not impugned Jefferson's manhood, but only that of a native population whom Jefferson and his fellow colonizers, when they were not killing them outright, were energetically displacing. Buffon only offered the common rationale that the Indians were inherently inferior, since wild nature everywhere was degenerate. Surveying all the natural world for his *History*, Buffon shuddered when he looked at those deserted seashores, those sad regions where man has never lived, bristling with deep black forests . . . barkless and topless trees bent, broken, crumbling with age with even more others fallen to rot on already rotting heaps, and smother whatever seedlings would start to germinate. Nature, everywhere else shiningly youthful, appears here decrepit; and the earth . . . instead of blooming greenery, offers only cramped spaces crowded with ancient trees laden with parasitic growths, with lichens and mushrooms, the impure fruits of decay. (*Morceaux choisis*, 13; my translation)

Killing its seedlings and breeding decay and death, nature is here antithetical to fertility, which awaits man's intervention. Cultivation vivifies the earth, and plowing and mining transform the land into a landscape that blooms with farms and cities.

This vision, bespeaking man's natural franchise over nature and more particularly that of European civilization over any wilderness it encountered anywhere, was a commonplace of the age. Montesquieu's thesis about the relationship of climate and civilization (such that the most vigorous and creative cultures arose in the earth's temperate zones, where they were neither enervated by jungle heats nor numbed by cold) was just one familiar corollary of an omnibus rationale for modern imperialism. The question is why Jefferson not only did not espouse it, but took such pains to refute it.

The Abbé Raynal was notorious in America for summing up the arguments of Buffon and his fellow "degenerationists" that the Indians' comparative lack of artifacts and monuments, the depressing and inconvenient omnipresence of thick virgin forests, the shallow fertility of the soil, as well as the stunted character of the flora and fauna generally, were "so many tokens of a world that is still in its infancy" (quoted in Chinard, "Human Habitat," 36). Not everyone took this badly, it is true. J. Hector St. John de Crèvecoeur, the other well-known herald of American agrarianism, was so far from feeling insulted that he dedicated his *Letters from an American Farmer* (1782) to Raynal as one of the continent's staunchest friends. But significantly, unlike Jefferson's *Notes*, the *Letters* are almost entirely given over to descriptions of the domesticated landscape. Crèvecoeur glories in a fertility he has activated with his plow. His ideal land is already turned over and he does not feel at all diminished by pre-Columbian degeneracy; on the contrary, Crèvecoeur is gratified by the opportunity to measure his improvements. For him, American destiny manifests itself in the possibility of universal domestication. The very wasps on *his* land, which was cleared of trees as of Indians, had been trained to perform the useful service of plucking flies from the eyelids of his sleeping infants (*Letters,* 41). It was just as Buffon had envisioned, with the denizens of nature that were either threatening to man or useless exterminated, and the useful brought under his yoke.

But Crèvecoeur was an exception, who, it should be recalled, opposed the Revolution. Most of his American readers, like Jefferson, took personally Buffon's hostility to America's poisonous insects and reptiles and his contempt for Indians. Conversely, but still more surprisingly, when the Europeans praised their domestications and improvements, the Americans essentially denied that they had changed anything. This perversity was especially marked in relation to the American climate. As Montesquieu's focus on it indicates, a temperate climate was an important factor in the evaluation of a land's suitability for civilization, and the relatively extreme variations of the North American climate were an early disappointment. Since it was generally assumed that climate was a matter of latitude, Europeans had expected temperatures in North America to range between those of London (around Newfoundland), and those of the south of Spain (in Virginia). In fact, while summer temperatures were approximately commensurate, American winters were far more severe. Complicating this basic pattern was the "little ice age" of the sixteenth and seventeenth centuries, which made not only the winters particularly cold but the whole pattern erratic.[3] So if there was some disagreement over the fertility of the soil, the vigor of the natural life, and the perils of life in the wilderness, there was substantial agreement that the North American climate was a problem.

With the gradual end of the little ice age in the eighteenth century, conditions improved somewhat. Since this coincided with a significant degree of cultivation, the conclusion that cultivation was the cause seemed inescapable. In the *Notes* Jefferson reported that "a change in our climate . . . is taking place very sensibly. Both heats and colds are become much more moderate within the memory even of the middle-aged" (206–207), and explained this as most probably the result of the clearing of forest lands. In this respect at least, he seemed to be agreeing with such observers as Chasseboeuf de Volney, who proposed the converse of the Montesquieu law: not only did a moderate climate empower European civilization, but the latter had the power in turn to engender a more moderate climate. What was happening rapidly in America was the same thing that had happened in Europe over centuries. Of course, as far as America had yet arrived in the transition from wild to civilized, the change was not all to the good. More temperate, the climate also fluctuated more. Writing later than Buffon, Volney found American nature still immature. But like Raynal, Volney, who was a close friend of Jefferson's, expected all good things to come of the civilizing of America. Like a moody adolescent, the present uncomfortably erratic climate would improve with maturity.

If this seems to have satisfied Jefferson, it did not at all please Volney's translator, the novelist Charles Brockden Brown. He felt obliged in fact to suspend his translator's neutrality and append a long footnote to the account of the climate, first denying that it fluctuated as much as Volney claimed and then counterattacking. Volney had cited Montesquieu's thesis to explain the primitive state of pre-Columbian America. Brown was greatly surprised "that notions, so crude and so generally exploded, should be countenanced by our author" (*A View of the Soil*, 225n). In fact, he asserted, the contrary was more likely true. He had himself "often observed men working diligently in the field, in a heat of 87, and has himself walked five miles, in a dusty, shadeless road, at noon day, with a black beaver hat on his head, when the heat was 91, in the shade of an adjacent wood" (108n). If this tended to substantiate the tales of extreme heat, it also illustrated "the influence of constitution and bodily habit to enable the natives to support them" (225n). Montesquieu had had it backward; only "weak and effeminate forms" were discomposed by the weather, and these "a mild and serene climate is more likely to produce than a bleak and churlish one" (225n).

51

This is a defense, to be sure. But Brown, who has now conceded that the climate of Cape Cod is "bleak and churlish," and that at Lichfield, Connecticut, "at nine o'clock in a July morning, the writer's hand has literally been *burnt*, by laying it by chance on the tire of a cartwheel" (108n), seems not to notice that Volney had stipulated that these unfortunate conditions were rapidly changing. Brown claims no improvement, and seems in fact reluctant even to acknowledge it. Thus, at least with reference to what all considered a central issue in the habitability of the New World, the Europeans, who believed America to be naturally an inferior environment for the building of civilization, were certain it was improving. The Americans, in contrast, were skeptical of any change and not much excited by its possibility.

Not that the Americans were not concerned. Noah Webster's "Dissertation on the Supposed Change of Temperature in Modern Winters," first presented to the Connecticut Academy of Arts and Sciences in 1799, draws on years of research and debate. Webster approached the problem with characteristic energy. He would once and for all get at the truth of this "popular opinion that the temperature of the winter season, in northern latitudes, has suffered a material change, and become warmer in modern, than it was in ancient times" (119). (Sometimes couched only in terms of winter temperatures, this is the same issue as that of general moderation of climate.) Everyone he has consulted seems to believe it, "indeed I know not whether any person, in this age, has ever questioned the fact" (119), and the references he cites show that he searched everywhere for a doubter. But it is simply not true. Starting with biblical evidence, Webster pursues his investigation all the way to his own day, along the way refuting the gullible Jefferson, to conclude firmly that it would be "extremely unphilosophical to suppose any considerable change in the annual heat or cold of a particular country" (145).

Logically, Webster points out, "we have no reason to suppose that the inclination of the earth's axis to the plane of its orbit has ever varied: but strong evidence to the contrary. If this inclination has always been the same, it follows that the quantity of the solar rays, falling annually on a particular country, must have always been the same" (145). What *has* happened, to give rise to rumors of change in America, as in previous sites where civilization has been under construction, is that the clearing of the forests has caused greater vibrations of the temperature of the air, so that there are times in the winter when it is in fact warmer. *But* "so far is it from truth, that the clearing and cultivation of our country has moderated the rigor of our cold weather, that the cold of our winters, though less steady, has been most sensibly increased. There is not a greater amount of cold during the winter, but the cold at times is more severe than before our country was cleared" (147). At most, the change amounts to a redistribution of a set quantity that no civilization, not the most actively transforming, can ever affect. Jefferson and also Benjamin Rush had thought some alteration had occurred, but nothing very significant and certainly nothing to herald an altogether new moderation. Webster chided them even for such concessions.

Then, in 1806, Webster returned to the Academy to supplement his "Dissertation" with the fruits of further investigations into what he considered a crucial issue, namely "to ascertain, if possible, the real fact, whether the industry and improvements of men, by destroying forests and cultivating the earth, have occasioned a material alteration of climate" (*Dissertation*, 148). This became the definitive American position on the subject:

> From a careful comparison of these facts, it appears that the weather, in modern winters, is more inconstant, than when the earth was covered with wood, at the first settlement of Europeans in the country; that the warm weather of autumn extends further into the winter months, and the cold weather of winter and spring encroaches upon the summer; that the wind being more variable, snow is less permanent, and perhaps the same remark may be applicable to the ice of the rivers. These effects seem to result necessarily from the greater quantity of heat accumulated in the earth in summer, since the ground has been cleared of wood and exposed to the rays of the sun; and to the greater depth of frost in the earth in winter, by the exposure of its uncovered surface to the cold atmosphere. (162)

"But," he concluded, "we can hardly infer with perfect scientific pitch, from the facts that have yet been collected, that there is, in

53

modern times, an actual diminution of the aggregate amount of cold in winter, on either continent" (162).

Clearly, in the intervening years, his case had weakened. The real interest in its later, more cautious statement lies not in the case itself but in Webster's resistance to a conclusion that had come to seem more likely, and that would seem to have been a more useful stance for any American. By 1806 there was a strong argument to be made that Americans were transforming nature and literally building themselves a better new world. But far from so claiming, they were in fact inclined to fear the opposite, that they were making it worse. Jefferson himself was grumpy about the change in the climate, observing that if settlement was indeed responsible, it had only "produced an unfortunate fluctuation between heat and cold, in the spring of the year, which is very fatal to fruits" (*Notes*, 207). More seriously, these alterations seemed to be proving fatal also to men. "The first settlers received these countries from the hands of nature pure and healthy," Benjamin Rush told the American Philosophical Society, and "fevers soon followed their improvements" (quoted in Chinard, "Human Habitat," 46). These fevers resulted from the clearing of forests, which produced the fluctuating climate and let loose upon the land and its new inhabitants impure miasmas, the gaseous emanations of bogs and swamps, which had been contained and absorbed by the leafy cover.

To repair the damage, Rush did recommend "a higher degree of cultivation," such as "draining swamps, destroying weeds, burning brush and exhaling the unwholesome or superfluous moisture of the earth, by means of frequent crops of grains, grasses, and vegetables of all kinds" (quoted in Chinard, "Forestry," 454). But this by no means placed him in Buffon's camp. Whereas for Buffon nature was primordially diseased, for Rush it was initially "pure and healthy"; civilization's corruption was what a more enlightened cultivation, and, in fact, a stricter compliance to original natural ways, would have to overcome.

Rush delivered this paper in 1785. Endemic fevers had been too literally plaguing American settlers from the first landings. Their incidence was increasing, however, especially and most dangerously in urban areas. There would be an epidemic of yellow fever in 1793 in Philadelphia and another two years later in New York. These were cities comparable to those of Europe, and they were being ravaged by tropical diseases that, elsewhere in the colonial world, signaled the colonies' permanent dependency. European observers drew the obvious conclusions. "Autumnal intermittents [fevers] prevail in this country to a degree scarcely credible," lamented Volney, and together with the bilious yellow fever, he said, they rendered the New World an unlikely site for civilized living. This did not mean America should be abandoned, but it did point to the extreme youth of the American enterprise, which would take a long time yet to transform the climate into the congenial state it had achieved centuries since in Europe. For now, life in the New World was inordinately straitened by the need to defend against the wasting fevers, not to mention colds and tooth decay, whose frequency entitled them "to be considered as the direct offspring of the soil and climate" (*A View of the Soil*, 224–225).

Charles Brockden Brown, translating faithfully, could not, at this point, resist one brief comment. "An infinite proportion of the diseases which exist in the world," he had observed, "are owing to absurd modes and vicious habits." In America, one such absurdity was the way "the dress and diet of Europe are assiduously copied." And while it was owing to the climate that these were more injurious in America than in Europe, the climate was really only a secondary factor. "If the influence of evil moral and pernicious physical habits were subtracted from the causes of disease, the climate would be next to nothing" (225n).

The thrust of this argument appears more readily in the positive form in which Rush had already put it:

> Perhaps no climate or country is unhealthy where men acquire from experience, or tradition, the arts of accommodating themselves to it. Those inhabitants of Pennsylvania, who have acquired the arts of conforming to the changes and extremes of our weather, in dress, diet, and manners, escape most of those acute diseases which are occasioned by the sensible qualities of the air; and faithful enquiries and observations have proved that they attain to as great ages

as the same number in other countries. (Chinard, "Human Habitat," 46)

Common sense, but also a new sense, pointed still more sharply six years later in Webster's preface to a "Collection of Papers on the Subject of Bilious Fevers Prevalent in the United States for a Few Years Past":

> I am persuaded that the Americans may be convinced by *facts,* that even in our climate, Epidemic and Pestilential Maladies may be generated by local causes. If they can be convinced of this, that sources of disease and death may be found among themselves created by their own negligence, it is a great point gained; for until they learn this, they will . . . still wallow in filth, crowd their cities with low dirty houses and narrow streets; neglect the use of bathing and washing; and live like savages, devouring in hot seasons, undue quantities of animal food at their tables, and reeling home after midnight debauches.

The "improvements" that infected Rush's "pure and healthy" country, fresh from nature's hands, Webster identified as depraved urban ways copied from Europe *and* the Indians. The sources of America's plagues were (already full-blown in the eighteenth century) a trio of its most powerful nemeses: cities, the sins and excesses of Old World fleshpots, and dark-skinned "savages."

The healthy alternative is clear: life in an unpolluted countryside neither modeled on overcivilized Europe nor indulgent of the lower instinctual impulses that governed this continent's pre-Columbian inhabitants. Neither of these is the American way, which here is emerging with great precision as a harmonious coming-together.[4] Neither the continent nor the immigrants by themselves are American. This is the rationale for the insistence that settlement has not materially changed the land. An American land transformed by European civilization would be Europe's permanently dependent derivative. Instead, Jefferson, Webster, Rush, and Brown argued that settlement had only fulfilled an inherent potential. This argument had the obvious implication of justifying independence from the Old World. It had a still more important effect in enabling Americans to claim the New World in a new way.

As modern individualists—men with the power to make worlds who, because that power is universal, have no world that is permanently and inarguably theirs—Americans would find the stance of implementor actually more empowering than that of creator. As the creators of the New World, they would henceforth be vulnerable to political challenge and to the erosions of the historical process. For a man-made world is always open to question. The settler's implementation of the continent's permanent contours and conditions, in contrast, vivifying the land from inside in the way Thoreau called "mining," places the emerging social structures beyond debate, in the realm of nature. Those who assist the emergence of those structures, moreover, wield the power of nature itself.

In the terms used by John Stilgoe in his study of the forms of continental domestication, America might be said to have come into being already a "common landscape," that is, as land shaped by a common sense (Stilgoe, *Common Landscape*, x). It was never "the [prior] chaos from which landscapes are created"; but neither did it ever become exactly, or only, "shaped land, land modified for permanent human occupation" (3). Perhaps it was more nearly land modified *by* permanent human occupation, but that description leaves out the crucial factor of the land's own agency. In Jefferson's vision of the genesis of the Blue Ridge landscape, the land is the agent of its own transformation; and in Webster's and Rush's accounts, it is a participant ignored or countered at one's peril. Again I should qualify, however, for the American landscape was not the product of interaction, but of mutual fulfillment. In contrast to Keith Thomas's *Man and the Natural World* (1983), which is about English conceptions of nature, one would not entitle chapters in a book about American conceptions of nature "Civilization or Wilderness?" or "Conquest or Conservation?" In a book about America, the *or*s would be *and*s.

As they refused to claim the remaking of the continent, so American writers tended not to see cultivation as particularly problematical. For instance, William Bartram, second-generation naturalist and conservationist, happily envisioned the complete domestication of a scene he had just apotheosized as nature's wild essence:

57

This vast plain, together with the forest contiguous to it, in possession and under the culture of industrious planters and mechanics, would in a little time exhibit other scenes than it does at present, delightful as it is; for by the arts of agriculture and commerce, almost every desirable thing in life might be produced and made plentiful here, and thereby establish a rich, populous, and delightful region; [he then lists the crops and animals that might be raised so plentifully and easily on this land, which] lying contiguous to one of the most beautiful and navigable rivers in the world . . . is most conveniently situated for the West India trade, and the commerce of all the world. (*Travels of William Bartram*, 199)

When this vision is juxtaposed to one with the same content projected by the Abbé Raynal, foremost "degenerationist," the difference between the American and the European views is dramatic. Raynal's is, so to speak, a song of the Re-Creation, an intended paean to his American friends, who had unfortunately taken his earlier accounts of their infantile world as slurs. He still could not deny that at the dawn of European settlement, all in the New World was chaos and confusion. "But man appeared," he rejoiced, "and immediately changed the face of North America."

He introduced symmetry by the assistance of all the instruments of the arts. The impenetrable woods were instantly cleared, and made room for commodious dwellings. The wild beasts were driven away, and stock of domestic animals supplied their place while thorns and briars made way for rich harvests. The waters forsook part of their domain, and were drained off into the interior part of the land, or into the sea by deep canals. The coasts were covered with towns, and the bays with ships; and thus the new world, like the old became subject to man. (Chinard, "Human Habitat," 36–37)

There are few such heroics in American accounts, and the reason is clear in Raynal's next sentence: "What powerful engines have raised that wonderful structure of European industry and polity?" Bartram does not understand the coming of civilization as Europeanization, but instead as the fulfillment of an inherent American character. The replacement of wilderness by agriculture, or even by a commerce that vaguely implies urbanization, is so without violence or event that it seems just the result of a more penetrating perception. Bartram looks once and sees the jungle marshes of Georgia's wetlands, looks twice and sees fields and markets, as if they had grown there, hardly even planted. And as the first stage metamorphoses into the second, so the foreground extends, again without overcoming obstacles or crossing boundaries, toward an infinite global horizon. Bartram envisages as little conflict in America's expansion as in her settling, neither, for him, having to do with external limits but only with a kind of potential that melds inner and outer, landscape and land, soul and body.

The concept is that of Jefferson's road to Fredericktown, of a nature that is not only, as in European Natural Law philosophies, the prior setting of an individual's birth, whereby he is gifted with rights and attributes that are prior to (and beyond) societal definition, but also itself socially informed; so that natural man in America lives in a natural society. Hence, as I suggested in the Introduction, not in society but in a civilization that is the human dimension of nature.

In Bartram's vision and in the earlier texts, the identity of land and landscape, of America and the continent, the incarnation of the idea of the former in the body of the latter, has achieved a fundamental reconciliation. It is true, as we will see in later chapters, that natural man and natural (rather than historical) society can also confront each other catastrophically. But these confrontations are divisive in proportion to the accord that can be derived from the identity of all three aspects of America: the land, the people, and the society. This identity, moreover, was as much social and political as philosophical or metaphysical. Incarnation reconciled not only man and nature but man and man. The world Bartram envisioned that day in the Georgia swamp would not only emerge free of inherent opposition but remain so. In short, the accord of nature and civilization implied as well an internally homogeneous society: without original conflict there need be no later conflict, and different classes, religious groups, nationalities, and even races can come together on the basis of a more profound sameness. The ground upon which American political pluralism rests is the continent itself.

This aspect also of the incarnation was fully articulated in the eighteenth century, best among others by Benjamin Franklin, who in his role as America's first advocate of machines (of technology, commerce, and cities), appealed to nature and nature's God as readily as did his agrarian counterparts, thus demonstrating the broader resonance of the concept of nature. Conceptually, Franklin's urban artisan is as much a man of the American soil as Jefferson's yeoman. I would suggest that the opposition between them has been overstated. If Jefferson defended the nature of the New World because he saw it as incarnating the national spirit and ideology, Franklin did the obverse, defending American ideology by appealing to nature.

In a remarkable letter written in 1753, Franklin laid out a model of American politics whose crux was a uniquely unoppositional relationship between the emerging society and its natural environment. The theme of the letter, addressed to an English correspondent, Richard Jackson, is the need of new social orders to establish an encompassing legitimacy. Franklin sees this issue arising in two guises: first and most urgently in the growing threat of German immigrants to dominate Philadelphia's life and culture, and secondly, as an ongoing problem of getting people to work hard in a nonauthoritarian society. To exclude the Germans from equal political participation and to force the poor to work, Franklin finds himself having to argue not only the benefits but the justice of inequality. At first he seems to be repeating an old argument, that hierarchy is simply the way of God and nature.

But as he elaborates this ancient opportunism, he develops a radically new argument for it, and resolves a potential contradiction in Natural Law philosophy. The problem is how to ensure social stability and preserve the existing order without impinging on individual rights. The possibility that the social and the personal will conflict arises unavoidably when basic human rights are established in nature, outside of society. Since, being naturally endowed, the individual cannot and must not be forced to abandon his ontological freedom, he must be persuaded to cooperate voluntarily. This he does, in fact, because it is in his interest. Social contracts are expedient. Rousseau assumed "that men have reached a point [some time in their history] at which the obstacles that endanger their preservation in the state of nature overcome by their resistance the forces which each individual can exert with a view to maintaining himself in that state. Then this primitive condition can no longer subsist, and the human race would perish unless it changed its mode of existence" (*Social Contract*, 17). The human race therefore makes the change of its own free will, which is thus affirmed even in the acceptance of limits.

Franklin invokes this vision, a set piece of enlightenment political philosophy, to come to a radically different conclusion: "I am apt to imagine that close societies, subsisting by labour and art, arose first not from choice but from necessity, when numbers, being driven by war from their hunting grounds, and prevented by seas, or by other nations, from obtaining other hunting grounds, were crowded together into some narrow territories, which without labour could not afford them food" ("Letter," 137). Though Rousseau described a necessity, the certainty of death unless a different way were adopted, his point was to demonstrate human power to choose; Franklin's account opposes necessity and choice to prove the latter *not* a primary power: "first not from choice but from necessity." In the spirit of this syntax, the whole passage stresses prohibitions. For Rousseau, the response to necessity remained existentially a choice; Franklin implies that even choice is necessity: "as matters now stand with us, care and industry seem absolutely necessary to our well-being" (137).

When he immediately goes on to advocate the establishment of workhouses to employ the idle poor as a warning to others that they had better "work voluntarily . . . rather than run the risk of being obliged to work at the pleasure of others for a bare subsistence, and that too under confinement" (138), he has reversed the political logic of Natural Law doctrines, which seek to limit societal authority. He transforms the right to choose into an instrument of state control: the poor will work voluntarily so that the state does not need to make them work.

On closer inspection, however, the contrast between Rousseau's and Franklin's views is less philosophical than ideological. Both posit the individual's natural autonomy, but they have opposite views on how to implement it. Rousseau sought a way of freeing the individual from a society to which he had basic objections, while Franklin, on the contrary, wanted to confirm a social order he fully endorsed—hence Rousseau's emphasis on the dependence of all political systems on the consent of their constituencies, and Franklin's insistence that this consent was an absolute necessity.

The difference is one of historical context. In America, in contrast to France, it was not individual autonomy that seemed endangered, but, in the middle of the eighteenth century, a newly established government with only delegated authority. White English middle-class rule rested rather obviously on the power of the rulers, and, in its growing numbers and wealth, the German middle class was challenging that power. Franklin thus needed an argument that depended neither on relative power, in population or in property, nor on Rousseauean or Lockean liberal principles, since these could also imply a transfer of authority to the more numerous Germans. The argument he constructed devolved neither from old rejected notions of the right of the mighty nor, really, from the new democratic postulates.

It begins by acknowledging the democratic case for German rule. German and English immigrants differ considerably in their economic behavior, the former working even harder when, as in America, they are better rewarded, while the latter react by sloughing off. Since "the English are the offspring of the Germans," and "the climate they live in is much of the same temperature," there is "nothing in nature that should create this difference" (134). Therefore it must have a social origin, and Franklin proposes that this source is the unlike constitutions under which the two groups previously lived. "I have sometimes doubted whether the laws peculiar to England, which *compel the rich to maintain the poor,* have not given the latter a dependence, that very much lessens the care of providing against the wants of old age" (134). Note that the argument has shifted, from examining the growing challenge to the English middle class from its German counterpart, to debating the relations of rich and poor. But Franklin had not forgotten the first issue and would return to it much better able to deal with it for the detour.

The first step of the detour brought him from a historical explanation to a natural one, or rather it revealed the historical to be more profoundly natural. That the Germans and the English differ not in nature but in history actually points to a natural law based on the culminatingly transcendent fact of mortality. Thus progressed, Franklin has now entered the realm of universal necessity, and he speculates that it is the "order of God and Nature" itself that "has appointed want and misery as the proper punishments for, and cautions against, as well as necessary consequences of, idleness and extravagance." And, he warns, "whenever we attempt to amend the scheme of Providence, and to interfere with the government of the world, we had need be very circumspect, lest we do more harm than good" (135).

The quixotic "laws peculiar to England," which made the rich support the poor, are here juxtaposed to "the government of the world," not to mention "the scheme of Providence," and handily outweighed. But this is only an interim stage in Franklin's argument, which means to establish the legitimacy of the rich (the propertied) and ultimately of the English on other and in fact surer ground than the divine will. He goes on to illustrate with a short fable his warning about meddling with cosmic orders:

> In New England they once thought *blackbirds* useless, and mischievous to the corn. They made efforts to destroy them. The consequence was, the blackbirds were diminished; but a kind of worm, which devoured their grass, and which the blackbirds used to feed on, increased prodigiously; then, finding their loss in grass much greater than their saving in corn, they wished again for their blackbirds. (135)

If the ecology those impulsive New Englanders destroyed was originally the scheme of Providence, it is now, like Milton's representation of God's plan for mankind, separated from the Creator and become the responsibility of its enactors. In transferring his political principles from history to nature, Franklin retained free will; only it no longer implied the freedom to transform society.

The blackbird ideology is a natural social order: not just in harmony with nature but *of* nature, as natural man prior to and beyond his social contracts is of nature. And this implies the same thing about society as about the individual: its basic rights and the laws of its being are as inalienable as his. Thus established as not only in but *of* nature, white, male, middle-class English rule could not be more powerfully legitimated. It is in these terms, by citing their different relations to Philadelphia not as a political or economic entity but as a place, that Franklin then justifies the denial of its rule to the politically and economically more entitled Germans. He is entirely open about the politics of the matter, and urges "Measures of great Temper" (139) to divert the "Stream of [German] Importation" lest they "soon so outnumber us, that all the advantages we have, will not in my Opinion be able to preserve our Language, and even our Government will become precarious" (140). He can be thus explicit because, as he presents the case, it is not English rule of Philadelphia he defends, but Philadelphia itself. When that city was threatened by French invasion, he recalls, the German inhabitants refused to arm themselves, "at the same time abusing the Philadelphians for fitting out Privateers against the Enemy, and representing the Trouble, Hazard, and Expense of defending the Province, as a greater Inconvenience than any that might be expected from a change of Government" (141). For "Philadelphians," of course, one should read "English," and therein lies Franklin's argument. Incarnate in its very soil, "Philadelphia" is not an English colony or any other political entity, but Franklin's whole world. The Germans do not see it as a world, but only as a colony, a place they are in but *not* of. It is therefore not of them, and therefore not theirs.

Though the issue of political legitimacy as among European colonizers was especially delicate, it had a precedent that Franklin could not ignore. For if the English had a better right to Philadelphia than the Germans because they identified more with it as a place, then the Indians, who were there and of it first, would seem to have had the strongest claim. To argue that they had, on the contrary, no claim at all, Franklin refines his thesis to specify kinds of identification and possession that, still naturally, deed the land to some and not to others. Again, he begins with a historical-cultural distinction. Although "they are not deficient in natural understanding," the Indians differ in important ways from whites and (exercising their universal natural right as men to choose) "have never shown any inclination to change their manner of life for ours, or to learn any of our arts" (136). The primary difference between the two manners of life is that one involves hard work while the other emulates the lilies. In a word, the Indians are lazy. Fully supporting the principle that all men are created equal, Franklin does not impugn the Indians' innate nature. (Interestingly, he does not make the racist argument.) The unhappy fact is that all men are lazy, and one need look no further for proof that the white race and the red are equal in this respect than the eagerness with which white persons who, upon being captured by Indians, embraced their "manner of life" to the extent of refusing to be ransomed; while Indians in the same situation virtually never wished to remain in the white world.

He concludes with an anecdote that is a companion to the parable of the blackbirds. He was once told of an instance "where the [white] person was brought home to possess a good estate; but, finding some care necessary to keep it together, he relinquished it to a younger brother, reserving to himself nothing but a gun and a matchcoat, with which he took his way again into the wilderness" (137). As some freely choose not to keep their estate, others take it by the same natural right. The natural tendency of men to be lazy and not to take possession of the land is the first premise in a syllogism that concludes with the natural right of white men to possess America.[5] More generally, this grounds the right to acquire and to own property in nature itself, which is thus no longer precontractual but, on the contrary, the very source of fine print.

This last provision, for the competitive acquisition of property, makes it clear that Franklin's natural society is of modern times, and, despite its concern for the maintenance of order, not, like its monarchic and aristocratic predecessors, statically hierarchical. The laws of the blackbird economy, which must themselves not be tampered with, nonetheless justify active, even confrontational social policies. As the parable of the renegade white man justified taking the land from the Indians, so the parable of the blackbirds elevates class domination, the exploitation of the lower class by the higher, into universal law. This is a point that is sometimes missed, as it was by one French scholar and admirer of Franklin who found the blackbird story a touching instance of scientific modesty on the part of one who was already then known in Europe as "a new Prometheus." But its abnegation of a Promethean stance had a different motive and meaning. For in rejecting the posture of nature's transformer, Franklin expressed an even greater ambition. He annexed all nature as it was, as Whitman would put it later, "without check, with original energy" ("Song of Myself," l. 13), whole and infinite, precisely in its immutability. Vico had imagined that lightning, terrifyingly, incomprehensibly alien, drove aboriginal men and women into caves, where they married and banded together into society to protect themselves against nature. Franklin's kite, seeking out and drawing down the lightning, is an opposite myth, invoking cosmic energies as the life-force of a natural civilization.

Franklin probing the sky and Thoreau, with his divining rod, the earth are emblematic figures that connect directly to this cosmic energy, which, to repeat, is as physical as it is spiritual. Indeed, in the writings I will consider next, this energy is mostly a matter of the body, actually generating food for Americans who have the sense, much as did Thoreau, that they plow, plant, and harvest as if they "mined" the land from within.

The theme of this chapter is well summed-up in the title of a farming manual written at the turn of the century and published posthumously in 1825: *Nature and Reason Harmonized in the Practice of Husbandry*. Its author, John Lorain, was interested mainly in the workings of fertilizers, and particularly lime, as his very first sentence urges, because "a sufficiency of lime to answer every purpose in the economy of plants and animals, exists in animated nature, and is intimately blended with all soils, whether they be calcareous, or otherwise." Where lime will not do, the farmer must use one or another kind of manure; and Lorain is severe with "the perpetual ploughers and croppers" who "seldom suffer the grounds to lie sufficiently long to be well covered by the slow but certain hand of nature, even with weeds" (185). Through the seventeenth and eighteenth centuries, such practices had exhausted large tracts of land, as settlers moved on, wasting resources they took to be infinite. Enlightened agriculturalists like Lorain were sharply critical of the common ways of farming, from first clearing to final abandonment. Turning forests into fields "by the destructive and truly inconsiderate and savage practice of burning," Lorain complained, destroyed in a day or two "by far the greater part of the animal and vegetable matter which nature had been accumulating for a great length of time." After a few undeservedly bountiful crops that used up the stockpiled fertility of centuries, "when they had worn out one piece they cleared another, without any concern to amend their Land" (335–336). The contemporary literature is full of such reproaches and of warnings that, as Cecelia Tichi has remarked, constitute a precocious conservationism. So in themselves, these manuals and homilies are readily explained, and their advice to be more careful of the soil and more responsive to its needs and rhythms is hardly peculiar to America. One of the most popular handbooks imported into New England was that of the Irish farmer Jethro Tull, inventor of a popular plow, who went so far in consulting nature that he argued against rotation of crops and aggressive fertilization on the grounds that nature did not practice it, and that forests seemed to do quite well by manuring themselves just with fallen leaves.

Still, Lorain's title does point to a characteristic American perception: that the first principle of good farming, which guides the application of fertilizers, the combining of crops, the proper feeding of livestock, is *harmony*—meaning, not just learning from nature in order to achieve civilization's goals, as Tull advocated, but the delivery of the land's own potential, which was identical with human goals. Indeed, the uncultivated land is governed by principles that are the equivalent of those which govern only the more advanced stages of human civilization. In his more primitive states, man is less rational, less civilized than the wilderness. Lorain inveighs against certain agricultural methods in just these terms:

> Hilling, ridging, and moulding up plants, must have originated in barbarism, or but few removes from it; like the practice of planting fruit trees as though they were fence posts. The latter practice, however, has been abandoned by enlightened cultivators, and the former will share the same fate, when nature and reason are harmonized in the practice of husbandry. Hilling, ridging, and moulding up plants have been the too general practice of the world from time im-

67

memorial. It is, however, as much opposed to reason and observation, as it is to the economy of nature, and these ought to govern all our agricultural pursuits.   (176)

In a similar vein, he urges "fermentation" as nature's superior way of fertilizing and chides heedless farmers: "We might . . . have long since seen the impropriety of the usual mode of cultivation, merely by walking through these parts of our woods which still remained well set with timber, and other native vegetation . . . We might likewise have seen that nature did not cut, rend, or mangle either the tops or the roots of the plants, and by this means debilitate, and procrastinate the growth of them" (129). In the wild, nature was a supreme cultivator, and was supremely cultivated. It is not surprising that Lorain, though he knew temperatures and seasons first hand as a farmer, scoffed like Rush and Webster at the notion that the climate might have recently moderated. Those who believed it had were taken in by the old folks boasting, as usual, of how much tougher things had been in their day. But nature was as nature had always been.

Jared Eliot's vision of the reclamation of a swamp, in contrast, is at first sight strikingly like Buffon's. Eliot was no ordinary tiller of the soil, but the son of a well-educated missionary and himself a clergyman and physician as well as a successful farmer. He had many friends in Europe, and it was to one of them that he wrote, as he is most frequently quoted, that the first settlers "began the world a New." The following passage does represent bringing virgin land under cultivation as a replay of Creation.

> Take a view of a Swamp in its original Estate, full of Bogs, overgrown with Flags, Brakes, poisonous Weeds and Vines, with other useful product, the genuine Offspring of stagnant Waters.
>
> Its miry Bottom, an Harbour to Turtles, Toads, Elfts, Snakes, and other creeping Verm'n. The baleful Thickets of Brambles, and the dreary Shades of Larger Growth; the Dwelling-Place of the Owl and the Bittern; a Portion of Foxès, and a Cage of every unclean and hateful Bird. Now take another Survey of the same Place, after the Labour of Clearing, Ditching, Dreining, Burning, and other needful Culture has passed it.

Behold it now cloathed with sweet verdant Grass, adorned with the lofty wide spreading well-set Indian-corn; the yellow Barley; the Silver coloured Flax; the ramping Hemp, beautified with fine Ranges of Cabbage; the delicious Melon, and the best of Turnips, all pleasing to the Eye, and many agreeable to the Taste; a wonderful Change this! and all brought about in a short Time; a Resemblance of Creation, as much as we, impotent Beings, can attain to, the happy Product of Skill and Industry. (*Essays upon Field Husbandry*, 96–97)

The lyricism of this elegy to the powers of cultivation is especially striking in contrast to Buffon's march-time invocation of wilderness clearing: "let us dry up these bogs, animate these dead waters by making them flow, transforming them into streams and canals; let's employ that active and devouring element which was hidden from us and which we owe only to ourselves (N.B.); let us set fire to this superfluous undergrowth, to these ancient forests that are already half consumed; let's finish off with steel that which the fire has not altogether consumed" (*Morceaux choisis*, 15–16). The "wonderful Change" heralded by Eliot requires no such ravage; the land is not raped, slashed, and burnt into useful fruition; it blossoms. Indeed, the passage from primeval slime to flowering garden is, in the telling, almost instantaneous, and the one sentence perfunctorily listing the actions that bring it about is not only abstract but without agent.

The difference between Eliot's and Buffon's views of creation must have been in part temperamental, but it was also conceptual. The relish with which the Frenchman imagines the wilderness falling to his axe and torch was sanctioned by the assumption that a wholesome new nature can emerge only when the old has been absolutely erased. Harrowing nature's underworld, Buffon is an angel of destruction; the creation represented by cultivation is an entirely separate and discontinuous procedure that comes later. Eliot, however, did not separate them so easily, as is evident from the fact that his attitude while actually witnessing the transformation of nature from wilderness to garden is even less aggressive than when he only imagined it. The near sight of desert and bog, instead of inspiring him to take charge of their reclamation, makes him reflective: "When I have travelled the Road, I have seen on one Hand large Sand Hills, where the small Spires of Grass struggled to rise an Inch in Height, and on the other side a gloomy Bog, that produced only Frogs and Reptiles, and have been at a Loss to know what Use they could be put to," which leads him not to plot their destruction but on the contrary to seek deeper, until he discovers the use they put themselves to: "a few Rods further hath convinced me, that the Rains which have washed the Sand of the Hill on the cole heavy Soil of the Bog, hath begun a fine Piece of English Meadow" (*Essays upon Field Husbandry*, 155–156).

In the earlier passage Eliot spoke of labor and culture as from a long distance, and yet he was describing activities he himself probably engaged in and certainly directed. But here natural evolution is an immediate and concrete reality; while the business of farming was a general abstraction called "Skill and Industry," nature's own process is precise and material. The formation of the meadow is a

> hint which Nature hath kindly given, full proof that Sand is a proper Dressing for low wet Ground: But the soil of the Bog will not always do for the Sand Hill, because when the Water which always kept it moist in its original State, is thoroughly drained off, it will then retain no more Moisture generally than the Sand itself. This Bog Soil, when it has lain in a Heap to ferment one Year, makes a good Manure for ploughed Lands that fall heavy, by keeping such Lands light, that the Roots of Vegetables will be able to range under Ground for their Food. (155–156)

From wilderness swamp to meadow to garden, an inherent dynamic, implemented by men who can take nature's hints, proves that "Nature hath not made any Thing in vain." Eliot insists on this, foretelling Lorain's strictures about lime and manures: "We should turn our Thoughts to the Melioration or mixing of Soils, and we shall then find that every Thing is good for some Thing" (155). In fact, Eliot assigned part of the credit for the propagation of fields and gardens to the wilderness itself, and much to the point, to bogs in particular. Thankfully, he supposed that "Peat may be found in all parts of the country, yea all over the World;

which is an Evidence of the Care, Wisdom and Goodness of Providence, in preserving as it were in Pickle, the Wood which grew before the Flood for our use, and that the Ruins of the old World should supply the Wants and Wastes of the present" (46). Providence probably cared for Europe, Asia, and Africa too, but the American "present" was the last come and therefore inheritor of all the preserved wealth and energies of the Old World. Hearing that seashells had been dug up high in the Appalachians, Benjamin Franklin exclaimed, with an heir's proper appreciation, "it is certainly the *wreck* of a world we live on!" (quoted in Eliot, *Essays upon Field Husbandry*, 221). The wreck deeded the new builders was an infinitely valuable stake they would mine forever.

Thus the difference between Eliot and Buffon was not merely that between a grateful beneficiary of the land's resources and a dyspeptic urban academician. Ireland's bogs were proverbial on both sides of the Atlantic, but an Irish farmer writing at about the same time, George Rye, could see no good at all coming from them. "A considerable Part of the Kingdom is render'd useless by the boggy marshes covering the Land which generally should be our Meadows and finest evenest Plains." Instead of continuities, Rye saw clear oppositions: nature had made bogs and it was men who would have to make meadows. And that activity more broadly involved the imposition of an orderly society. A bog was for Rye a "Harbour for Wolves and Tories," a corrupter of water when its putrid mud ran off into adjacent streams, and a refuge for thieves. The drainage of bogs was the responsibility of "private gentlemen on their Estates" who for "such laudable Actions" would deserve the high esteem of everyone. For thus, "in one Age, the great Fastnesses of all *Ireland* might be destroyed, and even the most barbarous Parts, yet not Amenable to the Law, and Civil Power, rendred habitable" (*Considerations on Agriculture*, 84–85).

This last passage points to the central difference between American and European attitudes to farming, a difference of conceptual structure.[6] For George Rye, the noxious effects of bogs are wolves, Tories, and thieves; they corrupt not only the community's water but its morals. In a parallel sense, Sam Pierson warned against "a neglect and disuse of the Plow by the *Tiller* and a Restriction from *Tillage* by the Landlord, because by bad Husbandry and ill Plowing, the Land is destroy'd, the Farmer beggar'd, and the Landlord not paid his Rent" (*The Present State*, 3). As the proper cultivation of the soil created civilization, so it was explicitly a moral activity on behalf of the good society. The terms are distinct and dialectical: cultivation (civilization) or the wilderness; the legitimate or the criminal. Jethro Tull saw the farmer beset not only by the weather and the land but also by "the Wickedness of Servants and Labourers," by "Hedgebreakers" and "Takers away of our Corn at Harvest" (*The New Horse-Houghing Husbandry*, xii). The ideal European farmer (as he came to be seen in the eighteenth century) is constantly engaged in confrontation with a wild and unproductive nature that both represents and foments social disorder.

Remarkably, no such dichotomy organizes the American agrarian concept. Jared Eliot thought primeval marshes were useless and even unclean, but he did not therefore cast cultivated land as their opposite, in the sense that it could and should be chosen and the marshes discarded. Rather, he imagined how the marshes might be developed to their own next stage of evolution, a process they engaged in of themselves at times, as in the making of English meadows. The ideal eighteenth-century American farmer, Jefferson's yeoman or Lorain's, was not, as was the English, Irish, or French farmer, the positive term of a dialectic; rather, the American farmer was the mediator of a complementarity, causing order to emerge out of chaos and civilization from the wilderness.

Moreover, as it has been frequently observed, "society" is not an explicit term in the American agrarian concept, but the implicit product of the virtuous relationship of each yeoman to his land. So that in this role, too, as civilizing settler, the American farmer was not confrontational in the way his European counterpart was, and, instead of imposing the values of the Christian middle class on the wilderness, he manifested them *in* it.

In draining swamps, then, the American farmer saw himself not so much as (re)claiming the landscape as implementing in it the natural harmony of the wild and the cultivated; cultivation here meaning development, nurturance. And this sense of himself as nature's agent, creating nature's kind of civilization by cultivating not a telos (which connotes a predetermined program) but an infinite entelechy, empowered him, as we saw earlier, far beyond his counterparts to the south and the north.

But there was a catch to this exaltation. When action is understood as implementation rather than as radical transformation, it ceases to be one's own. So that even as one is convinced that one can do anything, one has little sense of *doing;* and in return for universal permission and cosmic potency, one gives up agency. This exchange—essentially of one kind of power for another—is my recurrent subject in following chapters. For the ideology of implementation poses an ironic problem. Such an ideology works ideally so long as the object is to drain swamps, but it almost precludes *deciding not* to drain them. If the reigning consensus is that swamps are intended to be drained, he must drain them, or rise to global dissent in order to argue that they are intended not to be drained. In short, the conviction that farming brought reason and nature together (since man and nature had the same reasons), inspired cultivation as such and as already defined, but made it particularly difficult, in fact, contradictory to contemplate basic changes of agrarian policy.

On the other hand, one could argue that, from the standpoint of national survival and expansion—though, to be sure, not of all individuals and groups in the nation—it was precisely cultivation as such that was the major concern of the eighteenth century, or even of the nineteenth, rather than the capacity to project alternative forms. It is important to recall what we saw in relation to Franklin's stress not on the contractual nature of society but on its necessity: that achieving a country of its own all but reversed for the middle class in America the ideological problems of its European counterpart. In this context, the European agriculturalists' confrontational posture, and their assumption that farming is also involved in social conflict, arise from the same perception. Men farm as they live, and for George Rye and his colleagues that meant as individuals against the world. In America, however, men and their individualist civilization seemed of the land. Just as the wilderness was understood to be only a less desirable version of one integrated nature, and not its opposite term, so society also seems not so much divided between upholders and subverters of the laws as graded along a continuum: Franklin's poor were not

73

Tories or thieves but only lazier rich, with only the Germans, who were precisely *not* Americans, altogether outside the (new) world. Thus identity with America permitted an unprecedented pluralistic tolerance (of which the same Franklin who wanted the poor marched into workhouses was a foremost exponent). But certain reforms were as indefensible as the suggestion not to drain the swamps would have been—since in the same way as the Virginia mountain pass happened to decline into a road to Fredericktown, swamps already tended of themselves to fill in and become meadows. Identity with the continent, then, empowered both individual *and* society, imparting to the latter what it lacked at its most historically and politically powerful in Europe: the axiomatic force of physical law.

This concept of America, as a natural world animate with human purpose, was an extraordinary vision, projecting an individualism that, for being lord of its own global acres, was literally universal, at the heart of everything that happened everywhere, incarnate in the dynamic of bog-into-meadow, as in Dylan Thomas's "force that through the green fuse drives the flower." If it disclaimed the creation of its new world, this was because as the universal life-form (as well as force), the source of everything, it did not *do*, but much more potently, though with the catch that it could not really refuse to be as it was, it *was*.

Was: this means received and fulfilled. A wonderful culminating passage in John Spurrier's handbook *The Practical Farmer* (1793) celebrates the fertility of the land, precisely as an incarnation whereby the spirit of life is made flesh in the earth it animates to feed mankind, equally in the flesh.

> This globe of the earth that affords unto us the substance not only of ourselves, but of all creatures sublunary, is impregnated with a spirit most subtile and etherial, which the Original or Father of nature has placed in this world as the instrument of life, and motion of everything. The spirit is that which incessantly administers to every animal its generation, life, growth and motion; to every vegetable, its original and vegetation. It is a vehicle that carries with it the

sulphurious and saline parts, whereof the matter, substance, or body of all vegetables and animals are formed and composed. —It is the operator or workman that transmutes by its active heat, the sulphurious and saline parts of the earth or water into that variety of objects we daily behold or enjoy. It continually perspires through the pores of the earth, carrying with it the sulphurious and saline parts, the only treasure the farmer seeks for. (19–21)

The spirit that "perspires through the pores of the earth," bringing the farmer mineral fertilizers, emanates but remains immanent. The *Spiritus Mundi Americanus* built man a real world.

3 ✳ Necessary and Sufficient Acts

$\mathcal{J}$ ohn Spurrier dedicated *The Practical Farmer* (1793) to Thomas Jefferson. Thirty years later he might have inscribed it as well to Ralph Waldo Emerson. More accustomed to trace the New England path from Jonathan Edwards to Emerson, we might find it interesting to imagine him also descending that road from the Blue Ridge pass, and, anticipating Whitman, taking passage to more than Fredericktown.

For rather than trudging along a dirt road, even one leading like Jefferson's all the way to the horizon, Emerson is more often pictured in vertical levitation, or in his own words, "uplifted into infinite space." The sentence containing that phrase, however, opens with a dependent clause which is both a basic stipulation and a point of departure: "Standing on the bare ground,—my head bathed by the blithe air and uplifted into infinite space,—all mean egotism vanishes" (*Nature,* 10). Once he is projected into infinite space, moreover, what Emerson's unobstructed vision enables him to perceive is "the analogy that marries Matter and Mind" (26). The bare ground has not been left behind but itself lifted up. Emersonian Transcendentalism is the idealization not only of the philosopher but of his world, of nature along with man, of the mundane with the empyreal.

76

Such transcendence abstracts only to absorb, and discovers infinity inside the finite: rather than any withdrawal from engaging "the meal in the firkin; the milk in the pan" ("American Scholar," 69), it is an intensification of consciousness so powerful that the material universe dissolves into the observer's universal knowledge. (A knowledge that claims, beyond interpretation, to be simply vision.) By the same process, and creating its own complement, this universal knowledge renders its object infinite, so that by knowing the continent (in the supreme exegesis of the biblical sense of "knowing") the infinite spirit renders it infinite. In short, Emersonian Transcendentalism is the philosophy of the American incarnation, and its fulfillment in an unlimited individualism whereby the self transcends its mortal limits by taking total possession of an actual world.

Emerson thus completed the development of the modern concept of individualism, as I have discussed it in earlier chapters, by projecting an individual who possesses the world in his own image. To disencumber himself of the definitions of others, and to establish his own priority, the old-world ancestor of this individual had to distinguish between a prior natural being and a partly acquired, partly imposed social identity; to own himself wholly, he had to share the world with socially defined others and with their common past. However, in an America perceived as begun by each man anew, each man could representatively own the world *as* himself and as the image of a global autonomy that finally completed his revolution. Pursuing the logic of the discovery concept to its conclusion, by fully identifying the discovered continent with its discoverer, Emerson envisioned each individual discovering his own new world.

In retrospect, Jefferson's survey of the West Virginia landscape extended only part of the way to this horizon. Jefferson saw a meaningful landscape expressing inherent order and purpose and counted it a great privilege to be related to that landscape. He delighted in the land as in a magnificent opportunity or gift, or as a rich man might delight in his mansion, taking pride in it and feeling himself enhanced by it, while projecting, in its aggrandizement, his own as well. Franklin argued that the English but not the Germans were Philadelphians and Americans, because

77

only the English associated themselves with the place itself. More-over, Franklin's parable of the blackbirds derived political principle directly from nature so as to collapse categories that remained distinct in Europe: like Eliot, Rush, Webster, and Bartram, Franklin took "America" to be an exceptional entity that was at once, and necessarily, nation and continent. As Americans, these writers participated in this exceptionality; they guarded and imple-mented it.

But none of these spoke of their participation as a personal matter, that is, as defining their inner being. To be sure, they were entirely absorbed by the remarkable situation they inhabited and which they had a mandate to deserve and develop; but even those who believed themselves chosen to restore the kingdom of God in the New World defined their election instrumentally, as an external imperative. It was a mission, an "errand," which tested their personal worth, but it did not constitute *them*. Behavior was at issue, more than being. Rush harangued the good citizens of New York and Philadelphia to sweep their houses and bathe more often, and Franklin laid out a program of self-improvement that would enable his compatriots to seize the day, and also the title to America. But the self he improved was a mannequin even to its owner, who straightened its clothes and its ways because its progress was his most important product. So, all the while Words-worth was learning "to recognize/In nature and the language of the sense,/The anchor of my purest thoughts, the nurse,/The guide, the guardian of my heart, and soul/Of all my moral being" ("Tin-tern Abbey," ll. 106–111), American nature seemed to address rather a public than a private self. Perhaps Americans were at first too occupied with looking out to look in.

Emerson's great idea was that the power to act—not just to think, but to act—lay not in the individualist's hands but in his mind and soul, so that he would look out most effectively precisely by looking in. For Emerson was not less concerned with action than Franklin. Not unlike the indefatigable Poor Richard, "The true scholar grudges every opportunity of action past by, as a loss of power" ("American Scholar," 60). The important difference lies in the nature and locus of this power. For Franklin, it is a matter of competence and public strength possessed as a sort of personal commodity traded on the open market; but for Emerson it is rather a question of capacity (potential competence) and inner force that enables the individual to transcend the market, even as he corners it. This is the point he is making in "The Method of Nature" when he wishes that "each man should know himself for a necessary actor." Indeed, the very term "necessary actor" epitomizes Emerson's innovative understanding of the personal implications of the American fusion of continent and nation. In retrospect, it is the conclusion to which Jared Eliot's notion of the farmer's "needful Culture" clearly tends. From an activity in which farmer and land are externally in harmony, Emerson develops it into a mutual fulfillment of inner being:

> A link was wanting between two craving parts of nature, and [the necessary actor] was hurled into being as the bridge over that yawning need, the mediator betwixt two else unmarriageable facts. His two parents held each of them one of the wants, the union of foreign constitutions in him enables him to do gladly and gracefully what the assembled human race could not have sufficed to do. He knows his material; he applies himself to his work; he cannot read, or think, or look, but he unites the hitherto separated strands into a perfect cord.   ("Method of Nature," 123)

Not through any conscious manipulation—he neither reads nor thinks nor even looks—but simply by *being*, the necessary actor brings about something that is as inherent to the universe as his fulfilling power. The "perfect cord" he weaves out of "separated strands," like the orderly cosmos an enlightened understanding assembles out of the world others see as a "dull miscellany and lumber room," is already potential but cannot emerge without him. For his part, he exists, not through self-consciousness or a will to civilize—not through history—but as the world's active principle. He is unconscious of himself only for lack of an external perspective: he "knows" the universe and that way imparts meaning to it. He *is* the spirit incarnate in nature.

Thus arrived at its destination in Emerson's indwelling transcendentalism, however, liberal-individualist ideology abutted on a new contradiction. Emerson signaled this contradiction himself in the oddly violent description of the necessary actor's ostensibly reconciling birth. "Hurled into being as the bridge over that yawning need," he invokes unity and harmony less than he does Milton's description of the cosmic disjunction when Satan was "Hurl'd headlong flaming from th' Ethereal Sky . . . To bottomless Perdition" (*Paradise Lost*, I. 45–47) out of the oneness of Creation into the gulf of infamy that he would bridge by building Hell. Emerson's passage ends with the knitting of the "perfect cord," and although this image too has a paradoxical resonance (recalling the Fates weaving a determinism that encompasses them as well), it does assert an ultimate oneness. Nonetheless, the darkness, the rebellion and evil generally thought to be missing from Emerson's vision of things, might be seen implied in the violence with which the instrument of order and unity goes to his task. Indeed, with the same power, he could separate as readily as knit: in the image of the necessary actor bridging a yawning gulf, Emerson represents and simultaneously suppresses a potential unbridgeable, unresolvable opposition. Beyond Milton's arch-rebel, who was only the highest angel, Emerson's definition of man would permit an American poet to imagine a rebel God.

To prevent this, such Miltonic palliatives as the doctrine of the fortunate fall (offering the ultimate bribe for staying loyal) or the ambiguous concession of a free will based on not knowing what God knew, were inadequate, and Emerson, in effect, proposed sterner measures. Going back to a founding theology therefore more appropriate to America, he proposed an Augustinian solution: as we will see later in more detail, in Emerson's world there is only one positive presence, that of man at one with nature and the world. There is no alternative, but only a more or less complete realization of the one. The "other"—Satan, evil, or just another way—is thus cast as the absence of this "one," not a substantial negative but a negation. In his formulation, the fact that America was not only a historical entity but a physical place was crucial: the assertion that there was the "Me" and the "not-Me," natural and unnatural, America and not-America, was literally carved in stone.

America and the American thus incarnated the good (the affirmative and confirming), while the evil, the rebellious, was definitively *dis*embodied.[1] Emerson's Augustinian solution exonerated and preserved individual omnipotence as earlier Augustine had preserved divine omnipotence—by positing that no other power had positive existence. This proposition, earlier applied to God, was the more radical where the all-encompassing term was man, since, in relation to God, man had always been at least a subsidiary, if not a second term. When man is God, however, monotheism achieves absolute hegemony. The all-encompassing man encompasses God as well, and overcomes the opposition between subject and object by absorbing the object whole.

In so doing, this man-God represented a unique development in Western thought, a stable, indeed a permanent, ontological unity. The nineteenth-century Hegelian dialectic interprets dynamically a dualism that Judeo-Christians trace back to the radical schism of the Fall. Thus, there is a general sense that this dualism, while inescapable, is also in a sense aberrant—that the ideal state is unity. For, while it drives history's motor, the Hegelian dialectic is also, conventionally, the philosophical source of the radical instability of the middle-class world, and of its cosmic anxiety. In a world divided by antagonistic contradictions, equilibrium is stasis, but growth entails inevitable destruction, not just decay but an aggressive undoing. One appeal of pastoral ideologies in modern times has been their substitution, for this never-ending entropy, of a cyclical system in whose embrace even life and death are ultimately reconciled. Seeking such reconciliation in the future rather than in the past, Marx himself imagined a utopian culmination of social history in which the dialectic would be reconciled.[2] One tends to forget that Emerson and Marx were contemporaries reacting to the same nineteenth-century conditions. Yet the central motive of both their inquiries is to solve the paradox of capitalist progress which created poverty and wealth simultaneously—poverty of spirit and material wealth, poverty for many and wealth for a few. However, while Marx assumed that any resolution would have to redistribute scarce resources, Emerson envisioned a continental abundance whose infinite stores could give to the rich without taking from the poor. This amplitude encompassed all dualities, which were therefore not contradictory. The "polarity that ranges [every trifle] instantly on an eternal law" no more implies contradiction than the left hand implies a contradictory right. The American incarnation fused continent and civilization, nation and citizen, man and nature to constitute a universe where oppositions amounted to different versions each of which was the other's cathartic, so that their difference was itself transmuted into "necessary" means to the emergence of the single and unchanging truth. Internalizing the American incarnation, Emerson had achieved its double potential: to empower the individual fully, and to repair in him the old crack in his world.

The peculiarity of the Emersonian "dialectic" has been widely remarked, setting the terms for later analyses. Stephen Whicher wondered in *Freedom and Fate* (1953) at the oddly fluid character of Emerson's dualities, with their tendency to flow together or come apart without event: "[Emerson's] was a baffling monistic dualism or a dualistic monism . . ." (31). Though Whicher did not pursue the matter, focusing on the content of Emerson's oppositions rather than on their formal relations, what he had seen was fundamental: that transcendental dualism was characterized by a relationship between the opposite terms such that, at a deeper or higher level, they are revealed to be really complementary. Their opposition has been a delusion, a misapprehension born of incomplete knowledge. Thus in the "necessary actor" passage, the "two craving parts of nature" align themselves as opposites by craving each other. They are a pair, as are the "foreign constitutions" that parent the actor, and even the "unmarriageable facts": all of them are "wants" that want each other. As for the "separated strands," immediately identified as "strands" and thus part of the whole "perfect cord," they represent division even more constructively, as a pluralistic dualism whose parts add up to a total of One and then merge into Totality. The paradox that Whicher called "monistic dualism" is that the separate and opposite parts of Emerson's world actually fulfill themselves, in themselves, by coming together. They are reconciled entire and without self-contradiction.

Whicher had an excellent reason for not staying long with the subject of the formal oddity of Emersonian dualism, namely that, despite an easily available reconciliation, Emerson himself dwells on the dualistic state. "Ever the dualist," Kenneth Marc Harris calls Emerson; Harris also does not question the nature of this pervasive structure, apparently taking it as unproblematical (*Carlyle and Emerson*, 146). It is doubly problematical, however, first in its complementarity, which distinguishes it crucially from its European antecedent, and then in its pervasiveness when it would seem, for not representing any historical dynamic but only a transitory perception of nature, unproductive. If, in other words, an implicit transcendent unity makes Emerson's dichotomies matters only of form, why does he use the form so consistently, so insistently? For while the terms of his dualities are perfectly complementary in their substance, rhetorically they are as opposed as if no reconciliation were in sight. In "The Method of Nature," for instance, Emerson sets out the basic dichotomy of language and its mute objects: "Here about us coils forever the ancient enigma, so old and so unutterable. Behold! there is the sun, and the rain, and the rocks: the old sun, the old stones. How easy were it to describe all this fitly; yet no work can pass. Nature is a mute, and man, her articulate speaking brother, lo! he also is a mute" (129). The relation between language and the world that is its object is not contradictory: nature is not necessarily unutterable, not defined, that is, by its unutterability. On the contrary, it awaits expression as fulfillment. It should be easy to describe nature, it will be easy, it just is not yet done. Then why not directly affirm the coming fulfillment, why dwell on what is only a stage of things, when this stage differs from the next only in being incomplete? The answer lies in the next sentence: "Yet when Genius arrives, its speech is like a river; it has no straining to describe, more than there is straining in nature to exist." Not that the arrival of Genius actually changes anything, since it only articulates what already existed; there was no real opposition between language and object before, and neither has had to change for them to coexist now. And as Emerson goes on, it is clear that Genius does not add anything to the equation but simply transcends dichotomy into an encompassing unity: "Genius . . . advertises us that it flows out of a deeper source than the foregoing silence, that it knows so deeply and speaks so musically, because it is itself a mutation of the thing it describes. It is sun and moon and wave and fire in music, as astronomy is thought and harmony in masses of matter" (129). Matter is thus not transformed but described by thought, and Genius does not create. But what it does do is reveal to us unknown dimensions, which, though they were there all along, we could not know without the activity of Genius. This is the crucial thing: ironically, or rather, paradoxically, if we had already solved the enigma of nature, we could not know we had solved it.

Emerson develops and dwells on the merely formal dualities of incomplete transcendence because although merely formal they are nonetheless the necessary ground for the activity of Genius— for activity in general. In other words, it is the dualistic stage of transcendence, the dualism Whicher observed in Emerson's monism, that permits action. And while the Emersonian man need not (in later chapters we will see that, more important, he *must* not) *produce* his world in the sense of defining and forming it, he does need to *re*produce it—to continue and expand it. This he can do only when he and the world are in their formally dualistic stage. For the transcendental state is beyond activity, beyond—this is its one contradiction—the means of its own realization and fulfillment.

On the other hand, the activity that is made possible by a rhetorical, nonantagonistic dualism is extraordinarily energetic. Unlike its dualism, the vital energy of the "necessary actor" passage is not merely rhetorical: Emerson's sense of uniquely destined individuals hurled into being (hurling themselves into being) to do deeds that the assembled human race could not do is richly substantial. The deeds Emerson envisions are real deeds, of expansion and conquest, of industrial production and growth: they are deeds of social and national reproduction, building roads to the horizon. That the world's apparent conflicts, as between the good and the bad or the rich and the poor, can be readily transcended, is a conviction that frees the builders for pure activity. By believing that his acts enact the universal purpose, the Emersonian actor feels free, not only from the tax of ethical or political considerations, but free to invoke all the powers that be, to his and nature's end. He views his power as literally infinite and himself as not merely a force in the universe but the embodiment of the universal force. Emerson imagines him a conduit for the divine current: "his health and greatness consist in his being the channel through which heaven flows to earth." This seems to set a moral imperative: to be healthy and great a man *should* be a channel for heaven's flow to earth. In a parallel sentence in the same essay, the ethical stance is even more pronounced: "His health and erectness consist in the fidelity with which he transmits influences from the vast and universal to the point on which his genius can act." But the moral thesis of both statements is tautological, stating that if a man is a conduit for universal power and greatness he will be powerful and great. The real argument in these sentences is not about morality but about power. It asserts that the power of the entire universe can flow into an individual; and that he is then all-powerful by virtue of being an instrumental incarnation of the All-Powerful, he "whom the stalwart Fate brought forth to unite his ragged sides, to shoot the gulf, to reconcile the irreconcilable" (124–125).

Let me repeat that this last phrase, "to reconcile the irreconcilable," does not imply a Hegelian dialectic. The necessary actor reconciles simply by perceiving the oneness of the irreconcilable, by finding its unity already there in himself, and interchangeably, in the universe. To put it another way, the self and the universe are dichotomous in Emerson's conception as one's self and one's consciousness are dichotomous in the allegory of self-consciousness. Perceiving oneself as if from the outside, one is nevertheless of course *one* self. So Emerson's individual agent of heavenly unity brings the "irreconcilable" and the "unmarriageable facts" together, not through the *process* of historical action, but by the *agency* of his consciousness. The happy future that Emersonian idealists envision will emerge of itself from itself. It requires neither good deeds nor a revolution.

There is a negative side to all this enabling, the side denied by what I have called Emerson's Augustinian solution. For the necessary actor is a paradoxical being whose willful intervention either to hasten the future's advent or, worse still, to redefine it, can only distort the perfect order that already exists implicitly, and thus delay its explicit realization. Not only are deeds and revolutions not needed, they are forbidden, doomed to failure and worse, along with all "manipular attempts to realize the world of thought" ("Experience," 492). And because Emerson's sense of

85

transcendent oneness is absolute, this is an absolute prohibition, enforced by an absolute penalty: the wages of opposing the existing structure of things—since if it exists it must comport to nature's design—are death. (Such opposition would in fact create an antagonistic dualism.) I shall say more about this prohibition later, as it emerges in the writings of Hawthorne and Melville; let us consider first the positive or, more precisely, the enabling implications of conceiving oneself an agent of nature—not a natural man dialectically engaged with society as Rousseau imagined, but, in an essentially prophetic mode, the voice and hand of nature molding the clay of history to its own pattern.

Being nature's agent implies that the individual embodies activity itself—he is not only the worker but the work. If modern individualism increasingly identified men as what they did and understood, identity not as being but as becoming, Emerson's individual and his world are entirely composed of doing and becoming:

> All is nascent, infant. When we are dizzied with the arithmetic of the savant toiling to compute the length of [Nature's] line, the return of her curve, we are steadied by the perception that a great deal is doing; that all seems just begun; remote aims are in active accomplishment. We can point nowhere to anything final; but tendency appears on all hands: planet, system, constellation, total nature is growing like a field of maize in July; is becoming somewhat else; is in rapid metamorphosis. The embryo does not more strive to be man, than yonder blur of light we call a nebula tends to be a ring, a comet, a globe, and parent of new stars.   ("The Method of Nature," 121)

This incandescent and characteristic passage renders both the philosophy and the psychology of the necessary actor; and it also makes the crucial distinction—crucial for an understanding of the ideological power of the idea of the American incarnation—between innovative action and reproductive enactment. Everything here is in a state of becoming, developing, unfolding, emerging, growing; all the earth's mass has been transmuted into the energy of life. But it is not becoming "somewhat else," it is becoming more itself: the embryo evolving into man, and the nebula into "a ring, a

86

comet, a globe, and parent of new stars." It is precisely because things are becoming themselves and *not* changing that they can be all nascent, doing, tendency. With its pattern already sketched out, their becoming can be all execution, and, since the individual and his world have one common tendency, their friction-free progress can be all movement, so that all three, the ground, the road, and the traveler, flow ever onward together.

The individual self who carries the universal tendency dwarfs the most aspiring European hero. Not even Hegel's "great men in history whose own particular purposes contain the substantial task which is the will of the world spirit," ("The Philosophy of History," 17) could so transcend the limits of interaction. In fact Hegel's example of a great man was Julius Caesar, whom he saw fulfilling the will of the world spirit through a dialectical contradiction: if he brought Rome to its "necessary destination . . . in the history of the world" (17), he did it almost inadvertently, through "the execution of his purely negative, defensive purpose" (17). Hegel's Caesar thus differs from Emerson's necessary actor crucially by his negativity; for even when the necessary actor "cannot read or think or look," he "knows his material" and performs his task, if unconsciously, still positively. And while Emerson certainly knew that the world had its negative aspects, he argued that even these had a directly positive effect: poverty, for instance, made one work harder. And the work resulting from poverty is immediately positive. Not so Caesar's action, which arrives at its positive outcome only dialectically, having had, on the way, to transform its antithetical negativity, the defense of one man's power, into the positive synthesis of "monocratic rule."

Even Nietzsche's Dionysian might envy Emerson's ability to harness cosmic energy, as Emerson envisions merging with it in the ultimate embrace of total vision: "I am nothing; I see all; the currents of the Universal Being circulate through me; I am part or particle of God" (*Nature*, 10). For Nietzsche, who once named Emerson as the single man he admired fully, the utmost fusion with the unfathomable chaos of Reality still entailed some inevitable loss: of personal identity, of reason or reasons, of control. There was always some contradiction to be overcome, which tithed the cosmic potency transmitted, so that it fell short of the total force of the World Spirit or of Reality. Even in the most world-defying heroism, there was some persistence of costly contradiction, because of which a man, doing his all, still could not do All.

Not that Emerson meant that an individual could do all in practice. But the theoretical differences between the following two passages have important practical implications. The first is from *Sartor Resartus*, the work Carlyle called his "New England book," and features Carlyle's Tailor in full flight of inspiration:

> Be no longer a Chaos, but a World, or even Worldkin. Produce! Produce! Were it but the pitifullest infinitesimal fraction of a Product, produce it, in God's name! 'Tis the utmost thou hast in thee: out with it, then. Up, up! Whatsoever thy hand findeth to do, do it with thy whole might. Work while it is called Today; for the Night cometh, wherein no man can work. (148–149)

Now Emerson, calling his compatriots forth to what he and Carlyle apparently took to be the same task:

> Build, therefore, your own world. As fast as you conform your life to the pure idea in your mind, that will unfold its great proportions. A correspondent revolution in things will attend the influx of the spirit. So fast will disagreeable appearances, swine, spiders, snakes, pests, mad-houses, prisons, enemies, vanish; they are temporary and shall be no more seen. The sordor and filths of nature, the sun shall dry up, and the wind exhale. As when the summer comes from the south, the snow-banks melt, and the face of the earth becomes green before it, so shall the advancing spirit create its ornaments along its path, and carry with it the beauty it visits, and the song which enchants it; it shall draw beautiful faces, warm hearts, wise discourse, and heoic acts, around its way, until evil is no more seen. The kingdom of man over nature . . . he shall enter without more wonder than the blind man feels who is gradually restored to perfect sight. (*Nature*, 48–49)

But it was not at all the same task. Emerson's building amounts to production only in the strictest Latinate sense, meaning a leading forth of what already exists, and not in Carlyle's interpretation, in which it signifies making something new. Emerson's revolution is really a revelation. And this difference implies another, between Carlyle's vision of exalted but limited potency, aggressive but finite, and Emerson's idea of truly Godlike and infinite power through which he acts simply by being, never needing to do.

This then is the extraordinary paradox of the necessary actor who carries out nature's purpose. The world he builds according to the pure idea in his mind is already fully formed in the inarticulate mind of nature. Strictly speaking, he *en*acts. From one perspective, this describes a diminished power, or a lesser creativity. But from another perspective, since the world is still new, at least in the New World, Emerson's is the more active or activating conception. In the sentence "a man should know himself for a *necessary* actor," when one italicizes necessary, one retroactively italicizes *should* as well. It is a double imperative. *Because* a man enacts destiny, he *must* do it; he must cosmically, demonically violate his cosmic, divine identity. Pleased to observe that the road to Fredericktown traced out the landscape's natural contours, Jefferson saw affirmed his conviction that the national destiny was inherent in the continent. With Emerson, that conviction achieved its full potential by projecting outward to a vision of the entire universe and inward to a universal definition of self. And if the function of ideology is to inspire and enable action, and also to stabilize—so that a certain social system may both expand and retain its basic form—it is difficult to imagine a more effective ideology than this one, as it was simultaneously personalized and generalized by the concept of the necessary actor.

Thus in *Nature*, Emerson culminatingly idealized the ideology of liberal individualism. From a historically limited thesis, it became a truth whose universality was manifest in its reconciliation of history and nature, and of the ideal and the material. This is the explicit argument of the "Commodity" section of the essay, which, in treating the material world of social, political, and economic commerce, sets the policy of refusing to distinguish between the real and the metaphoric, or the physical and the ideal (12–13). All of nature's "goods" will be considered together: those which "support" man—"beasts, fire, water, stones and corn"—and those which "delight" man, "this zodiac of lights, this tent of dropping clouds, this striped coat of climates, this four-fold year."

"Commodity" makes it especially clear that *Nature* is not an argument for abandoning the world. On the contrary, the assertion that nature is a material commodity enables Emerson to absorb the category of commodity, of commerce and trade, into the world of the transcendent. The notion that the life of the spirit trades in use-values, just as does the marketplace, renders nature itself a sort of commercial enterprise, and establishes enterprise as part of the natural, the cosmic, the divine. To the ambient materialism of middle-class life, this entrepreneurial spirit dictates not the abandonment of commerce but commerce in better goods. With commodity idealized, the entrepreneurial order becomes the only one imaginable; commodity transcendent transcends argument—such as whether nature *should* be traded in. For it was a commodity before any merchant ever thought to trade upon it, a potential "use" before anyone actually used it. "Commodity" is in full a basic category of the universe: "Whoever considers the final cause of the world will discern a multitude of uses that enter as parts into that result." The only question is how to use it well; that it *be* used is a universal necessity, and by that the more inevitably a human one as well: "A man is fed," the section ends, "not that he may be fed, but that he may work." This "man" is the necessary actor, with the necessary actor's peculiar symbiotic mission: a man at work in the fields of nature realizes nature's status as all-commodity and his own as all-user; instrumental to a universal purpose that includes him, he fulfills his own universality along with nature's.

On the other hand, although the commodity of nature is entirely intended for man's use, it is not thereby the less self-defined. It is a resource rather than a raw material, differing markedly, for instance, from Buffon's nature. Recall Buffon's passionate invocation of man transforming—razing, cutting, burning, draining, ploughing, paving—the earth, and compare it to this from the "Commodity" section of *Nature:*

> All the parts [of nature] incessantly work into each other's hands for the profit of man. The wind sows the seed; the sun evaporates the sea; the wind blows the vapor to the field; the ice, on the other side of the plant, condenses rain on this; the rain feeds the plant; the plant feeds the animal; and thus the endless circulations of the divine charity nourish man.

Again, it is all for man but not by him. This symbiosis, moreover, is universal, for Emerson makes little distinction between man's relation to agriculture and to industry: "The useful arts are *reproductions* or new combinations by the wit of man, of the same natural benefactors" (emphasis added). And what follows is an excellent representation of furiously energetic activity that is nonetheless all enactment:

> [Man] no longer waits for favoring gales, but by means of steam, he realizes the fable of Aeolus's bag, and carries the two and thirty winds in the boiler of his boat. To diminish friction, he paves the road with iron bars, and, mounting a coach with a ship-load of men, animals, and merchandise behind him, he darts through the country, from town to town, like an eagle or a swallow through the air.

However his contemporaries felt, Emerson does not seem to have viewed the railroad as an engine of nature's devastation. On the contrary, a man on a train has the natural capacity of eagles and swallows. A technology that reproduces nature is precisely the necessary actor's catalyst, enabling a kind of change that is really the blossoming of more and better of the same. So this is how, for Emerson, "the face of the world has changed" through the "aid" of the steam engine and the railroad:

> The private poor man hath cities, ships, canals, bridges, built for him. He goes to the post-office, and the human race run on his errands; to the book-shop, and the human race read and write of all that happens, for him; to the court-house, and nations repair his wrongs. He sets his house upon the road, and the human race go forth every morning, and shovel out the snow, and cut a path for him.

Not the agent but the recipient of progress, this "private poor man" has entered into the modern world as into a larger, better-equipped apartment. So far is Emerson from casting him into the role of creator of his modern world, that here, at the end of "Commodity," he pictures the individual as an essentially passive consumer. Yet he insists that this consumer is also preeminently a producer: "A man is fed, not that he may be fed, but that he may work." In "endless" but ever widening circulations, he works to *re*produce the world he consumes.

The difference between this and working linearly to produce a continually changing world may be apparent only at the two ideological horizons. Emerson's horizon describes a full and therefore closed circle. The Western European thought I examined earlier looks to a different sort of horizon that only seems to curve because of the distance. Indeed, rather than a circle, this horizon is the vanishing point in the ongoing conflict between the individual and society. Self-fulfillment is thus inevitably, structurally problematical; it is in fact the great social problem. But when Emerson writes that "Whoever considers the final cause of the world will discern a multitude of uses that enter as parts into that result," he is thinking at once of the many uses and the final purpose, both of which already exist. If anything, the "final cause" is the better fixed site; it is the reference point that defines the commodity value of the "multitude of uses," each of which partially reproduces it.

Thus, by rendering the "temporary and mediate" relation of man and nature—the "mercenary benefit" of nature for man—as another aspect of his global spiritual nature, Emerson elaborated the discovery made by Franklin, Jefferson, and the eighteenth century: not only was an ideal use inherent in the land; the land entered *in all its materiality* into that ideal use. Nature and nation, and self with both, were now not just fused but merged. The ideological burden of the "Commodity" section lies in its co-option, for nature, of history's usual constituency: "low," everyday, "mercenary" life. Finally, the point to be derived from all this, as a starting premise for the close reading of *Nature*, is that the ideological argument in *Nature* is made first and most potentially through *its* materiality—its organization and rhetoric. Its ideas are expressed organically, and, as overt statements, can be deceptively bland and self-evident—which may be why what Huck Finn would have called the "interesting but tough" statements of *Nature* and of Emerson's other writings have been so readily translated to greeting cards and calendars. Emerson's message is incarnate in the body of his essay, as the meaning of America is in the body of the continent, that being precisely its major argument.

The transcendent idealism of *Nature* implies an ideology; in fact this idealism *is* ideological. To read the ideology, then, one needs to explicate the idealism, much the way one explicates a text. This is not quite the same as a general explication, and it may be useful to specify the difference at the outset. The central question in an analysis of ideology has a particular focus: it asks, about concepts, not so much what they say in and for themselves as what they mean for the understanding and the possibility of action; how they interact with and realize themselves inside the world they address. An ideology is never wholly abstract, because it always retains action itself as a substantial content. (It is in this way that ideologies are organically political, whereas ideals need not be.) Reading *Nature* ideologically, therefore, tends to evoke not any specific content but content as a category, and thus, in constant juxtaposition to its idealism, limits. When the essay calls on man to do everything he can, an ideological analysis will tend to name the act; but more importantly, it will point to the limits of "everything"—to what he *cannot* do. Because I am concerned, more than with concepts per se, with the conceptual situation they construct, my reading of *Nature* has a polar organization, defining ideas by both what they enjoin and what they prohibit, or what they enable and what they prevent. I have two reasons for this approach, the first of which makes it appropriate and the second useful. An ideological approach is particularly appropriate to Emersonian thinking, because of the immanence of his idealism, his characteristically American assumption of a real world, which particularizes his most abstract thought. Although this assumption is what permits him to universalize his ideas, it is also a latent presence in his universalities, and thus ground for an immanent analysis.

The opening sentence of the Introduction of *Nature*, almost as well known as the first sentence of *Moby-Dick*, is "Our age is retrospective" (7–8). The essay ends with a vision of entering "the kingdom of man over nature," which is the place of transcendence, the place of the spirit's ultimate emergence as the one true fact of reality. From the past to the future, man moves not from nature

93

to civilization but from history to nature, and himself evolves in the same direction; in history, he is encompassed all around by conventions, traditions, and other men, but his coming dominion over nature will seal his absolute independence. Yet, despite the self-assertion of such evolution, it amounts linguistically to an abandonment of active verbs. Syntactically, the retrospective age, which might have been expected to be passively observant, is aggressively active: "it builds" (albeit the "sepulchres of the fathers"); "it writes" ("biographies, histories and criticism"); "it gropes" ("among the dry bones of the past"). The emphasis in these sentences is on the object, but even taking "builds" and "writes" and "gropes" ironically for the parodic character of their achievements only intensifies the rejection of activism. In pointed contrast to the feverish activity of the historically minded, the stance Emerson recommends, as we begin our return to nature, is contemplative to the point of passivity. We must learn to "enjoy" (an original relation to the universe); when we become "enbosomed"in nature, we will be surrounded by "floods of life" that "stream around and through us, and invite us . . ." The argument for our thus relaxing is a world that declares itself without a conscious subject: "the sun shines . . . There is more wool and flax in the fields. There are new lands, new men, new thoughts." Not "we think new thoughts" or "we can think new thoughts," but "there are . . . new thoughts." And when, in the next sentence, Emerson does call us to action, this action is peculiarly indirect: "let us demand our own works and laws and worship." Not "let us construct them," but "let us demand" them. From whom? To demand is to be active, certainly, but not in the sense of building or writing. Demanding is not a directly creative activity, and the phrase "let us demand" here connotes direct action still less for the parallel constructions that soon echo its intransitivity: "let us interrogate . . . let us inquire . . ."

The object of man's righteous activity, in other words, is not to make but to acquire. Commodities, knowledge, poetry, philosophy, religion: why, Emerson asks, should we not *have* our own versions of these? Indeed, not only are they all, as answers, given us, but so are the questions that evoke them, both being projected from within a prior completion we have only to assume: "We must trust the perfection of the creation so far as to believe that whatever curiosity the order of things has awakened in our minds, the order of things can satisfy." And while we are to be satisfied, the determination of that satisfaction is no more ours to make than was the formulating of question or answer: "Whenever a true theory of nature appears, it will be its own evidence. Its test is, that it will explain all phenomena." Emerson does not say to whom it will explain. This is a theory that inhabits its own universe, grammatically, somewhat as the crash of a tree falling in an uninhabited forest inhabits a universe of sound sufficient unto itself.

Even though we are involved in the emergence of theory, truth, or artifact, we seem not to contribute to it. First, we are often involved unconsciously. The "inquiries" a man "would put" to the universe have solutions to which his understanding is immaterial; he lives them out before he ever apprehends them as truth. But even when we consciously manipulate nature, our "operations taken together are so insignificant, a little chipping, baking, patching, and washing, that in an impression so grand as that of the world on the human mind, they do not vary the result." This statement, with which the Introduction ends, requires close attention. It would be easy to substitute for it the more familiar and much less interesting one that man only scratches the surface of the earth and is impotent to change the deep laws of nature. In Emerson's actual statement, it is not the world itself that man's art leaves essentially unchanged, but the "impression . . . of the world on the human mind." The reason the impression does not vary is that its source in the real world is essentially unaltered by all the arts that construct "a house, a canal, a statue, a picture." But Emerson skips this step in the argument, collapsing perception into the reality of an "impression" made by the world upon the mind. This collapsing of the object of sight into vision is significant because the distance between perception and reality is the ground for interpretation and judgment, indeed for art and for mental creation generally, at least as creation has been elsewhere understood since the seventeenth century. Emerson's subject in the essay will be the "impression . . . of the world on the human mind," but with the odd proviso implied, by the translation of reality into its "impression" and perception into imprinting (or into imprint),

95

that the human mind has nothing to do with the generation of its perceptions. Indeed he says this explicitly: both the energy and the model for man's ideal way of life issue entirely from nature, in "floods of life" that "invite us by the powers they supply, to action proportioned to nature."

"Action proportioned to nature" is prescriptive in quite another sense than, say, action that harmonizes with nature or even action that imitates nature. The latter types of action continue to assume a distance between nature and the actor, who, in making his action harmonious, still translates nature into the distinct terms of his medium, or in imitating nature, sees it apart from the perspective of his own separate identity. In contrast to these, the concept of action proportioned to nature begs the question of the distinction between nature and the artist, the natural and the artificial. Now the action simply complements, fits in with nature, shares nature's proportions; the apparent differences between man's actions and nature, which arise from man's having to reuse nature to reproduce her—as in the construction of house, canal, or statue, from wood, water, and stone—amount only to different idioms within a single language.

Thus in the Introduction Emerson forecasts his central point: the good life, the virtuous, the intelligent, the worthwhile, and also the natural life, is a life in total accord with "all that is separate from us . . . both nature and art, all other men and my own body . . . NATURE." For the "Soul," which is the other party to this accord, has no program of its own, but seeks its truth, its "idea of creation" in nature's "true theory." In the total communion with nature and with one's own natural self that this accord permits, the flowing of one's blood and the action of one's hands have a single rhythm that is also the rhythm of plant growth and seasonal rotation. Breathing *and* writing, "language, sleep, madness, dreams, beasts, sex," are all seen as avatars of a single life-force. Emerson's ecstasy, his "perfect exhilaration" in the woods, is of another order entirely from Wordsworth's in nature. Emerson's is really the opposite experience, not a heightening of his own separate and autonomously creative consciousness but a merging into universality. When he describes becoming that "transparent eyeball," losing "all mean egotism," he projects, by that very dissolving, an intensification of the self. Poetic in its perceptions and reflections, this self is yet not actively a poet.

Emerson, in fact, never proposes to make anything more out of his exhilaration; he does not need to, his feelings are already acts. In returning to "reason and faith," and loving "uncontained and immortal beauty," he manifests a shared "power to produce this delight" which resides in a "harmony" of nature and man. In a word, Emerson finds in nature not only the inspiration and the material for poetry but the poems themselves. (Recall from "Commodity": "Nature, in its ministry to man, is not only the material, but is also the process and the result.") His thinking about writing poetry is organized by the thesis that nature is a poet, that "in its forms and tendencies" it is already "describing its own design." He imagines that what nature said in the hieroglyphics of "natural facts" was equivalent as statement to what men might say in words. Far from postulating the poet-creator or Promethean man, he suggests that man's truest and best creations are, as it were, dictations from nature.

This does not leave poet and man much to do. There is a stillness at the heart of Emerson's relation to nature, a great calm into which his very prose seems to sink back with a sigh. When he writes wittily that "the greatest delight which the fields and woods minister is the suggestion of an occult relation between man and the vegetable," one notices that all his nature is indeed botanical, that there is very little movement in those woods but an occasional waving of boughs or possibly the lengthening of shadows. And from one perspective the transcendent moment when he feels "the currents of the Universal Being circulate through [him]" and he is "part or particle of God" might well describe a return to the primordial sea, to that molecular soup of the origin of life, where our "original relation to the universe" was first defined. There is the same loss of self-locomotion, whether physical or spiritual, attending arrival at the place of ultimate reunion.

This is no Buddhist self-abandonment, however. The stillness and the pull of oceanic surrender are there in *Nature*, but so is a thrusting energy that can at any moment turn Emerson's movement out of himself, all the way around, and make God part or parcel of *him*. This energy is conveyed, in the parts of the essay discussed so far, especially in the notion that "the most abstract truth is the most practical" and in the sole caveat to Emerson's entire acceptance of whatever life and the world may bring him— that his sight be spared. In these two statements, he establishes sites for the individual self short of the oceanic spirit, sites whose construction follows the geometry described earlier: they are built of paired and complementary opposites.

"The most abstract truth is the most practical," Emerson writes. By the "most abstract truth" he means an "idea of creation" that we still lack. When it appears, however, its "test" will be "that it will explain all phenomena." For "now many are thought not only unexplained but inexplicable; as language, sleep, madness, beasts, sex." So "abstract," in his use of the term here, means all-encompassing, universal; "practical" means whatever is applicable, useful. That a universal truth be the most useful is only logical. Then why does he stress their opposition, insisting by the form of his sentence that we read them as opposites? The reason lies, as earlier, in the capacity of a nonantagonistic dualism to generate activity despite the absence of a dialectical impulse. This activity is reproductive rather than productive, an enactment instead of a true action. Nonetheless it constitutes movement, whereas transcendent unity implies stasis. Thus while the abstract-practical dichotomy is not really contradictory, it suggests the need to develop both terms in relation to each other. Indeed, Emerson does develop them, showing logically how the abstract, since it is universal, is universally practical, and how the practical . . . "language, sleep, madness, dreams, beasts, sex," in short the tangible world we actually experience—being universal, is also the stuff of abstraction. Thus the abstract has been made active and the practical has acquired an added dimension in its connection to the universal and the infinite. Viewed at a higher level of transcendence as aspects of a single unity, without the rhetorical dualism that sets them at formal odds, the abstract and the practical would have merely blended in inert fusion. With the rhetorical dualism, their ersatz opposition produces more energy for practical action than their real opposition would have, since the real opposition of the practical and the abstract would limit the significance and the reach of each. The division of the everyday from the transcendent limits both, and therefore limits our activities in each realm. The outright fusion of the everyday and the transcendent renders our activities in either realm moot. The nonantagonistic and transitory separation of the mundane and the spiritual inspires, indeed implies, practical actions in order to realize their infinite potential.[3]

In the same way, the nonantagonistic dualism of self and nature actually enhances the power of the self, which, were it fully transcendent and united with nature, would be totally paralyzed. Just short of this ultimate dissolution-in-union, however, it is as totally potent. For before Emerson becomes a "transparent eyeball" through which light passes unfiltered, he is a most active observer. Indeed he claims, in the untitled second section of the essay (9–11), to see better than others because of his insight: as he is a "lover of nature," his "inward and outward senses are still truly adjusted to each other." Ordinarily, "few adult persons can see nature," and "most persons do not see the sun. At least, they have a very superficial seeing." Now, when his eye penetrates "into infinite space," he will lose his seeing in infinite sight. Then the problem will emerge in other guises. As he writes necessarily short of transcendence, he also sees short of transparence and, here as before, projects what is really a stage on the way to transcendence, in the rhetoric of dualism. Again the opposition between the two poles arises out of incompleteness, in this case the partiality of most people's seeing. Unable to see "the integrity of impression made by manifold natural objects," they think the world is composed of distinct solidities identified by their distinct uses. So the woodcutter sees a stick of timber, and the farmer a fenced-in field that is either his property or not his property. But the poet, "whose eye can integrate all the parts," sees a tree that is to him a sign of all nature, and in "some twenty or thirty farms," a "charming landscape" that "is the best part of [the] farms" but to which "warranty-deeds give no title."

This is orthodox idealism—with one addition. This idealist moves away from the material land to the landscape only to return to the land with enhanced power; he has "a property in the horizon." Of course Emerson is speaking of property metaphorically, but his metaphor is just the point. He might as easily have written that the reason "none [of the farmers] owns the landscape" is that

99

no one does, since the landscape is an idea and therefore not a property. What he wrote instead was that the poet does own the landscape, because he has the power to own an idea. In this account of the poet and the landscape, there is no conflict and not even an indirection between seeing, all the way to the landscape's infinite horizon, and having, all the way around the whole countryside. Not that the poet actually owns the countryside. But he could, the better and the more completely for his better sight. His particular practical living is thus infused with the energy that is potential in universal transcendence. And best of all, there is no contradiction between the lives (the truths, the goals) that these two realms require of him. Their coming together is only a matter of adjusting his inward and outward senses. Once adjusted, they will report identical truths, and—this is how Emerson perfected the invention of America—this identity will enable both conceptual status and unchecked entrepreneurial development. In its completed perfection, nature is already ideally suited to man's needs; therefore, since it is in man's nature to produce, in a natural world he can produce ideally. "A man is fed, not that he may be fed, but that he may work." In context, this does not mean that a man is fed only so that he can work, but rather that nature demonstrates in this way a complementarity that keeps it eternally stable and ever reproductive: a timeless and forever new world.

So at the end of this second section of the essay Emerson has arrived at a beginning, he has led man out of history and the work of history, into nature. There man will find all his needs and all the potential ways of his being already fulfilled, so that he has no use for history or society and may be wholly free of them. But this will make him neither hermit nor shepherd. The leitmotif of nature is how nature *works*, how useful it is to man; the organization of the whole essay is by "use"—as "Commodity," as "Beauty," as "Language," as "Discipline." Its triumphant conclusion will be the call to "build . . . your own world." By the conclusion of "Commodity," Emerson has distinguished between the sort of work he wants to urge and the kind he deplores, the rebuilding or building-on that proceeds inside history—that *is* history. And the rest of *Nature* sets out the dimensions and properties of natural work.

Emerson conceives of beauty as a property of work in the realm of nature (14–19). If we seek beauty for its abstract feeling and sight in the "shows of day, the dewy morning, the rainbow, mountains, orchards in blossom, stars, moonlight, shadows in still water," they will "mock us with their unreality. Go out of the house to see the moon, and 'tis mere tinsel; it will not please as when its light shines upon your necessary journey." Not because beauty is extraneous or unimportant or unreal, but because it is real as an aspect of the "totality of nature," and therefore seems unreal when perceived apart from this greater unity. There, within that unity, it realizes itself through its function, which is to body forth the "perfectness and harmony" that pervades all creation. "Nothing is quite beautiful alone: nothing but is beautiful in the whole. A single object is only so far beautiful as it suggests this universal grace." Beauty is a mechanism of transcendence and its manifestation.

It is both organic and functional; more, it is also enabling, even generative of a certain kind of action. As an aspect of the whole, beauty is an energy the artist taps: "The poet, the painter, the sculptor, the musician, the architect, seek each to concentrate this radiance of the world on one point, and each in his several work to satisfy the love of beauty which stimulates him to produce." Indeed, beauty does more than fuel the production of art; it is something like a circuit in the machinery of all production.

> The intellectual and the active powers seem to succeed each other, and the exclusive activity of the one, generates the exclusive activity of the other. There is something unfriendly in each to the other, but they are like the alternate periods of feeding and working in animals; each prepares and will be followed by the other. Therefore does beauty, which in relation to actions . . . comes unsought, and comes because it is unsought, remain for the apprehension and pursuit of the intellect; and then again, in its turn, of the active power. Nothing divine dies. All good is eternally reproductive. The beauty of nature reforms itself in the mind, and not for barren contemplation but for new creation.

Not for "barren contemplation" but really not for "new creation" either, for *new* creation does not emerge from the eternal reproduction of the divine good, nor is it formed so much by re-forming as by transformation.

Of course, mortals must make do in their building with the materials already provided. Emerson's conception, however, posits a creation that lacks even the categories of reorganization and rearrangement. The thrust of each "new creation" for him is to achieve a better, more encompassing representation of the one truth, to "throw a light upon the mystery of humanity"—not to engender new men or invent new ways of lighting. "A work of art," he writes, "is an abstract or epitome of the world. It is the result or expression of nature, in miniature." This should not be read too quickly as expressing a general Romantic attitude proclaiming the primary relation of art and nature; for one may thus miss its implication of a very particular kind of relation between art and nature.

This relation is elaborated most fully in the next section of *Nature*, which sets out nature's third use for man, language (20–25). When Emerson says that language is one of the uses of nature, he means it precisely. Surprisingly so. It was only after the third reading of the second sentence, which begins "Nature is the vehicle of thought," that I recognized its first word. I had been reading "Language is the . . ." Therein—in my mis-expectation—lies Emerson's argument. Nature functions linguistically quite directly, not needing, except as a recorder, the intermediation of man: language is not for Emerson an artificial human construction, as it is defined in philosophies that view nature and civilization as opposites. Nature being inherently meaningful, language articulates its meanings: "Words are signs of natural facts." This is the first way nature provides man with language: "Every word which is used to express a moral or intellectual fact, if traced to its root, is found to be borrowed from some material appearance." This appearance is not a matter of interpretation but of fact, as *"Right* means *straight; wrong* means *twisted."* It is not only single words that we derive from individual natural facts, but whole paragraphs of moral and philosophical meanings that nature literally (not to say literarily) speaks to us in "things" and situations.

An enraged man is a lion, a cunning man is a fox, a firm man is a rock, a learned man is a torch. A lamb is innocence; a snake is subtle spite; flowers express to us the delicate affections. Light and darkness are our familiar expression for knowledge and ignorance; and heat for love. Visible distance behind and before us, is respectively our image of memory and hope.

We must not confuse Emerson here with Swift's Projector, who found the perfect substitute for speech in a vast collection of objects he displayed in lieu of words. Indeed, Emerson's is really the opposite conception. The "radical correspondence" he sees "between visible things and human thoughts" arises from their common transcendent spirituality. Far from reducing language to a mechanical equation, this correspondence enables him to read the whole world as one great poem.

But what does it do to his ability to *write* a poem *about* the world? The man who mines his language from nature, whose "picturesque language is at once a commanding certificate that he who employs it, is a man in alliance with truth and God," has found the key to "good writing and brilliant discourse" through the images he culls from nature. There is no mistaking Emerson's association of the use of a natural language not only with truth or beauty but more especially with power. The section ends with striking force: when we put "unconscious truth" into words, we acquire nothing less than "a new weapon in the magazine of power." This and similar statements have inspired the critical consensus that Emerson's conception of language was unambiguously empowering—that it claimed for the New World writer the ability to create new worlds of his own imagination.[4] The view I shall propose and develop here and in the next two chapters is that considering language as one of nature's uses does inspire unparalleled poetic energies, *but that it also forbids the creation of new worlds*. In its enabling capacity, the concept of what one might call an inherent linguicity functions like the general conception of a nature that contains an implicit civilization: it permits the poet, as it does the explorer or the settler, to construct his world with all of nature's resources. The power of language, the power with which it endows the poet, can be infinite because it does not arise in society, where it would be the "artificial" product of the "curtailed life of the cities." The only limit to linguistic potency is personal merit: "A man's power to connect his thought with its proper symbol, and so to utter it, depends on the simplicity of his character, that is, upon his love for truth and his desire to communicate it without loss." Those who write and speak well may know that they are good people, without further appeal to social judgment or artistic tradition. The naturalization of language thus makes possible not only an unmediated and untaxed empowerment, but also a moral self-justification entailing no involvement with social morality; it permits one to be righteous among men without the constraints of engaging with them. More ambitious than Wordsworth, the Emersonian poet is at once laureate and prophet.

But in another sense, he is forbidden to be either; this prophet-laureate gains infinite personal power at the price of never using it for anything personal. For if the poet's power can be infinite because the language of truth and beauty is not man-made but natural, this means also that it is not the province of man to make language. The poet receives his poetry as natural "forms"; his "thought" already has "its proper symbol" extant somewhere in nature, speaking its own truth. Indicting the "perpetual allegories" of these forms is "proper creation. It is the working of the Original Cause through the instruments he has already made." It is precisely this instrumentality that yields the poet "the keys of power." His power depends upon the fact that he has not created the allegories but only deciphers them; it flows to him unchecked because this "relation between the mind and matter [whereby natural facts signify moral and philosophical truths] is not fancied by some poet, but stands in the will of God, and so is free to be known by all men."

This last sentence represents the situation perfectly: considered as a natural resource, language gains an infinite capacity to articulate all of God's creation; but moral creation, now recast as "some poet's fancy," suffers a commensurately infinite loss. When nature and the divine can project their own image, the poet's image will always be inauthentic. On the contrary (and just as logically), Romanticism elsewhere accorded artistic creation the *only* authenticity.

Compare Wordsworth's invocation of memory in "I wandered lonely as a cloud" with this sentence from the "Language" section of *Nature:* "At the call of a noble sentiment, again the woods wave, the pines murmur, the river rolls and shines, and the cattle low upon the mountains, as he saw and heard them in his infancy." The experience in nature that Emerson recalls was complete in itself and returns as the memory of a wholly self-sufficient perception. In contrast, it is only *after* his sojourn among the daffodils that Wordsworth, with a now heightened consciousness, understands what he saw, "what wealth the show to me had brought." Reflection has nothing to do with the wealth Emerson's poet recaptures; on the contrary, it comes to him when he is not reflecting. Deadened by "the roar of cities or the broil of politics," he finds that unbidden "solemn images [of nature] shall reappear in their morning lustre"; these images are autonomous although they appear in his imagination, not only undimmed but as if unmediated. They do not so much "flash upon that inward eye" as replace or rather subsume the outward sight. Wordsworth too thought that he culled from nature spiritual truths organic to her. But they did not constitute his poetry, they only inspired it. Thus Wordsworth's purpose in gathering impressions from nature, a purpose that significantly is not accomplished at the time or for that matter at the site but back in the poet's study, is to create later and elsewhere a new linguistic imaginative situation that culminates the experience: "when on my couch I lie . . . / They flash upon that inward eye . . . / And then my heart with pleasure fills, / And dances with the daffodils." Emerson, who tells us he has to "retire from his chamber" in order to be fully with himself, in effect seeks the daffodils themselves, as inherently linguistic. Nature's "noble race of creatures," its "profusion of forms," its "host of orbs in heaven," "furnish man with the dictionary and grammar of his municipal speech." So while the poet, by having full access to "this grand cipher," can say anything he can decipher, which is potentially anything in the universe, he has literally no language to say anything else. This is not a matter only of form or words (of grammar and vocabulary), but of content, organized all the way to complete statements. The "memorable words of history, and the proverbs of nations" are acquired through a selection among meanings inherent in natural facts. Emerson offers these examples: "A rolling stone gathers no moss; A bird in the hand is worth two in the bush; A cripple in the right way, will beat a racer in the wrong; Make hay while the sun shines; 'Tis hard to carry a full cup even; Vinegar is the son of wine; The last ounce broke the camel's back; Long-lived trees make roots first." Indeed, Emerson seems here almost to be suggesting, in the structural unity he finds between form and content that (essentially the opposite of the current view) the forms of both nature and language carry their meanings organically, so that one might say they speak us rather than we them. Such a suggestion would be astonishing: how could a writer so committed to freedom and self-determination develop this determined conception of language?

The answer lies on the other face of the same coin. Reading one face, the speaker is forbidden to say anything that is not already implicit, but reading the other he finds himself permitted to say *everything* that is. So, if nature is a metaphor before the poet ever gets to it, it is nonetheless "a metaphor of the human mind." Uncreative himself, man is still the focus of all creation: "He is placed in the centre of beings, and a ray of relation passes from every other being to him." And this is the crux of the matter: "Neither can man be understood without these objects, nor these objects without man." The "radical correspondence between visible things and human thoughts" renders determinism and passivity as freedom and activity; and the reverse is simultaneously, organically also the case.

Emerson's poet is an avatar of the necessary actor: he is the *necessary speaker*. He speaks what needs to be spoken, he mediates complementary pairings through symbol, analogy, correspondence, allegory—all forms of nonantagonistic, rhetorical dualism, enabling speech in a situation where its outcome awaits only articulation. The speaker's role and identity are as absolutely determined as they are absolutely free—and in Emerson's world that is not a contradiction. It is determined that he will speak with total effectiveness to realize himself totally. Recalling more of the earlier discussion, the necessary speaker can be seen as one whose personal power to speak is realized in the reproduction of the language of nature. He can no more produce new speech than he can create the stone that gathers moss. Still, by discovering the stone's message, he acquires "a new weapon in the magazine of power."

This leads the essay directly and logically to its next section and the "new fact" that "nature is a *discipline*" (26–31). By "discipline" Emerson means a teaching, essentially what we mean in calling history or anthropology an academic discipline: "Space, time, society, labor, climate, food, locomotion, the animals, the mechanical forces, give us sincerest lessons, day by day." These lessons all point one moral, he says: "the unity of Nature,—the unity in variety,—which meets us everywhere." For "All the endless variety of things make an identical impression." "The river as it flows, resembles the air that flows over it; the air resembles the light which traverses it with more subtle currents; the light resembles the heat which rides with it through Space. Each creature is only a modification of the other; the likeness in them is more than the difference, and their radical law is one and the same." In its substance, the discipline of nature seems, contrary to its "moral," to be the study of differences; and unlike the nameless differences between the opposites that the necessary was meant to reconcile, these differences are identifiably solid, real entities. For if the "lessons of difference" are said to point toward unity, this unity is abstract; while the specific characters of the "particular" and the "manifold" project tangible presences that make up the real stuff of the writing.

> Therefore is Space, and therefore Time, that man may know that things are not huddled and lumped, but sundered and individual. A bell and a plough have each their use, and neither can do the office of the other. Water is good to drink, coal to burn, wool to wear; but wool cannot be drunk, nor water spun, nor coal eaten. The wise man shows his wisdom in separation, in gradation, and his scale of creatures and of merits is as wide as nature.

Nature as a whole, out of the infinite capacity of its oneness, tunes itself to an infinity of differences: "Proportioned to the importance of the organ to be formed, is the extreme care with which its tuition is provided,—a care pretermitted in no single case." And what the reader actually reads, in the process of being taught that all manner of people "have each an experience precisely parallel" because "all organizations are radically alike," are the names that differentiate them (sailor, shepherd, miner, merchant). For that matter, the earlier passage asserting unity is constructed of difference: the river may "resemble" the air, the air the light, the light the heat, and each creature every other, but there too, what is *named* is their separateness.

In this way, the "Discipline" section constitutes the most important representation in the essay of Emerson's nonantagonistic, rhetorical dualism, of his characteristic insistence on separation in the service of an affirmation of unity. Why and to what effect is he so dualistic specifically in relation to the concept of nature as discipline? The most probable answer seems to be that discipline, having to do with what one has to understand and accept in order to function, represents an unacknowledged examination of limits. The examination cannot be acknowledged because a conception of limits is in fundamental contradiction to the notion of transcendence. Still, even the term "discipline" acknowledges that the attainment of transcendence is not without cost. To counter the implication that transcendence therefore has its limits, the dualisms of this section of the essay not only affirm an ultimate transcendent reconciliation of all apparent oppositions; more important, they preempt the emergence at this vulnerable junction of the irreconcilable and the really contradictory.

I do not suggest that in writing *Nature* Emerson schemed to co-opt dissent. But effective defenses are seldom consciously invented, arising rather from conviction of more or less global rectitude. Emerson's assumption of his world's rectitude was absolutely global. So although he was not coldly calculating how to control opposition, he was thinking politically in this section, as seems clear from his making here the most directly political statement of the essay, the assertion that "Property and its filial systems of debt and credit," along with space, time, climate, and the animals, are nature's benevolent guides to intellectual truths. The argument is unusually concrete:

Debt, grinding debt, whose iron face the widow, the orphan, and the sons of genius fear and hate;—debt, which consumes so much time, which so cripples and disheartens a great spirit with cares that seem so base, is a preceptor whose lessons cannot be forgone, and is needed most by those who suffer from it most. Moreover, property, which has been well compared to snow,—"if it fall level today, it will be blown into drifts tomorrow,"—is the surface action of internal machinery, like the index on the face of a clock. Whilst now it is the gymnastics of the understanding, it is hiving in the foresight of the spirit, experience in profounder laws.

Poverty, especially when expressed in debt, is an extreme representation of social difference as inequality. The debtor and his freedom are inevitably diminished by the extent of the debt. Debt, rather than immanence, is in fact the real opposite of transcendence. Moreover, debt signifies a substantial difference between people, literally a difference of substance. Against the transcendentalist, the debtor argues untranscendable material differences; against the individualist, inescapable ties. In "Discipline" Emerson brings up the two strongest objections to the notion of a transcendentally benevolent world: poverty and death. In the closing sentences of the section, he appends a discussion of death, represented movingly in the loss of friends. Loss of property and loss of life, both real and the former as insurmountable, to Emerson's mind, as the latter: these are the classical reasons for rebellion— one the oldest justification to rise against the human order, the other to rail at the divine.

The function of "Discipline" is to disarm these reasons. Emerson will demonstrate that just those aspects of the world which seem most to imply a malignant lack of care for man's fate are in fact the means by which man's best interests are carefully and lovingly protected. Such a reversal is the culmination of ideological hegemony, showing that the state of things is not only natural but good. This is what "Discipline" proves, and in this sense, it concludes *Nature*'s account of the secular universe. After this section come "Idealism," "Spirit," and "Prospects," in which Emerson can assert the possibility of transcendence—of freedom and omnipotence—because "Discipline" has co-opted the material reality of limits and powerlessness. The facts that some are indebted to others and that all owe the final debt of mortality have been made to testify to the primacy and infinite power of the individual in an infinitely benevolent universe.

The individual not only transcends death and taxes; he seems to rise above nature itself. In the image of the transparent eyeball, Emerson projected fusion with nature as an equal coming together. In "Discipline" he writes, "Nature is thoroughly mediate. It is made to serve. It receives the dominion of man as meekly as the ass on which the Saviour rode." In the earlier section man and nature became as one when both dissolved in Universal Being: here man's "victorious thought comes up with and reduces all things, until the world becomes, at last, only a realized will,—the double of the man." But this is a difference in rhetoric, not in substance. The nature that man conceives in his image is revealed to be already informed throughout by a prior moral law:

> every globe in the remotest heaven; every chemical change from the rudest crystal up to the laws of life; every change of vegetation from the first principle of growth in the eye of a leaf, to the tropical forest and antediluvian coal-mine, every animal function from the sponge up to Hercules, shall hint or thunder to man the laws of right and wrong, and echo the Ten Commandments.

Once again man has not created freely but only realized the cosmic blueprint. Still, the difference in rhetoric between the earlier and later versions of the unity of man and nature is significant, and signals that by the end of "Discipline" Emerson's construction of secular individualism is essentially complete. From the premise that "perpetual youth," "reason and faith," and "decorum and sanctity" inhere in "the woods," Emerson has now fully derived the infinitely empowering conception of individual action as universal enactment. The progress of the child from the "successive possession of his several senses up to the hour when he saith, 'Thy will be done!' " defines action as fulfillment and fulfillment as action. "The exercise of the Will, or the lesson of power, is taught in every event." Emerson has returned Satan to the right hand of God.

As most students of Emerson have noted, *Nature* is not a

rigorously logical work. Nonetheless, it is organized more purposefully than might at first appear. This is especially evident in the placing of "Idealism" right after "Discipline," and the joining of them by the essay's most explicit transition (32–39): "Thus is the unspeakable but intelligible and practicable meaning of the world conveyed to man, the immortal pupil, in every object of sense. To this one end of Discipline, all parts of Nature conspire." This translation of sublunary limits into avenues to cosmic transcendence was the burden of "Discipline." Here it is successfully carried on high: having been translated into "the immortal pupil," and his several physical senses and multitude of worldly experiences having come together in their "one end," man is now apotheosized as the world's "Final Cause."

This idealization of the argument of "Discipline" resolves some potential contradictions that could have arisen in Jefferson's idealistic but not fully idealized horizon. One is the contradiction between actual and ideal frontiers, which seems somehow not to be perceived when Americans at once regret the closing of the actual frontier and continue to celebrate "America" as the site of perpetual frontiers. Emerson resolved this possible conflict by defining the landscape not through its actual farms but through his vision of them, which was permanently safe from time, tide, and man. Paradoxically, this idealization completed the work of the incarnation, embedding the historical United States in an idea of the physical American continent.

"Idealism" begins, then, by posing an ultimate question implied by everything that has come earlier: does the fact that the universe is so perfectly wrought to work man's good not suggest "a noble doubt . . . whether nature outwardly exists"? Emerson's world is here so far from standing dualistically separate from him that one might reasonably ask whether it is separate at all, or only appears so "in the apocalypse of the mind." The sensible answer Emerson provides is "be [the world] what it may, it is ideal to me, so long as I cannot try the accuracy of my senses."

This is the commonsense answer, but it also undermines the possibility of common sense, and Emerson hastens to deny that the subjective nature of knowledge in any way implies that *truth* is subjective. "The stability of nature" is not affected by idealism.

Nature's laws are permanent, and God will never permit them to be altered. "We are not built like a ship to be tossed, but like a house to stand." "The wheels and springs of man are all set to the hypothesis of the permanence of nature." Such permanence is essential for the daily conduct of life and society, and "the broker, the wheelwright, the carpenter, the tollman" rightly balk at all intimations of mutability. The product and point of idealization is incarnation.

In "Discipline" Emerson listed, as aspects of nature, "space, time, society, labor, climate, food, locomotion, the animals, the mechanical forces." A little later he cited the laws of property accumulation as natural principles in which debt instructs the poor. No distinction exists, then, between the laws of nature and those of society. The laws of both are immutable, and our task is only to observe them. A world whose laws changed would not "stand" but would become unmanageable. Inconsistency would mock man's efforts; fortunately, "God never jests with us, and will not compromise the end of nature, by permitting any inconsequence in its procession." Yet elsewhere Emerson celebrated nature's "uncontained beauty" as an inspiration to transcend the petty rules of logic: inconsistency, goes his best-known aphorism, is the hobgoblin of little minds.

He reconciles these attitudes by distinguishing between the "permanence of natural laws" and "the absolute existence of nature." The first, he writes, does not necessarily imply the second. On the contrary, "It is the uniform effect of culture on the human mind, not to shake our faith in the stability of particular phenomena . . . but to lead us to regard nature as a phenomenon, not a substance; to attribute necessary existence to spirit; to esteem nature as an accident and an effect." The laws in themselves are absolute. But that their *existence* be the projection of a generating mind, a Mind in which all individual minds participate, implies a priority by which the self, the "I" or, in the current idiom, the "subject," is sprung free to manipulate laws it masters by realizing them.

Emerson describes this hierarchy of consciousness through the example of a man accustomed to walking, who, riding through his own street, sees it become "a puppet-show." "The men, the women,—talking, running, bartering, fighting,—the earnest mechanic, the lounger, the beggar, the boys, the dogs are unrealized at once, or, at least, wholly detached from all relation to the observer, and seen as apparent, not substantial beings." Their substantial reality awaits his projection. Not that he has reduced the people to puppets simply by withdrawing that projection. Their loss of reality does not change them (*he* does not change them), but only renders them, as it were, latent. While the world remains as it must be, it is man who causes it to become what it is. In that way he is its master and creator, and his activity in mastering and creating emerges as the whole purpose and meaning of life, indeed, as the condition for the actual existence of the world. The mounted man is bold and fears no inconsistencies—knowing them one in his perception—and rejects all social constraints, knowing that, as with the "talking, running, bartering, fighting," he can unrealize them at his will. And all this freedom is possible precisely because of the permanence of nature's laws and the inherence of the landscape's purpose and meaning: they permit a man to do everything without endangering anything.

Idealism makes man the reference point; he is no longer in motion but the prime mover. From this self-sufficient perspective, he can see the various and changing representations of the "spectacle" about him as so many manifestations of one transcendent reality—his own. He sees this with "a pleasure mixed with awe": the pleasure of knowing that, as a viceroy of the ideal world, he can turn the kaleidoscope of nature any way he wills; and the awe of understanding that, however many permutations and combinations of colors he evokes, an infinite number remain because they are all one in an infinity of light. And he, as a transparent eyeball, is the prism at the center of that infinity.

For all this triumphant idealizing, however, Emerson does not reject the material world. "Some theosophists," he notes, "have arrived at a certain hostility and indignation towards matter." Not he; in fact, "I own there is something ungrateful in expanding too curiously the particulars of the general proposition that all culture tends to imbue us with idealism." That proposition implies a rejection he is far from feeling: "I have no hostility to nature, but a child's love to it. I expand and live in the warm day like corn and melons. Let us speak her fair. I do not wish to fling stones at my beautiful mother, nor soil my gentle nest." The warm charm of this passage (and of others like it scattered throughout *Nature*) should redeem some of Emerson's well-known personal detachment and abstraction; more to the point, this passage makes it explicit once more that transcendentalism is directed *toward* the world. "I only wish to indicate," Emerson explains, "the true position of nature in regard to man, wherein to establish man, all right education tends; as the ground which to attain is the object of human life, that is, of man's connection with nature." Indeed, the real political problem with Emersonian idealism is not its abstraction, but this connection: not that Emerson remains aloof from social reform but that the naturalization of his ideals renders them immutable.

Hence the opening sentence of the next section, "Spirit" (40–42), which seems to try to correct this: "It is essential to a true theory of nature and of man, that it should contain somewhat progressive." The closing paragraph of "Idealism" has brought its conservatism into sharp focus. The "ideal theory" is useful above all because it enables one to perceive "the whole circle of persons and things, of actions and events, of country and religion," as one vast picture. "Therefore the soul holds itself off from a too trivial and microscopic study of the universal tablet." The particulars of history here become inessential, almost insubstantial: the soul

> respects the end too much, to immerse itself in the means. It sees something more important in Christianity, than the scandals of ecclesiastical history or the niceties of criticism; and, very incurious concerning persons or miracles, and not at all disturbed by chasms of historical evidence, it accepts from God the phenomenon, as it finds it, as the pure and awful form of religion in the world.

What actually happened, or will happen, in the ways of the world is so trivial a representation of the ultimate meaning of things that there is little point in disputing it—and as little point in clarifying it: the soul "is not hot and passionate at the appearance of what it calls its own good or bad fortune, at the union or opposition of other persons. No man is its enemy. It accepts whatsoever befalls, as part of its lesson. It is a watcher more than a doer, and it is a doer, only that it may the better watch." In a world where actual life is the shadow of reality, watching is the most adequate response.

But if watching preserves, it does not accomplish—and this brings us back to the opening sentence of the "Spirit" section: "It is essential to a true theory of nature and of man, that it should contain somewhat progressive." The "somewhat progressive" element, whose insertion into the theory of *Nature* is the burden of this section, is, literally, movement. Everything in "Spirit" is in motion. The "one and not compound" spirit of the world moves throughout the universe and into each man, diffusing unending vitality and energy.

> As a plant upon the earth, so a man rests upon the bosom of God; he is nourished by unfailing fountains, and draws, at his need inexhaustible power. Who can set bounds to the possibilities of man? Once inhale the upper air, being admitted to behold the absolute natures of justice and truth, and we learn that man has access to the entire mind of the Creator, is himself the creator in the finite.

Thus *man* moves out into all the universe, extending an imperial consciousness over all he surveys.

If the ideological task of "Idealism" was to stabilize, that of "Spirit" is to *mobilize*, by rendering mobile. Not in just any direction; the right path and the wrong are already well marked, and the right (like the road to Fredericktown) leads through a nature that constitutes a system of signposts, "a projection of God in the unconscious." Nor may the posts be rearranged. God himself has laid out nature, and "its serene order is inviolable by us." We are prime movers, then, along a marked path whose direction is absolutely set, and when we go astray, nature "is a fixed point whereby we may measure our departure." Thus freedom and destiny are reconciled in "Spirit" at the highest level of abstraction, as they have been all along at each stage of the argument, by a larger, more encompassing identity, this one an identity of man and God whereby an individual realizes his existential freedom by harnessing destiny to his own cart. For while destiny would limit and even obviate history, it can be seen, from a certain perspective, to liberate the individual from requiring others in order to fulfill himself. The unfolding of an indigenous concept of necessity—from Franklin's invocation of natural necessity as an incentive to work, to Jared Eliot's notion of a "needful Culture" that was man's role in the New World, to Emerson's own "necessary actor"—is here complete in the paradoxical but by now perfectly logical projection of necessity as a personal resource. The world each one enters is not his to make, but the more because of that, it is his to take.

This distinction becomes clear at the close of the section when Emerson suggests, essentially, that not everyone is equally fallen. Humanity as a whole has wandered from the natural path, and "as we degenerate, the contrast between us and our house is more evident." Unworthy settlers in God's world, we live a false and necessary dichotomy: "this may show us what discord is between man and nature, for you cannot freely admire a noble landscape if laborers are digging in the field hard by." But Emerson's vision condemns to the status of view-blocking laborer only those who lack the consciousness to rise from it. Anyone can return to primeval harmony "freely," and is prevented only by other men: not by anything he has in common with them, any common limitation or state of guilt, but by the presence of their lesser consciousness. "The poet finds something ridiculous in his delight, until he is out of sight of men." Men have fallen into community. Alone, a man is at once God and all-men, and his individual elevation is the "somewhat progressive" moment at the beginning of "Spirit." With this conception, the infinitely stable universe of "Idealism," which rendered the material limits of "Discipline"as structures of the mind as well, and therefore as the limits of possibility, becomes in "Spirit" the personal, private province of the individual.

Accordingly, *Nature* ends with a section, "Prospects" (43–49), that projects the essay toward a distant horizon that all our questions and speculations barely adumbrate. Still, "the highest reason is always the truest. That which seems faintly possible—it is so refined, is often faint and dim because it is deepest seated in the mind among the eternal verities." And although his "little book" has been a sort of anatomy of natural philosophy, Emerson emphasizes now that anatomy has not been its point, nor has any specific description or definition. He has sought the ineffable wholeness of things rather than any of its parts, the only worthy mediation being finally "the manly contemplation of the whole." The only question the true philosopher asks is "why all thought of multitude is lost in a tranquil sense of unity." Thus, the great purpose of *Nature* has been to point along the line of sight toward Jefferson's small catch of smooth blue horizon, where history and prophecy come together. The great discovery of *Nature* has been that that horizon is here within the self, indeed, that it *is* the self.

Jefferson looking west was invested with a mission; Emerson looking into infinity becomes the mission. The fusion of self, nation, and universe complete, he embodies it personally and is thus far more powerful than Jefferson the observer. When Emerson wrote that the soul "is a watcher more than a doer, and it is a doer, only that it may the better watch," he meant by watching something *more* effective than doing, beyond process, an instantaneous emergence, whereby a man sees his vision into being. Mere doing, by comparison, is ineffective, the groping in the dark of those who lack vision: "he that works most [in the world] is but a half-man, and whilst his arms are strong and his digestion good, his mind is imbruted, and he is a selfish savage." The laborers in the vineyard earn scant respect from Emerson: a man must be literally the vineyard's overseer. To sow and reap is "such a resumption of power, as if a banished king should buy his territories inch by inch"; in watching, on the contrary, the king "vault[s] at once into his throne." Watching is action unlimited by time or space—no buying of territory inch by inch but an instantaneous assumption of the whole land, as far as the eye can see.

This vaulting into thrones is the modern equivalent of the music of the spheres. It is a mode of production in which the product is an expression of the world itself, encompassing worker and work so that, rather than being interactors, they together make up action itself. But while this melding is the ultimate ideal, pretranscendentally, at the stage at which the world needs the reconciling ministrations of an "actor," the actor's vision and the world's can appear widely at odds. What we have seen is the ideological power of the concept of incarnation as Emerson developed it, which lay essentially in its ability to relate these two states nonantagonistically, as stages. Or, in Emerson's words: "The ruin or the blank that we see when we look at nature, is in our own eye. The axis of vision is not coincident with the axis of things, and so they appear not transparent but opaque. The reason why the world lacks unity, and lies broken and in heaps, is because man is disunited with himself" (*Nature*, 47). The basic program projected by Transcendentalism is the restoration of congruence. The difference between this and the basic program of European liberalism is profound, the latter remaining dialectical at its most idealistic, and therefore, instead of congruence or correspondence, proposing a synthesis that inevitably transforms. Emerson, on the contrary, envisages man's rebuilding of the world this way:

> As fast as you conform your life to the pure idea in your mind, that will unfold its great proportions. A correspondent revolution in things will attend the influx of the spirit. So fast will disagreeable appearances, swine, spiders, snakes, pests, mad-houses, prisons, enemies, vanish; they are temporary and shall be no more seen. The sordor and filths of nature, the sun shall dry up, and the wind exhale. As when the summer comes from the south; the snow-banks melt, and the face of the earth becomes green before it, so shall the advancing spirit create its ornaments along its path, and carry with it the beauty it visits, and the song which enchants it; it shall draw beautiful faces, warm hearts, wise discourse, and heroic acts, around its way, until evil is no more seen.   (48–49)

Beyond its reiteration of the material power of spirit, and, in fact, of the lack of any basic distinction between the material and the spiritual as they cooperate in the production of the real world, this passage is distinctly American in a way that is more readily apparent when it is compared, for instance, to Carlyle's vision of world-building. Here is Carlyle's Professor Teufelsdröckh in a moment of equal enthusiasm:

> it is with man's Soul as it was with Nature: the beginning of Creation is—Light. Till the eye have vision, the whole

members are in bonds. Divine moment, when over the tempest-tost Soul, as once over the wild-weltering Chaos, it is spoken: Let there be Light! . . . The mad primeval Discord is hushed; the rudely-jumbled conflicting elements bind themselves into separate Firmaments: deep silent rock-foundations are built beneath; and the skyey vault with its everlasting Luminaries above: instead of a dark wasteful Chaos, we have a blooming, fertile, heaven-encompassed World. (*Sartor Resartus*, 148)

The difference between Carlyle's radical transformation of Chaos into a "blooming, fertile" earth and Emerson's vision of the cleansing and renewal of an inherently orderly nature is deepest in the opposition of their conclusions. This is Emerson's:

The kingdom of man over nature, which cometh not with observation,—a dominion such as now is beyond his dream of God,—he shall enter without more wonder than the blind man feels who is gradually restored to perfect sight. (*Nature*, 49)

And Carlyle's:

I too could now say to myself: Be no longer a Chaos, but a World, or even Worldkin. Produce! Produce! Were it but the pitifullest infinitesimal fraction of a Product, produce it, in God's name! 'Tis the utmost thou hast in thee: out with it, then. Up! Up! Whatsoever thy hand findest to do, do it with thy whole might. Work while it is called Today; for the Night cometh, wherein no man can work. (148–149)

For Teufelsdröckh, the force of the human spirit is the power to engage the limits of the "infinitesimal . . . utmost" that may be all he possesses; for Emerson, the exercise of spirit aims not at an enhanced "infinitesimal" but at the full value of the infinite. Emerson is not more ambitious than Carlyle. But while Carlyle urges man to do whatever he can with his own two hands, Emerson means, by such self-reliance, manipulating the power of the universe—because *his* hands extend from a universal body. Carlyle's hands, on the contrary, are his own because they are *not* God's or the country's.

Over many years of correspondence, Carlyle and Emerson unfolded this difference the more fully because they thought their visions were so similar. After proofreading the English edition of Emerson's *Essays*, for example, Carlyle wrote Emerson that the book was "a *sermon* to me . . . a real *word* . . . in a world all full of jargons, hearsays, echoes, and vain noises, which cannot pass with me for *words*." But, he continued,

> I have to object still, that we find you a Speaker, indeed, but as it were a *Soliloquizer* on the eternal mountain-tops only, in vast solitudes where men and their affairs lie all hushed in a very dim remoteness; and only *the man* and the stars and the earth are visible . . . It is cold and vacant there; nothing paintable but rainbows and emotions; come down, and you shall do life-pictures, passions, facts,—which *transcend* all thought, a[nd] leave it stuttering and stammering! (*Correspondence of Emerson and Carlyle*, 371)

Carlyle thus reproached what he took to be Emerson's withdrawal from the field of action. Emerson replied, essentially, that he withdrew *to* the field of action:

> Of what you say now & heretofore respecting the remoteness of my writing and thinking from real life, . . . I do not know what it means. If I can at any time express the law & the ideal right, that should satisfy me without measuring the divergence from it of the last act of Congress. And though I sometimes accept a popular call, & preach on Temperance or the Abolition of Slavery, . . . I am sure to feel before I have done with it, what an intrusion it is into another sphere, & so much loss of virtue in my own . . .   (373)

What transforms abdication into imperial claim is that Emerson's "own sphere" is really all-spheres, the All.

But this has a catch. The heavenly All cannot be altered short of the Götterdämmerung. So the real difference between Carlyle and Emerson lay not in how much each acted or advocated action but, more profoundly, in the nature of the action. Carlyle could do relatively little, or imagined he could, but everything he did changed the world. Emerson could do everything—so long as he left the world intact. That concealed opposing term is what transformed the ideal of untrammeled individualism into an ideology that harnessed (controlled and released) energy. When this term is made visible, much of what has been considered philosophically dubious in Emerson's thinking reveals its real rigor. For instance, when Frederic Carpenter sees "a clear logical flaw" in *Nature*, he seems to me to misinterpret Emerson's own concern, over the course of the writing, that there was a "crack" in the essay between discipline and idealism. For Carpenter, the flaw is "nothing less than Emerson's failure to solve the (so far) insoluble philosophic problem of mind and matter." Carpenter does not blame Emerson for not solving this perennial problem, but does find *Nature* itself flawed "by the impression given that he somehow had solved it" (*Emerson Handbook*, 53). In the context of the preceding discussion, however, that impression is not so misleading, for having redefined dualism as complementarity, Emerson is able to achieve at least a mediation whereby discipline enables action in the context of idealism, while idealism sets the limits of action.

It should be said that Emerson's mode of exposition contributed largely to the impression that he was unsystematic. Carlyle described *Nature,* memorably, as "a beautiful square bag of *duckshot* held together by canvas"; he complained delicately that its sentences "did not . . . always entirely cohere for me. Pure genuine Saxon; strong and simple; of a clearness, of a beauty—But they did not, sometimes, rightly stick to their foregoers and their followers . . ." (371). But because Carlyle's own system depended on the conception that history is man-made, he may have missed the point Emerson made at every turn: that order (relations between parts, structures of thought, and expression) is not temporal but simultaneous, not dialectical or dualistic but holistic, not man-made but universal. When one accepts that he *really* meant all that, his language becomes entirely rigorous. In fact, its lack of forward sequential argument, its continual return to flat assertion interspersed with nonprogressive illustrations, might be taken as the linguistic representation of the assertion that America is primordially and organically defined, and thus—from analysts, historians, or celebrants—awaits only articulation. Emerson was not trying to develop but to reveal the definition of America.

In other words, the issue for Emerson was not, after all, building his own world, but assuming it: "We are taught by great actions that the universe is the property of every individual in it. Every

121

rational creature has all nature for his dowry and estate. It is his, if he will. He may divest himself of it; he may creep into a corner, and abdicate his kingdom, as most men do, but he is entitled to the world by his constitution" (*Nature*, 16).

So the North American continent awaited the European's discovery that it was already his. To exemplify the prior and eternal oneness of man and his universe, Emerson imagined this scene: "When the bark of Columbus nears the shore of America;—before it, the beach lined with savages, fleeing out of all their huts of cane; the sea behind; and the purple mountains of the Indian Archipelago around, can we separate the man from the living picture? Does not the New World clothe his form with her palm-groves and savannahs as fit drapery?" (17). The answers are obvious.

4 ✳ Plain and
Fancy Fictions

*I*n the passage quoted at the end of Chapter 3, the answers to
Emerson's question are obvious because they are axiomatic: the
very concept of discovery posits the inherence of "America" in
the continent and therefore the identity of the new arrivals with
their new world. The central argument of *Nature* is essentially the
elaboration of this axiom, showing how the identity of the American with America endows the American with transcendent autonomy, or how through his identification with his world each
man becomes an autonomous universe in himself. In terms of
Emerson's conception of language, we can say that a man discovering his entire correspondence with nature writes himself universally large.

Yet in this version of that identity—the destined land first
coming under the interpretive gaze of its discoverer—what happens to Columbus is a little ambiguous. It is not clear that Columbus wholly or only gains by the merger. The situation itself is
unusual, however. Typically, Emerson imagines the coming together of man and nature as an interior spiritual process yielding
a heightened state of consciousness. Here the product of communion is external, a specific and concrete "living picture"; and
in becoming part of this picture, Columbus acquires a new costume, is clothed and draped. Thus nature not only aggrandizes

123

him but also alters him and is in turn altered by him when he becomes its organizing focus. In that way, each of them—Columbus and nature—seems actually to *lose* some autonomy.

Let us look at the passage again:

> When the bark of Columbus nears the shore of America;— before it, the beach lined with savages, fleeing out of all their huts of cane; the sea behind; and the purple mountains of the Indian Archipelago around, can we separate the man from the living picture? Does not the New World clothe his form with her palm-groves and savannahs as fit drapery?

Alert now to the partial transformation undergone by both Columbus and the landscape in the creation of the living picture, we can note additionally that this transformation takes place over time. Or at least *in* time: "when" Columbus approaches America, crossing not only space but time, the savages appear not only in the same place but simultaneously; the Europeans and the Indians, *now* juxtaposed against their backgrounds of sea and mountains, *then* make up a picture. It is a familiar picture, especially in our context: Columbus and the savages, the sea, and the mountains encompass all nature and all mankind, made one when Columbus as spirit and nature as flesh act out the American incarnation. And yet that acting out is just what makes this account unusual, for it represents the incarnation in progress, the subject not of an epiphany but of a story. Our initial suspicion that there was something odd about this particular representation of the coming together of man and nature is strengthened: if pictures are rare in Emerson's writing, stories are rarer still.

They are rare with good reason, as this picture/story demonstrates. Seen interacting, either in picture or in story, man and nature inhabit a universe that is necessarily larger than either of them. For if both were adequate to the whole of their shared world, they would be identical and there would be no story, while if one were thus commensurate with everything he would absorb the other and again there would be no story. The "living picture" transcends its components; it is a whole that is greater than the sum of its parts, let alone any one of them. But Emerson's central tenet is that every part, each individual and each aspect of nature, is equal to the whole, *is* the whole. Starting out to establish the identical wholeness of American/America by evoking the transcendent epiphany of their mutual origin, Emerson instead has described each term in the dialectical process of delimiting the other. While together Columbus and the New World add a new reality to the world, in that new setting each becomes less self-sufficient. Columbus's appearance is changed by the costume provided by the New World, and in turn the definition of that world is reorganized around him. All this amounts to describing the "discovery" of America, in a word, as an *invention*.

On a third reading, the passage, once seen as a story about two characters, man and nature (the "savages" being an aspect of nature), reveals a third character, the "we" to whom the rhetorical questions are addressed. And this "we" saves the day. It brings the living picture/story back under the aegis of an observing eye. This observant "we," a corporation of all-sufficient eyes and I's, restores wholeness and timelessness by fusing the interactive terms of man and nature in the coherence of the self. To this we/I looking retrospectively through the transparent eyeball of transcending Americanness, the living picture, the story of Columbus arriving in the New World, is not history after all.

But a final look at the passage reveals that its preservation of a transcendent American/America is costly. The cost is implicit in the very form of the emergence of the salutory "we," namely the suppression of dissent represented by the rhetorical question. That "we," really Emerson's "I," outlaws grammatically any answer but the one that affirms the perfection of the new America. The "we" does not enter into argument—lest it perpetuate the dialectical condition it is intended to transcend. This is a supremely authoritarian "we," essentially a divine "we" who, asserting epiphany, brings to an end both story and history.

None of this need present a problem for Emerson, whose constant message is the ultimate authority of the self. But his brief dip into the forms of art and fiction has brought to the surface an implicit difficulty in the identity of man and nature. We began to see this difficulty earlier, that the unlimited power of the Emersonian individual to fulfill all the possibilities in nature may preclude his creating new possibilities and changing nature. In fact, his identity with the universe implies their common perfection and makes him its natural guardian. The essay *Nature* as a whole celebrates the positive aspect of this bond, which bestows on the individual the capacity to build his world by realizing (enacting) the universal potential. But in the passage I have been discussing, the converse of such ideal unfolding occurs when the production of something new in the world (ironically, America is the new thing) implies the limits of the producer's power, since this power is not the identical force of nature but additional to it. That the producer's power is limited, moreover, implies that nature's power is also limited, that the existing state of things is not complete, since it can be added to. The act of creating has qualified or even called into question the original wholeness of creator and Creation alike.

The European artists who, when their God died, just took over his job, might take such impiety in stride, but for Americans it was blasphemy. Emerson especially could not condone the implication that either he or his world was incomplete—it denied the ground of his philosophy. But to reestablish that ground at the end of the passage, in effect he has to bind himself to it. For the all-encompassing "we," who appears to reaffirm unity, also refuses others the right to demur from that unity, to wonder, for instance, whether Columbus was in fact the rightful monarch of the New World or if possibly the "savages" were. Seen in this way, the authoritative American has an authoritarian cast. Activating the other term of the potential contradiction entailed by his identity with all the (new) world, this American not only enjoins enactment but forbids actions.

This aspect of the "we" would not concern Emerson, whose fundamental belief in a benevolent universe assured him that the utmost assertions of personal desire would enhance universal freedom. It is equally important that he was not a painter of pictures or a writer of stories. Rather than pictures he typically described visions, and he wrote essays and poems whose central characteristic is their monistic perspective. But for those of his contemporaries who had less faith in the world's inherent goodness, and for writers of stories, the contradictions in the identity of man and nature were much more serious. As I will show in the next three chapters, the unavoidable tendency of pictures and stories to project new worlds of their own was a central and ultimately insuperable problem for the founding fathers of the American novel. Their every living picture seemed to imply that the real New World of the real founding fathers might be itself a living picture. By inventing their Americas, they suggested that the discovery of America was also an invention; that Jefferson's *vision* of roads leading to the horizon was a *picture* he projected onto a terrain that would as readily have accommodated the paths of Indians.

Against such relativist and historicist implications, Emerson invoked the authority of the all-seeing self—and living picture dissolved into transcendent vision. A writer whose purpose it was to draw a picture, however, would need a different solution. Moreover, insofar as this writer's primary commitment was to pictures, his appeal to the self would tend to have the opposite effect from Emerson's. Indeed the writers whose work I shall discuss in the next chapters, by probing the ground of individualism, raised monsters of the absolute self that were absolutely set on the creation of pictures, satanic selves whose solution to the division of American reality implied by their pictures was to reconcile it in *their* image, so that in their work the vision of America would dissolve in the picture drawn by *one or another* American. All the components of this disintegration are there in the passage from Emerson: the picture/story's intimations of relativity, the stirrings of historical mutability that result from the dialectical interaction of relative beings, and the self's hypertrophy in defense of the monolithic universe that offers the self its own universality. What is not there is any mechanism for avoiding the disintegration, other than, as Emerson does, by a first-person grammatical fiat that closes the necessary dialogue of fiction. The very telling of the story of the incarnation seems to challenge its integrity, while the writer who properly realizes his creative power as an American in the telling may emerge thereby as America's archenemy.

The profundity of this dilemma is dramatically evident from its emergence in what should have been the most reconciling of contexts: Emerson imagining the coming into being of America. Yet it was enough for him to imagine the New World as a new reality for this to conflict with the timelessness and transcendence

127

that defined the New World's dispensation from change and historical vicissitude. This is a dilemma that penetrates to the basic structure of the ideology of incarnation, so that the invention of stories can stand here for any act, mental or material, that results in a new reality, whether imaginary or concrete. In that wider scheme, it suggests the possibility that the unequaled triumph of the self that I traced in *Nature* and ascribed to the individual American's identity with America may also through that same identity have incurred a greater interdiction. Build therefore your own world, Emerson urged the individual, for you are in yourself equal to any world; but (apparently) let it not be any world but this one.

In considering the possibility that the status of the individual in America, his last best home, is so profoundly paradoxical, it may help to recall something of his prior situations. Our concern is with the modern individual, the figure who rose to political and philosophical ascendancy in the seventeenth century. For while the individual, like the middle class, may appear to have been always rising, it was in the seventeenth century that a significant redefinition of the basic unit of society from the group to the individual marked the onset of modern history. Hobbes feared that this shift would result in a completely atomized society in which not even the bonds between mothers and children would be fully reliable, but Locke saw reassuringly that common economic and political interests would continue to create communities of class. Still, these communities would not generate the old sense of organic and inevitable togetherness; membership in a modern class reflects personal advancement, not communal identity, and leaving one's native class for another, higher one represents self-fulfillment. Thus, in the modern mind, individuals and groups appear to be antithetical entities, each defining the other restrictively.

The modern liberal culture, moreover, sides with the individual, whom it defends as if he were its own child. But the individual was around long before the modern era. Classical heroes were individuals as fully fledged, as distinctly characterized, as self-protective and aggressive, possibly even as internally reflective, as modern heroes. There is a crucial difference, however, between the individuality of wily Odysseus and rash Oedipus, on one hand, and that of Stephen Daedalus on the other: that of the classical heroes consists of a constellation of traits, complex but stable, while the modern man is who he is chiefly by virtue of his ability to change and by changing actively to mold his own identity. The familiar description of this difference dubs Odysseus and Oedipus types and Stephen Daedalus an individual, but this only brings us around a tautological circle back to the problem of defining "individual." On the way, however, we discover something that *is* peculiar to modern individuality, namely that the path to it leads away from the village common. Rousseau's *Confessions,* one of the classic texts of individualism, starts off full tilt down that path: "I am made unlike any one I have ever met," Rousseau insists at once; "I will even venture to say that I am like no one in the whole world. I may be no better, but at least I am different" (17). Achilles and Lear are not different from their fellow men, they are only more. Larger or smaller, better or worse, the ancient individual is defined comparatively, so that even the claim of incomparable heroism connotes only that he possesses a paramount quantity of the same ideal values that others also have. It is precisely the impossibility of comparison that defines Rousseau: he *is* those aspects of himself which presumably occur in no one else.[1] And the same antithesis individualizes his writing. The first sentence of the *Confessions* identifies the book to follow by separating it from all other books: "I have resolved on an enterprise which has no precedent, and which, once complete, will have no imitator."

The capacity for change that characterizes the modern individual thus has as its object the production of a unique being. But why is self-generated difference the mark of modern individuality?[2] It seems reasonable to suppose there is a correspondence between this new personal ideal and the new basis of economic and political identity that emerged at the same time. In the feudal societies prior to the Renaissance, changing one's class was nearly impossible, because land, the major category of property, occurred mainly in fixed and previously distributed amounts passed on by inheritance. Personal distinction in that context would consist of being like the others in one's class, only better. Being better, one might either merit more of what there was or be able to take more by force; overreaching, however, one would collide tragically with the world's fateful limits.

But the mercantile and capitalist modes of production that became dominant in the seventeenth and eighteenth centuries generated in capital a new kind of property, which individual enterprise causes to expand as if from within. Even if, as Marx explained, only labor actually produces new value, merchants and industrialists, by appropriating the labor of others, acquire a multiplied creative power that redounds to them personally. For the wealth whose production they command is additional, new. The capacity to create newly in the name of his unique person demarcates the modern individual from the ancient, who contended with his likes for a larger share of the common stock. Henceforth the individual is defined by, literally produced by, what he makes that is new—including, indeed starting with, himself. Rousseau identifies himself as what no one else has been or will be. (Note that the New World is as exceptional as Rousseau, as productive, in its substance, of its own essence, as without peer or precedent, as exceptional, as incomparable and inimitable.) In brief, viewing one's individual stake in life, starting with one's self, as capital capable of generating a self-sufficient economy of its own inspires a commensurate autonomy as the productive core of selfhood. The individual becomes an individual*ist* when he takes his individuality as his stake and sets about developing it into a whole world.

To corner the market or to co-opt all creation, just being different is not enough. It is possible to be unique and a sport, a freak, without access to the common currency of production, an illiterate or moronic Rousseau, a New World wasteland rather than wilderness. This possibility points to a paradox: the realization of difference in the production of the new (machines, ideas, or dresses) involves a separation from the existing state of things; set apart, the producer of the new may appear limited to *just* his newness, and be thus actually diminished by his difference. To prevent this, he needs to represent himself as globally different—capable of any and all differences. Rousseau therefore claims not only uniqueness but universality. Not only is he different from all others, he is also able to be, if he wishes, exactly and entirely like any one of them or, more ambitiously still, like all of them together. Rejecting the limiting definitions of class or nation, the modern individual becomes simply Man, able to attain anything the species can attain. This Man indeed is fond of claiming that nothing in nature or in other men is alien to him, understanding that otherwise some parts of nature and some forms of achievement open to others would be barred to him. Being universal, the unique individual is also representative of all (unique) individuals, and this makes him uniquely powerful. In a world where individual potential proves itself tangibly in the self-propagation of property, a man who encompasses all the possibilities of man may reasonably claim to be building whole worlds in his own—both exceptional and universal—image. There is a precedent, Jehovah, one God yet universal, a monolithic deity who made the whole world. The modern conception of the individual as at once unique and universally representative thus endows the individual with unprecedented potency to effect his own designs. All this is the case in theory. In practice, in the European cradle of individualism, continuing challenges to the individual's universality limited his empowerment. What Raymond Williams termed residual and emergent cultures both have persistently denied the bourgeois the right to project himself as the modern Everyman. In default of such representativeness, he has remained both class-identified and personally relative—neither entirely unique nor wholly universal.

The American middle class, by contrast, always had the stage effectively to itself. In posthistorical America, the individual could readily claim he was building his own world. If in its European form individualism created the modern world (to be sure, out of the stuff of nonmodern worlds everywhere), the incarnate individualism that, as the saying goes, made America great was still more potent for having generalized its individualism into a whole new world. We have already read the announcement of this apotheosis in Emerson's *Nature*.

But there could be a complication, whose emergence in the realm of fiction and art I began to explore earlier. Recall that this problem lay not in the definition of the individual as such but in the way he implemented his individuality. In the creation of new "pictures" or realities, he exercised a dialectical creativity at

131

odds with the notion that his world was already a complete whole. And by impugning this wholeness, he reopened the question of historical process, with its future that differed from the past. Ironically, the creative American threatened to subvert the American Creation.

Continuing the exploration of this problem, I want to emphasize that such subversion occurs not intentionally but by definition when a modern individualist creates at all and to any purpose. In contrast to previous literary visions, which could parody or denounce the deformations of their real worlds without challenging the basic order of things, the modern imagination, even when it means to confirm an existing system, questions it by constituting itself an alternative and thus a competitor. In sum, the competitive individualist turned artist is willy-nilly a revolutionary.

This is just the message conveyed by the familiar image of the rebel-artist in modern European culture. As familiarly, however, the rebel-artist fails to accomplish significant social transformations: his rebellion generates art *instead* of revolution. The rebel-artist is a popular martyr in a parable of the ultimate powerlessness of the individual to change the world single-handedly. Even his utopian visions, while they may prophesy eventual transformations, more immediately measure the inertia of the existing system. And that system's (historical) transcendence of *him:* when Stephen Daedalus sets out to create the conscience of his race, it is apparent even to him that there still are more things in the world than are contained in his philosophy.

But not more than are contained in Emerson's philosophy— and there is the rub. The American, and therefore the American artist, is identical with America and sufficient unto all of it. He incarnates America and encompasses its entire consciousness— but this means that his rebel-vision presents an entire alternative to America. The greater power of the American individualist is matched in an implicitly more powerful art. It was history that killed God in Europe; in America history in turn came to an end and a new god emerged, not out there in the heavens but right in here, looking out at his creation through Emerson's personal eyeball. What he saw outside therefore was also inside, and what he projected from inside would also be outside. The modern competition between art and reality could go on in Europe because neither party could win; and art, because it was an individual action, was finally the weaker. But in an America that was at once reality and art, the art of an American himself as large as America was another order of threat altogether. If the unique succeeds in claiming universality, it delegitimates the existing universe: the culmination of the modern individualist's evolution into an American would appear to render his art capable of doing just that.

This subversive potential was perhaps not present in all the forms of the American's art or all the genres of his literature. The dominant literary forms of each historical epoch are those which are not only ethically but aesthetically linked to contemporary issues. Thus, the genres of classical tragedy and epic, of mock epic and satire, of lyric and novel have been each in turn and in their time inherently political. Other genres, not at the moment dominant, certainly address the politics of the contemporary culture as well. But the predominant genre (or genres) speaks politically whatever it says. In our time the novel, or fiction more generally, has been the genre that is most organically of the epoch—to conceive of a novel is to imagine a middle-class society. Because the middle-class way of structuring the world is implicit in the structure of the novelistic universe, the one *naturally* entails the other. This conjunction is hardly mysterious, the novel having developed in response to the perceived cultural needs of the middle class, taking its constructions of being and of thinking as the imagination's givens. I should specify here that by "novel" I do not mean prose narrative in general but that version which became common in the eighteenth century through the writings of, for example, Samuel Richardson *(Pamela, Clarissa),* Jane Austen *(Pride and Prejudice, Emma),* Rousseau *(Hélöise),* and a little later Honoré de Balzac. Such novels posit, as a principle of character development, the ideology of individualism I have outlined; and as the social context in which their characters move, the fluid relations and multiplied possibilities of a market economy.

To note that a particular literary structure is imbued with the politics of its time is not to say that it celebrates them. Not even the *Iliad* or the *Aeneid*, though each announces itself as "singing" its subject, remains uncritical. The aesthetic of an epoch embodies the assumptions of the epoch but does not necessarily approve them, let alone their implementation. And in the case of the novel, the possibility of a critical stance is itself a structuring assumption, the modern individualist being by definitition critical. The novel, in comparison to earlier dominant forms, has tended to be hypercritical. I have already discussed how the insufficiency of middle-class ideological hegemony exacerbated this tendency. But as a form the novel is rebellious anyway, by its rebelliousness as well reflecting its originating ideology. This point begins to refine the definition of the problem we saw in Emerson's sketch of Columbus's discovery into the possibility of a fundamental conflict between the ideology of fiction and that of America, which would imply, as modern fiction implies modern reality, as basic a contradiction inside American ideology.

It became apparent earlier in this discussion that the basic demands of fiction conflict with the ideology of discovery: a novel has to project more than one point of view or it will have no plot. The congeniality of storytelling to the definition of modern individuality through difference is undoubtedly one of the reasons telling stories seemed to the early novelists the best way to represent their world. Moreover, since in Europe individualistic difference never entirely achieved universality, the multiple perspective implicit in storytelling continued to be both useful and relevant in representing the conflict of the still insurgent self with society. But in America individualism did achieve universal status. This achievement is precisely the point of Whitman's "Song of Myself," in which the author introduces himself in terms that seem to be the opposite of Rousseau's. In contrast to Rousseau's "I am made unlike any one . . . I am like no one in the whole world," Whitman says, "My tongue, every atom of my blood, form'd from this soil, this air. / Born here of parents born here from parents the same, and their parents the same" ("Song of Myself," ll.6–7). Whitman's uniqueness is fully representative. He is distinctly Walt Whitman, "now thirty-seven years old in perfect health" (l. 8), but at the same time, "what I assume you shall assume, / For every atom belonging to me as good belongs to you" (ll. 2–3).

That these two prophets of individualism boasted in such different languages dramatizes the extraordinary problem of the American novelist. For Whitman's poetic form permits him to claim difference and universality at once because he is the only character in the piece. But as the impersonality of the characters in his catalogs testifies, he could not have written a story that way.

Hawthorne's novel *The Scarlet Letter*, by contrast, typifies the apparently ineluctable tendency of fictional characters to blaspheme against America. This tendency is the crux of the plot. Hester Prynne arrives in America alone and sets out to build herself a new world. Exercising her naturally endowed freedom (the absence of her husband effectively returns her to a condition prior to the social contract), she proposes, individualistically, to live differently from the way she did in the Old World, more in accord with her nature. The man with whom she proposes to build her own world, however, already embodies an established order. Dimmesdale is the New World's moral guardian. The birth of the illegitimate Pearl reveals this blasphemous doubling: there is Hester's America and there is Boston's, and both claim the universal moral franchise. That Hester is an artist makes the representation almost superfluously explicit, for the exposition of the problem was already complete in her creation of a life of her own that differed from the conventional lives of her fellow settlers, a life that individualistically claimed universality.

Not only the characters in *The Scarlet Letter* blaspheme. If Hester's attempt to construct an alternative America threatens to dismantle this one, Hawthorne's construction of Hester is no less subversive. The author is more radical than the character: she rejects certain of Boston's moral tenets but he challenges its moral authority as such. In contrast to "Song of Myself," *The Scarlet Letter* is born not "of parents the same" but of parents necessarily other. It is Hawthorne who likens Mistress Prynne to Ann Hutchinson and links her to antinomianism; Hester herself makes a more limited case. But the novel could not begin without making the larger case, or rather it has already made it by beginning; for any individualist dissent is a divergence; an individualist, as Emerson insisted, builds worlds simply by imagining them. The *novel*, then, wears a scarlet letter, for by writing it Hawthorne too commits adultery, with another America. No amount of penitence on Hester's part can undo his act in having invented her. The sign on her bosom may come to mean "Angel" but *The Scarlet Letter* remains adulterous.

It seems clear from Hawthorne's handling of Hester's prophecy near the end of the novel that he knew he faced this dilemma. After Hester's return to Boston, she not only accepts its laws for herself but becomes their active advocate to others. She counsels resignation even to women who through no fault of their own bear "the dreary burden of a heart unyielded, because unvalued and unsought"; for in this seventeenth-century America rebellion is never justified, nor does it ever succeed. From a more hopeful perspective, this is because it has already succeeded: Hester assures the cheated women "of her firm belief, that, at some brighter period, when the world should have grown ripe for it, in Heaven's own time, a new truth would be revealed, in order to establish the whole relation between man and woman on a surer ground of mutual happiness." There is no need, therefore, of her or their laboring to bring change. Indeed by seeking change they only impede it:

> Earlier in life, Hester had vainly imagined that she herself might be the destined prophetess, but had long since recognized the impossibility that any mission of divine and mysterious truth should be confided to a woman stained with sin, bowed down with shame, or even burdened with a life-long sorrow. The angel and apostle of the coming revelation must be a woman, indeed, but lofty, pure, and beautiful; and wise, moreover, not through dusky grief, but the ethereal medium of joy; and showing how sacred love should make us happy, by the truest test of a life successful to such an end! (344–345)

The central but also the puzzling point in this passage is conveyed by the repeated image of a woman whose burdening sorrow is *not* guilty: earlier this woman bore the weight of a heart she would have gladly yielded had her husband sought it, and now her "life-long sorrow," though unspecified, is clearly distinct from either sin or shame. One wonders why Hawthorne adds unmerited suffering to the proscribed list, particularly as Hester's advice to these guiltless women to submit carries her apart from her own story and dilutes its ending.

After all, Hester herself *is* guilty, and so far her guilt has seemed to be the issue. Now it appears that she would have been tainted even had she not been adulterous, just by being an unhappy wife. In suggesting that the guiltless deserve punishment also, this definition of the problem is newly harsh. For in effect the passage tells anyone yearning for a better future that you can't get there from here. There is no path, no process that will lead to that better world. This is because in one sense we are already there, since the future is implicit if not yet evident. But in a more disturbing sense, it is also because the very consciousness of injustice corrupts the protest it inspires and essentially invalidates it. Had the sorrowful women been worthy, they would have proved it by being successful and happy; because they are not happy, they deserve no better. Jehovah himself was less jealous: though they have not like Hester distorted the patriarchal word, let alone struck the patriarchal rock, Hawthorne denies them the Promised Land, simply for finding the desert dry.

But Hawthorne had to be stricter than God because he was dealing with a more unruly subject—namely, another god, the Individual Self. Hester's last absolute prohibition forbids a divine activity, the conception of (better) worlds. The injunction reaches beyond Hester's own crime to Hawthorne's, exceeds the plot to encompass the enterprise of writing. The passage is curiously impersonal (as is the entire treatment of Hester after her return to Boston) and also mannered, allegorical. Its harshness may be less disturbing if we see that it envisions characters less than the very act of characterization. In sum, the absolutism of *The Scarlet Letter* is not so much an expression of the author's conservatism or even of his anxiety over the transgression he has evoked. It is not sufficiently explained, I think, by either a simple political motive or a psychological one. Rather, this final denial seems to me a necessity imposed by the very form of the novel, which requires a closure commensurate with its opening. Having by that opening questioned the foundations of the idea of America—of the (new) world—it can only end by affirming them categorically, even though this negates the novel's own categories, bringing Hawthorne, in denying the usefulness of Hester's suffering, to deny as well the value of his own authorial travail.

The very last line of the story, describing the "semblance of an engraved escutcheon" that ultimately marked Hester's tombstone, "On a Field, Sable, the Letter A, Gules," amounts to an abdication. The character Hawthorne brought to life is now dead. But, more significantly, so is her language: the letter "A" is reduced below the status of a character in narrative allegory, where it began its imperial expansion, to that of a lifeless cipher. In the story, the letter first appears on Hester's bosom, where it is more animate even than the infant Pearl (it is really the child who symbolizes the letter, in a reversal that represents the true relation between language and character). But even before that, in the account of the letter's discovery in the Custom House, Hawthorne has already insisted on its inherent vitality. When he placed it on his breast, "the reader may smile, but must not doubt my word—it seemed to me then that I experienced a sensation not altogether physical, yet almost so, of burning heat." Not only a letter but already a three-dimensional object, the letter is from the first autonomously powerful. *It* compels Hawthorne to ponder meaning that comes from within it, "some deep meaning . . . most worthy of interpretation, and which, as it were, streamed forth from the mystic symbol" (145–146).

Nothing streams forth from the last representation of the "A." Fixed forever on the slate tombstone and, still further from life, on the *semblance* of an escutcheon, the scarlet letter radiates only a deeper blackness: "so sombre is [the engraving], and relieved only by one ever glowing point of light gloomier than the shadow." It has become literally imponderable. At most a writer might decode it, a formula for a formula. With self-destructive irony, the story of Hester Prynne has its last incarnation in a disembodied "device, a herald's wording of which might serve for a motto and brief description of our now concluded legend. " Retrenched from symbol to herald's wording, the scarlet letter has withdrawn its

138

guilty challenge. When he imagined it first in the Custom House, Hawthorne must have already sensed it would come to this. It burned him like "red-hot iron," and he "shuddered, and involuntarily let it fall upon the floor" (146). But once he picks it up again and enhances its life-force with his own—not merely reading it in the real world of the Custom House but writing it into a world of his own creation—dropping it will not be sufficient to put an end to its satanism. Hester herself, purged in the last chapter of any potentially dissenting interiority, is definitively contained by the grave. (The foresight of the founding fathers cited in the novel's opening has been rewarded; sin and death now serve only to strengthen the social foundation.) But the letter, the all-powerful source of the story, is immortal. Not unlike a succubus, it has to be buried with the stake of Hester's tombstone through its heart.

Less dramatically, we can simply observe that Hawthorne ended his novel in the language of feudal romance; and that he prefaced his next novel, *The House of the Seven Gables,* with a warning that it would not be a novel at all but a "Romance." As he explained it, the essential difference between the two forms lay in their relation to the real world: the novel was bound "to aim at a very minute fidelity" (351) to reality, while the romance was freer to express its author's fantasies. Indeed, he claimed that what prompted the prefatory disclaimer was fear that the possible resemblance of the story's setting to the real town of Salem might inspire readers "to assign an actual locality to the imaginary events of this narrative." For such assignment "exposes the Romance to an inflexible and exceedingly dangerous species of criticism, *by bringing* [the author's] *fancy-pictures almost into positive contact with the realities of the moment*" (352; emphasis added). What were these dangers? One of them was the ire of living persons who saw themselves traduced in Hawthorne's stories. The preface to the second edition of *The Scarlet Letter* reports the strong resentment of certain persons who took themselves to be the models for the venal incompetents of the Custom House. But Hawthorne cheerfully refuses to withdraw a word of his sketch, on the ground that a careful rereading has only revealed its absolute accuracy. Since he thus renews the insult, the dangerous criticism he fears surely is not that of the insulted. Later, in a second conclusion to *The Marble Faun*, written under pressure from readers for a more positive elucidation of that story's mysteries, he complained that to drag these mysteries into the realistic light of day would make them absurd. This possibility seems a more likely motive for insisting that his stories were only "fancy-pictures," not to be taken literally. But to claim he was writing in another genre altogether seems a little overelaborate if the only issue is to win a little more imaginative latitude.

All the more in that elsewhere he complained that the romance was really not suitable to American subjects. This was in the preface to *The Marble Faun*, where he wrote that he had chosen Italy as the site of his story because he could that way avoid dealing with "actualities" which are "insisted upon, as they are, and must needs be, in America." He added, "No author, without a trial, can conceive of the difficulty of writing a Romance about a country where there is no shadow, no antiquity, no mystery, no picturesque and gloomy wrong, nor anything but a common-place prosperity, in broad and simple daylight, as is happily the case with my dear native land" (854). "Romance and poetry, like ivy, lichens, and wall-flowers, need Ruin to make them grow" (855); far from representing the American way of fiction, the romance was the form of expatriation.

To complicate the matter further, he had claimed earlier that he actually preferred the kind of writing he now described as more appropriate to America. In the Custom House sketch he regretted his sterile years as an inspector, wasted in yearning to create "the semblance of a world out of airy matter":

> The wiser effort would have been, to diffuse thought and imagination through the opaque substance of today, and thus to make it a bright transparency; . . . to seek, resolutely, the true and indestructible value that lay hidden in the petty and wearisome incidents and ordinary characters, with which I was now conversant. The fault was mine. The page of life that was spread out before me seemed dull and commonplace, only because I had not fathomed its deeper import. A better book than I shall ever write was there; leaf after leaf presenting itself to me, just as it was written out

by the reality of the flitting hour, and vanishing as fast as
written, only because my brain wanted the insight and my
hand the cunning to transcribe it.   (150–151)

We can discount much of the self-derogating rhetoric of this
passage but not its central point, that the highest task of the
writer is to reveal, through the everyday, life's essential spirituality. It is clear that he hopes his romances will accomplish the
same purpose. In this case the question of why Hawthorne
wrote romances (which in that form would have to be answered
mostly in terms of his personal temperament and talent) becomes, more particularly, Why did he *make a point* of writing
romances?

The words I emphasized earlier can begin to frame an answer:
that he sought in writing romances to avoid the exceeding danger
he saw in "bringing his fancy-pictures almost into positive contact
with the realities of the moment." The key phrase is "almost into
positive contact," projecting a fine distinction between two relations
of fancy to reality, this one destructive and the other ideal. The
ideal relation is described in the sketch on the Custom House as
"a neutral territory, somewhere between the real world and fairy-
land, where the Actual and the Imaginary may meet, and each
imbue itself with the nature of the other" (149). "May meet" and
"each imbue itself with the nature of the other" thus mean something qualitatively different to Hawthorne from "almost into positive contact"—so different that the last is essentially the end of
art and the first two are the beginning.

What is the difference between meeting on neutral ground
and having positive contact? I suggest that it is the difference I
drew in the preceding chapter between Emersonian complementarity and the dialectic: the first lifts duality out of its state of
contention by discovering a higher principle that renders its terms
mutually enriching; the second does almost the opposite by press-
ing the advantage of each over the other until both are transformed, and only in that way reconciled. Thus, when the actual
and the imaginary "meet on neutral territory" in a sort of interpretive armistice, the artist, like the *Scarlet Letter*'s prophetess
who will usher in universal happiness not by overcoming evil but

simply by being happy herself, realizes beauty without confronting ugliness; in fact by finding the beautiful in the ugly. On the contrary, in writing that brings the real and the imaginary into "positive contact"—for instance by claiming historical precedent for a fictional Judge Pyncheon—each tends to accuse the other or at least to test the other, so that the novel's success as a novel is in part measured by its success in enlarging our understanding of history.

But a large understanding of history can be a dangerous thing. Hawthorne explores its dangers in a short story, "The Prophetic Pictures." In this story a supremely skilled painter has acquired a reputation for doing just what Hawthorne in the Custom House sketch chides himself for not attempting: using his art to render surface commonplaces transparent to the deep meaning beneath.[3] "They say that he paints not merely a man's features, but his mind and heart" (456). On the eve of their marriage, Walter and Elinor commission their portraits. The paintings are brilliantly alive, and at first glance the likenesses are perfect. But upon closer inspection, there is a certain sadness in Elinor's picture and a passion in Walter's that seem lacking in the originals. Over the years, however, the originals come more and more to resemble the portraits. Walter's darkening mood causes the gentle Elinor great anxiety. Shuddering, she recalls at times a sketch with which the painter had amused himself while he worked on their portraits: it pictured a maddened Walter in the act of stabbing Elinor to the heart. After many years the painter returns to Boston and hastens to the home of Walter and Elinor, eager to see how his paintings have fared. He enters just in time to see his two models standing in front of their portraits, whose respective passion and melancholy they now entirely mirror. As the painter steps into the room, Walter turns toward Elinor, draws a knife, and cries, "Our fate is upon us . . . Die!" "The picture," the narrator says, "with all its tremendous coloring, was finished" (469).

In this interpretation of a familiar theme, Hawthorne, interestingly, has not worried about the most familiar issues. For instance, the problem in the painter's skill does not seem to lie in its potential abuse. He wields his brush honestly, depicting only what he sees and never attempting to benefit personally from his power. The tragedy of Walter and Elinor is not of his doing. Moreover, when Elinor recoils from the pencil drawing of her murder, he offers to change the action of the figures, "But would it influence the event?" (464). So the possibility that prior knowledge might of itself distort the order of things is also not what worries Hawthorne. In fact the tale closes with Cassandra's moral: "Could the result of one, or all of our deeds, be shadowed forth and set before us—some would call it Fate, and hurry onward—others be swept along by their passionate desires—and none be turned aside by the PROPHETIC PICTURES" (469). But this ending is really a misrepresentation. For while foreknowledge did not deter Elinor from a marriage she was warned would end in her death, in fact she does not die. Entering the room at the fateful moment, the painter prevents the destined outcome. He "interposed himself between the wretched beings, with the same sense of power to regulate their destiny, as to alter a scene upon the canvass. He stood like a magician, controlling the phantoms which he had evoked" (469).

In protesting the interference—"Does Fate impede its own decree?" (469)—the maddened Walter reveals the real problem. For as a moral man, the painter *has* to interfere when it is in his power to prevent a crime. Otherwise he would be complicitous, as is clear from his appearing at precisely the crucial moment: his knowledge has implicated him. He has literally entered into his models' consciousness. His choice then, the artist's choice, is to intervene in the course of history or to share the guilt for its injustices. Thus the fact that he uses his gift for good only sharpens the definition of the danger he both represents and incurs: it is not the danger of doing evil but the danger simply of doing. No one accuses him of worse. The good citizens of Boston who have grumbled that it may constitute "an offense against the Mosaic law, and even a presumptuous mockery of the Creator, to bring into existence such lively images of his creatures" (458), are clear that the sin lies in the creation of any icon, however saintly. The artist too makes the act of creation itself the issue. Approaching the house of Walter and Elinor on that last evening, he is more than a little satanic as he gloats:

Oh, glorious Art! . . . Thou art the image of the Creator's own. The innumerable forms, that wander in nothingness start into being at thy beck . . . Thou snatchest back the fleeting moments of History. With thee there is no Past; for, at thy touch, all that is great becomes forever present; and illustrious men live through long ages, in the visible performance of the very deeds, which made them what they are. Oh, potent Art! as thou bringest the faintly revealed Past to stand in that narrow strip of sunlight, which we call Now, canst thou summon the shrouded Future to meet her there?" (467)

And not surprisingly: "Have I not achieved it? Am I not thy Prophet?"

The problem, then, is doing, doing at a level of power that is precisely divine, for the painter's foreknowledge is that of Milton's God, which does not compel human behavior but predicts it (literally names it before it happens). Milton reasoned that since God exists outside of time, his predictions need not prevent the exercise of free will over time. But the painter is mortal and acts alongside his models; his intervention, reversing the outcome of their marriage, robs Walter and Elinor of their freedom. All for their good, of course, and in the name of art: to leave them their freedom, he would first have to refuse to paint them and later have to forbear to prevent the murder. By ending his story with the dictum that prophecy is really powerless, Hawthorne tries to escape an insoluble dilemma: When the individualist has transcendent divine power, how is he *not* to act as God? And if he declines, is this abdication not equally sinful? In the despairing phrase of Melville's Pierre, whose tragic attempt to resolve this dilemma I will examine in Chapter 6, these alternatives are "impossible adjuncts." Because "The Prophetic Pictures" is an allegory—an allegory only contemplating its novelistic potential in the marriage plot of Walter and Elinor, who never achieve any autonomy—Hawthorne extricates himself from his plight with relative ease. In a novel, the doomed couple would have had to live out their characters, and Hawthorne to face the full force, and the guilt, of his power.

When Emerson called on the American writer to "fasten words . . . to visible things," he did not envision these problems. In part this was because he was looking beyond the level of life on which husbands occasionally kill their wives, toward a horizon where the infinite and therefore all-encompassing self evokes a universe that is free of conflict and united in the unitary self's image. This horizon, however, lies beyond the world of Hawthorne's novelistic imagination, in the way that the monolithic Emersonian self precludes the necessary multiplicity of fiction. But if, for the purposes of fiction, Hawthorne could not define the self as all-powerful, neither could he as an American imagine the self to be historically limited, as the European novel projects it. The power and sufficiency of the Emersonian self were unimaginably transcendent for him, but something like Balzacian historicity would have been just as unimaginably immanent. The predicament of the prophetic painter is that in order to imagine him an artist at all Hawthorne has to endow him with blasphemous potential, so that his power has not only an upper limit but a lower.

The lower was still blasphemously high, as may be more clearly apparent by comparison to the limits of authorial autonomy within which a European novelist wrote. In Balzac's *Eugénie Grandet* the European limits are pushed back to their utmost. The following passage describes the houses of Eugénie's village of Saumur:

> It is difficult to pass by these houses without stopping to wonder at the enormous beams, whose projecting ends, carved with grotesque figures, crown the ground floor of most of them with a black bas-relief. In some places the cross beams are protected by slates which draw blue lines across the crumbling walls of a house which is topped by a high-pitched roof, which has bowed and bent under the weight of years, and whose decayed shingles have been warped by the long-continued action of alternate sunshine and rain. Worn blackened window-ledges catch the eye, whose delicate carving can scarcely be distinguished, and which seem too slight a support for the brown flower-pot full of pinks or roses, set there by some poor working woman. Further along the street one notes the doors, studded with huge nails, on which our ancestors recorded the passions of the age in hieroglyphs, once understood in every household, the meaning of which no one will now ever again unravel. In these symbols a Protestant declared his faith, or a Leaguer cursed Henri IV, or some civic dignitary traced the insignia of his office, celebrating the long-forgotten glory of his tem-

porary high estate as alderman or sheriff. The history of
France lies written in these houses. (33–34)

In an earlier critical era, Balzac was read as essentially the voice
of history itself, but from our perspective, the narrator who finds
it difficult to pass by the houses without wonder, and who, having
wondered about them, decides their meaning with the certainty
of that last sentence, represents an almost arrogant subjectivity.
The omniscient stance that is still more impersonal in French than
in English—the translation "one notes the doors" introduces an
agent not evident in "c'est des portes"—represents not total
knowledge but total judgment. But what is less apparent, and
perhaps apparent only by comparison to American writing, is how
little power Balzac's omniscience finally wields.

In this passage the limits of the author's entire knowledge are
signaled by as total an ignorance. The "hieroglyphes domestiques"
traced on the houses will never again be deciphered: this passage
of Balzac's writing contains, indeed *writes*, a writing "the meaning
of which no one will now ever again unravel." There are then
aspects or levels of meaning in the houses that Balzac's omniscient
vision cannot penetrate. This is of course because these meanings
are lost in the past—but that is just my point: having arrogated
the past entire, he becomes subject to *its* limits, the most stringent
of which is that it *is* past and irrevocable, sometimes to the extent
that we cannot call back even the knowledge of it. Hawthorne's
characteristic mysteries are profoundly different from this lost
knowledge. Time has nothing to do with their remoteness. They
might be called synchronic mysteries, pointing to depths of consciousness or heights of transcendent truth it would be impious
to penetrate. The irritation they often cause readers expresses the
readers' recognition that if he wished Hawthorne could tell all—
because he possesses all. On the contrary, Balzac could not and
did not. The European novelist's appropriation of history is self-
limiting: it can never transcend the temporal and social necessities
of the historical.

On one level, Balzac is the match of Hawthorne's painter, not
only portraying the faces of the houses but revealing their deeper
meanings; and in that way he is certainly no less appropriative

than his satanic colleague. But he appropriates a different entity. The last sentence in the passage quoted, ringing with entire confidence in the authority of authors, claims its authority in a form that would have appeared a renunciation to the painter who boasted, "Art . . . thou snatchest back the fleeting moments of History. With thee there is no Past." Balzac insisted, on the contrary, that "L'Histoire de France est là toute entière." The entire history of France is there: thus Balzac's art captures history, but the American artist's erases it.

And in its place, the American takes possession of a realm of meaning that does transcend the historical: "at thy touch," he celebrates Art, "all that is great is forever present." The "great"— the permanently significant, the essential—is entirely abstractable from the fleeting moment in which it arose, and thereby also entirely absorbable by art and the artist. History, however entirely Balzac's narrator inscribes it in his descriptions, remains in some portion external to him, if only because its essential meanings incorporate others, who are manifest, in the passage quoted, in *their* inscriptions. In other words, his subjectivity interprets everything without transforming anything. He claims all he can for the power of interpretation; but the world he interprets remains solidly its own reality, and its mortal conflicts, such as that between Protestants and Catholics, are not in his power to resolve. If Hawthorne's painter can prevent Elinor's murder, it is because his art has co-opted the couple's conflict, as it were, transporting it entire within himself. Or it is because their conflict is already within him, so that he can incarnate the whole meaning of things because he inhabits a world in which meaning is already incarnate in a universal self. And for the same reason, he also *must* incarnate the whole meaning of things or be himself unfulfilled.

Balzac's conception of himself as a novelist is as a historian, Hawthorne's (guiltily) as a prophet. Balzac casts himself as archhistorian and his stories claim "l'Histoire toute entière"; but Hawthorne's stories take in the whole world, conceived as a nature/civilization that transcends all history. The power implicit in these appropriations is relative to their reach. One expression indeed of the larger claim of the American novelist is his greater concern with power, which in this period is almost always a theme of

American fiction and seldom of European. Thus the stories of Eugénie Grandet and Hester Prynne have a common plot in the rebellion of young women against patriarchal authority, but while Hester enters her novel having already realized her revolt in an illegitimate child, Eugénie's defiance seems as early doomed. Henry James's complaint that Emma Bovary was too feeble a character to merit Flaubert's art might have been addressed as well to Eugénie, on behalf of Balzac, and with the same implications for the profound differences between American and European understandings of the nature of the interaction between characters and their worlds. For Americans—for Hawthorne in depicting Hester Prynne and for James, who was perhaps thinking of his Isabel Archer—this interaction amounts to a clash of colossi, and the diminution of the hero or heroine diminishes the interest and significance of the situation. Power is an explicit issue and a necessity of the plot. But for Balzac with Eugénie and Flaubert with Emma, the encounters of individuals with society are less about relative power than about the complex relations of personality and politics that evolve from permutations beyond the control of any of the participants. *Eugénie Grandet* and *Madame Bovary* are not, like *The Scarlet Letter* and *The Portrait of a Lady*, primarily "about" their heroines; instead, they are about the worlds their characters inhabit.

Which is not to say that their heroines are therefore less individualized or even less personally responsible. Eugénie's resistance to her odious father represents a personal, indeed an individualistic heroism; in the end Balzac describes her overcoming, in her historically contained way: "The true greatness of her soul lessens the effect of her narrow upbringing and the manner of her early life" (248). Remarkably, Eugénie's final role in the life-suppressing society of Saumur is not unlike Hester's in Puritan Boston: "It is her hand that binds up the secret wounds in any household. Eugénie's way to heaven is marked by a succession of deeds of kindness" (248). But the difference between the issues they represent is summed up by the fact that Eugénie is innocent, and blameless for the unhappiness she suffers: the point in her case *is* the burden of a heart unyielded because unsought. Therefore the point is not what she has done but what she and her

148

village society have prevented each other from doing; not transcendence but containment; and not the fact of containment, which would itself imply the theme of transcendence, but its content.

To repeat, this should not be taken to indicate that Balzac's story is less concerned with the individual Eugénie than Hawthorne's with the individual Hester. In her way, the virginal daughter is as uniquely self-defined as the adulterous wife, and she acts as individualistically. Antigone defied Creon in the name of familial duty, Medea avenged her violated wifehood. Eugénie and Hester both act on behalf of themselves, or of *their* selves.

So do their authors, Balzac as aggressively as Hawthorne. Balzac's ostensibly objective descriptions of "l'Histoire" are furiously personal; his impersonal omniscience is unpityingly judgmental. When he writes that Eugénie's father's face announced "a dangerous craftiness, a calculated rectitude, the selfishness of a man who, day by day, concentrated all his emotions on saving money" (44), he is as co-optive as the painter whose portraits resembled their models more than the models did themselves. Monsieur Grandet does not see himself in the mirror as we see him. "His nose, which was thick at the end, had a veined knob on it which was popularly said, with some reason, to be full of malice" (44). In this sentence no level of information has been left unmediated, neither the physical nor the social (the people say, and there is reason to suppose, that Grandet's unfortunate "knob" is grotesquely purulent).

If we keep Monsieur Grandet's nose before us, it will be clear that Balzac's realism permits a very high degree of authorial self-assertion.[4] It is Hawthorne writing romances who seems worried about his interventions. Depicting a similar flaw in Judge Pyncheon's physiognomy, he is skittish and protests too much. He reports that Judge Pyncheon tries to appear benevolent. "Owing, however, to a somewhat massive accumulation of animal substance about the lower region of his face, the look was perhaps unctuous, rather than spiritual, and had, so to speak, a kind of fleshly effulgence, not altogether so satisfactory as he doubtless intended it to be" (452). Hawthorne's uncharacteristically heavy hand here—the heaping of snide qualifications, the overcleverness of "fleshly effulgence" signaled by the coy "so to speak," the uncharacteristic verbosity of the conclusion—may reflect his particular unease with the judge as a character, but it also reveals a general anxiety, not evident in Balzac's writing, about the whole enterprise of character description.

Against the background of the earlier discussion of Emerson's vision of the infinite reach of individual creativity, Hawthorne's anxiety can be seen to respond to the greater power for creation deeded the American individualist novelist by his identification with the world he depicted. The prohibition against reinvention embedded in the notion that America was discovered already complete and implicitly perfect (as nature is complete and perfect) turned the American novelist into a blasphemer. I have suggested that the form of the romance represented an attempt to separate the fictional from the world so as to avoid the confrontation of art and reality implied both by the identification of the artist with the New World and by the image of the New World as tantamount to a work of art in itself.

As we will see in the next chapter, however, this separation entailed its own dangers, for while it avoided the sort of direct appropriation of reality Balzac attempted, by releasing the romance-writer from the limits of existing probability, it also permitted him to exercise more freely the very power he feared. So that although apparently not challenging the actual (as Balzac explicitly did), he contemplated far worse, replacing it completely. The stance of historian would not have interested an American, nor could he have imagined America in historical terms. But the posture of prophet—one who articulates, speaks, authorizes the world—was all too congenial. The great danger in that stance is dramatized by the fact that Hester's power always projects itself into the future, first in her child and later in her hopes for a better world. Unlike historians, who recapture what they can of the past *as past*, American prophets are able to capture the future because it already exists and is incarnate in America's eternal present. Thus because, as Americans, the prophets fuse in themselves the previously antithetical figures of God and of his people, they lend a new and culminating meaning to the always latent possibility that prophecy not only foretells but also determines the future. The American novel is a self-fulfilling prophecy—of the replacement of the original vision with a "living picture" that could be as different from the past as the "living picture" of the New World was from the Old World.

Hawthorne's description of placing the scarlet letter on his breast is an allegory that exactly reverses Emerson's injunction to the American writer to fasten words to visible things (*Nature*, 17)—reverses it and reveals the profound contradiction within it. For instead of carrying a word denuded of its prior history into nature—"innocence" to the lamb, "cunning" to the fox (15)—Hawthorne has gathered the "old" letter to himself and probed its old meanings. The results are similarly reversed: the "picturesque language" that proves Emerson's "alliance with truth and God" (17) depicts a (supposedly) self-evident and single verity: " 'Tis hard to carry a full cup even; . . . Long-lived trees make roots first" (18). The scarlet letter symbolizes an increasingly complex moral ambiguity that distances natural fact from interpretation and, therefore, preexisting "truth and God" from symbolizing author. The reversal in Hawthorne's gesture is really not a negation but the mirror image of the same thing Emerson urged: fastening the letter on himself, Hawthorne follows the logic of Emerson's identification of the self with nature and seeks the meaning of words and of history in himself (thus defining himself as a creative writer).

But Hawthorne, acting just as Emerson's necessary actor did to ravel and bridge and mediate, discovers implicit in those activities another one. The letter, already charged with Hester's interpretation, has an energy of its own, and he in relation to it is also not only a repository for cosmic energy but as well a creator of it. It is when he feels the letter's mysterious heat and "involuntarily" lets it drop that he first notices the "small roll of dingy paper," much like the musty old books that Emerson deplored, that accompanies the letter. Reading the letter's book inspires him to write his own. *The Scarlet Letter*, however, is no more a "Book of Nature" than Hester's scarlet letter was a cipher for adultery. Both begin with the given, but inexorably they transform it.

The word has revealed an organic life, and that in turn has revealed the autonomous life of the writer (the Custom House anecdote presents the process in that order). Both lives were entirely implicit before. But, activated by the narrative, from being implicit they become competitive. Hester's letter competitively asserts "Artist" and finally even "Angel"; Hawthorne's story not only contradicts Boston's morality but complicates Emerson's. Thus competitive, they deny the perfect oneness of their natural model. Emerson's necessary actor now has a nemesis in the usurping artist. With this development, the shadowy prohibitions that in Emerson's interpretation already limited the incarnation ideology become clearer and more threatening. For the usurping artist is the active version of the necessary actor, and he takes that form unavoidably when he acts innovatively (when he invents fiction or new ways of real life). In Chapter 3, reading Emerson, I found the individualistic ideology of the necessary actor extraordinarily enabling; in this chapter I have read in Hawthorne the possibility that it might be equally prohibiting. That Hawthorne's last novel, the one that contains his most fantastic "fancy-pictures," is entirely detached from America's "visible things" by being set in Rome bespeaks not one but two impulses—to invent freely to the utmost of the imagination, and to discover the universal terms of an ultimate American art. And these two impulses are contradictory.

5 ✳ Transgression and Transformation

*T*wo young Americans, a painter and a sculptor, travel to Rome to study. There they discover that art blasphemes and artists kill. So they give up art and return home to marry. This summary of the plot of *The Marble Faun* suffices to name the central problem to be addressed here: the apparently inextricable connection between creation and destruction that haunts the protagonists of American fiction and that they escape only by retirement and compliance. The protagonists of *The Marble Faun* place themselves in jeopardy when they reverse the discovery voyage and journey to the Old World in search of the art of its ancient civilizations. They save themselves by leaving art behind and coming back to the New. It does not seem to be possible to be a good artist and also good.

In Rome, the Americans Hilda and Kenyon meet two young Europeans, Miriam and Donatello, who act out a sort of morality play demonstrating this moral. The tragic story of the fall of Miriam and Donatello through Miriam's attempt to recreate herself and her world, while edifying, is also tempting to Kenyon, who for a time stands perilously close to the brink of an eternal precipice. How close becomes evident early in the story, when Kenyon shows Miriam a statue he has almost completed. Its subject is Cleopatra; in his ambition to encompass all of ancient culture in a culminating American art, Kenyon has gone back before Rome to the first ground of civilization, which he mines exactly in Thoreau's sense of the word. He has in fact taken entire possession of the Egyptian queen: "in a word," says the narrator, "all Cleopatra—fierce, voluptuous, passionate, tender, wicked, terrible, and full of poisonous and rapturous enchantment—was kneaded into what only a week or two before, had been a lump of wet clay from the Tiber" (958). Miriam is overwhelmed. Kenyon has made more than a statue: "What a woman is this!" she exclaims. "Tell me, did she never try—even while you were creating her—to overcome you with her fury, or her love? Were you not afraid to touch her, as she grew more and more towards hot life, beneath your hand? My dear friend, it is a great work! How have you learned to do it?" Kenyon's answer removes any doubt about the fatal implications of an art that can prompt such questions.

> It is the concretion of a good deal of thought, emotion, and toil of brain and hand . . . But I know not how it came about, at last. I kindled a great fire within my mind, and threw in the material—as Aaron threw the gold of the Israelites into the furnace—and in the midmost heat, uprose Cleopatra, as you see her. (958)

Fortunately the statue is not yet cast in bronze; the American Aaron has not completed his idol. There is time yet to avert that final step into the pit. But our starting point in this chapter is the sculptor's near approach to what Hawthorne describes explicitly as perdition—for what has brought Kenyon to this edge is nothing but the practice of his art.

What art can lead to continues to emerge when Miriam, clearly encouraged by the attitude she sees implicit in the statue, proffers another temptation. She asks Kenyon whether she might confide in him as a friend or as a brother, for she is lonely and bears the burden of a terrible secret. Since Miriam's story is somewhat complicated and involves other aspects of the plot, it will be useful here to add to the opening summary.

The second American, Hilda, described as a "fair Saxon girl" and alternatively as a "daughter of the Puritans," embodies an ideal femininity expressed in pure white dresses, an ethereal

154

lightness of foot, and an exquisite moral sensibility. Donatello, Miriam's fellow European, is the faun of the title. That is, he bears a marvelous resemblance to the statue of Praxiteles (Hawthorne later said that he had conceived of the story while standing in front of that statue). The likeness is spiritual as well as physical, for Donatello seems a wild child of the woods, full of joy and poetry but not quite human. A Tuscan nobleman, he has come to Rome with no apparent purpose other than the enthusiastic pursuit of life and happiness. Kenyon is in love with Hilda (who is, however, too chaste to be told) and Donatello with Miriam.

The four friends often spend their afternoons together wandering among Rome's treasures of art and history. In the course of a visit to the Catacombs, Miriam wanders away down some deeper tunnel. When she returns to her anxious companions, she is followed by the sinister figure of a monk, whom she seems to know but refuses to identify. Henceforth the monk follows her everywhere, and she grows daily more despondent. Donatello will do anything to free her of the specter, and finally, one night atop a cliff where the monk has as usual trailed them, Donatello interprets a look from Miriam as a command to hurl her tormentor to his death. Miriam, exhilarated by her release, now returns Donatello's passion, and briefly the two are ecstatically united. Soon, however, their common guilt rises up between them. Appalled by his crime, Donatello flees alone to his ancestral home in the Apennines.

Meanwhile the spirit-girl Hilda, who has observed the murder unseen, is distraught over her first vision of evil. Unable to support its weight in her gossamer soul, she tells a Catholic priest what she has seen. Her confession travels through murky labyrinths to certain quarters of Rome where Miriam is well known. Miriam, as she will later explain to Kenyon, belongs tò one of Italy's most powerful families. As a young girl, she was betrothed to the head of another reigning clan (there are intimations here of Medicis and Cencis), a man whose physical decrepitude was exceeded only by his moral corruption. She successfully resisted this marriage but shortly after became entangled in a heinous event Hawthorne does not specify. Although once again Miriam remained innocent in the midst of guilt, she understood that her environment would continue to implicate her in its crimes. She ran away, therefore, and sought to escape the family taint by living the chaste life of an anonymous artist. Vainly, for on that fatal visit to the Catacombs she had been recognized by one who was associated wih the old unnamed atrocity. He was seeking to draw her back to her family when, in despair, she signaled Donatello to kill him. With that she sealed her fate and her unfortunate lover's as well. In the end the powers of the world Miriam could never escape immure Donatello for life in some lost dungeon, while she is no less a prisoner in her vigil of hopeless remorse.

At the start of her story, however, Miriam appears wholly admirable. Trying to escape the iniquities of her family and to develop her considerable artistic talent, she is only following the path of virtue and self-help. Why do her efforts at rebuilding her world lead to such destruction? Hawthorne begins to suggest an answer very early in the novel; when Donatello visits her and asks why she keeps her studio so dark, Miriam gives him this explanation: "We artists purposely exclude sunshine, and all but a partial light . . . because we think it necessary to put ourselves at odds with Nature before trying to imitate her. That strikes you very strangely, does it not? But we make very pretty pictures sometimes with our artfully arranged lights and shadows" (885). Donatello would indeed find this practice strange, being himself entirely at one with nature. Miriam's transformation of the faun (the novel's first title was "The Transformation") begins here when she suggests to him that one "imitates" nature better from a posture "at odds" with her.

This initial separation implies everything that follows, all the way to the fall that comes as its logical conclusion. The artist who recreates nature by letting there be light only as she wishes it is the woman who only a little later tells Donatello that when "men that cumbered the world" were in ancient times thrown from precipices "it was well done" (994). From that to signaling the death of one such cumbering man is a very short step, as it is not far to the almost lubricious abandon with which she reassures Donatello immediately after the murder that they both remain innocent since "Surely, it is no crime that . . . one wretched and worthless life has been sacrificed to cement two other lives forevermore" (998). Moreover, Miriam is incorrigible. Later, even when she has come to repent bitterly her destruction of Donatello's childlike happiness, she nonetheless glories in the man he has become. In fact she asks only to be permitted to continue the process she has begun, by dedicating her life to "elevating" him further. Miriam is profoundly, essentially a creator: of "pretty pictures," hence of men. And this inextricably involves her setting herself at odds with nature—and killing other men.

In sculpting the Cleopatra, Kenyon takes the same stance with which Miriam begins her plunge: he too defines imitation as re-creation, and indeed re-creation as creation. And an inexorable logic finally brings him to suggest that recreating men might be equally desirable. The change in Donatello certainly seems for the better: "He perpetrated a great crime; and his remorse, gnawing into his soul, has awakened it; developing a thousand high capabilities, moral and intellectual, which we never should have dreamed of asking for, within the scanty compass of the Donatello we knew." In that case, Kenyon continues, speaking to Hilda,

> Here comes my perplexity . . . Sin has educated Donatello, and elevated him. Is Sin, then—which we deem such a dreadful blackness in the universe—is it, like Sorrow, merely an element of human education, through which we struggle to a higher and purer state than we could otherwise have attained? Did Adam fall, that we might ultimately rise to a far loftier paradise than his? (1236)

This notion, which Miriam had suggested to him, is familiar as the doctrine of the fortunate fall—the thesis that with the knowledge of good and evil man acquired free will and thus the power to choose good, a greater virtue than blind obedience. Kenyon's phrasing makes clear how heretical this doctrine can be. For the uses of knowledge he projects, while they may be ultimately dedicated to God, meanwhile redound to the glory of man. Indeed they render man essentially self-creating, certainly self-legislating, since his very lapses lead to his passing higher laws. What Kenyon really values in the changed Donatello, one sees, is only secondarily the enhanced likelihood of his final arrival in heaven. Looking at the transformed faun with the eye of a sculptor, he admires his new earthly stature and seems, in his enthusiasm for the improvement, almost to contemplate its deliberate production.

Luckily Hilda is there to stop him. "Oh, hush!" she cries, "Do not you perceive what a mockery your creed makes, not only of all religious sentiment, but of moral laws, and how it annuls and obliterates whatever precepts of Heaven are written deepest within us?" (1236). Hilda has all along been the keeper of the primordial faith, here in terms of religion but earlier in those of art. For Hilda, by declining to create and thus by ascending, reverses the continuum of Miriam's fall through artistic creation into Hell. Hilda's way of pursuing art is the more clearly an alternative route in that she has actively chosen it over another. As a girl in New England, she had shown "a decided genius for the pictorial art," and had she stayed home "it is not improbable that she might have produced original works" (897). But "since her arrival in the pictorial land" she seems "to have entirely lost the impulse of original design, which brought her thither" (898). She has become a copyist. Hawthorne explains that when Hilda stood before the Old Masters she saw that they had already realized the entire potential of painting, and she resolved therefore to dedicate her talent to the dissemination of their art rather than to the creation of her own. Lest this decision in any way suggest a lesser artistic energy, Hawthorne assures us that in fact the opposite is the case. Hilda is perhaps the most artistic of the group: "She was endowed with a deep and sensitive faculty of appreciation; she had a gift of discerning and worshipping excellence, in most unusual measure. No other person, it is probable, recognized so adequately, and enjoyed with such deep delight, the pictorial wonders [of Rome]" (898).

A part of the girl's exquisite sensibility, no doubt, is inspired by Hawthorne's deservedly notorious notions of gender. Hilda the Dove, as her friends call her, does not really *see* art but feels it. "She bestowed upon it all the warmth and richness of a woman's sympathy; not by any intellectual effort, but by this strength of heart, and this guiding light of sympathy, she went straight to the central point, in which the Master had conceived his work" (898). But if her sex makes Hilda a likely representative of the faculty of appreciation, such an attitude toward both art and the world is presented through her as an ideal in itself. Indeed, Hawthorne had celebrated it before this in the prophetic painter who, having climbed "New England's loftiest mountain" to admire the majestic beauty of his native land, "did not profane that scene by the mockery of his art." On Lake George, he made "his soul the mirror of its loveliness and grandeur," but again did not attempt to paint, and upon visiting Niagara Falls, he "flung his hopeless pencil down the precipice, feeling that he could as soon paint the roar, as aught else that goes to make up the wondrous cataract" ("The Prophetic Pictures," 465).

Nonetheless, Hilda's total renunciation is remarkable, and Hawthorne himself is ambivalent about it, musing "we know not whether the result of her Italian studies . . . will be accepted as a good or desirable one" (898). Copying the classics of the Old World would appear to be the exact opposite of what an American artist needs to do. Pursuing the path of that thought, however, leads us back to the other American artist, Kenyon, whose aggressive appropriation and transformation of the Old World we have already seen tending to blasphemy. The dilemma that emerged in Chapter 4, between the American individual's transcending power to create and the possibility of his therefore wreaking utter destruction, is here fully fledged and permits of no resolution. In making Hilda a copyist Hawthorne expresses a desperate strait: he can imagine *no* form of creation that would not entail an ultimate destruction. Nor, in this context, is it imaginable.

The context, the situation that pushes the dilemma of American individualism to this final paralyzing extremity, is the fact of the novel itself. For by inventing fictions, Hawthorne himself engages in Miriam-style creation. As Miriam makes Donatello, Hawthorne makes all of the characters. On this level the sequence of errors I traced earlier are not only the characters' but their author's. As the Americans go abroad to pursue their art, so the author sets his story abroad; he first imagines the transformation of the Praxiteles statue into a living man, a more radical change than the man's subsequent education. In short, as the original title, "The Transformation," names Miriam's sin, it condemns her author equally. At the center of this hopeless quandary is the obvious fact that to write a story is to create a world and populate it.

159

Kenyon's account of how he made the Cleopatra is worth repeating here; as much or rather more than it identifies the blasphemous implication of the sculptor's art, it reveals the consummate trespass of Hawthorne's *Marble Faun*. "It is the concretion of a good deal of thought, emotion, and toil of brain and hand . . . but I know not how it came about at last. I kindled a great fire within my mind, and threw in the material—as Aaron threw the gold of the Israelites into the furnace—and in the midmost heat uprose . . ." (958). In Hawthorne's case, uprose the novel and Miriam, without whom, not coincidentally, there would be no story. Indeed, in Hawthorne's emphasis on the genuine improvement in Donatello that Miriam's criminality has brought about, one senses a certain artistic camaraderie: looking at her creation and seeing it good, Hawthorne covertly takes pride in his own. He will not deny that her work, which has caused such pain, has also created such beauty; and yet at the same time he damns her and her creation to hell.

One of the ways in which *The Marble Faun* develops to the fullest what I have identified as the peculiar dilemma of the American artist is by representing it through art and artists. The problem of authorial complicity thus arises explicitly. In the Cleopatra scene, when Miriam offers to tell Kenyon her story immediately after he shows her the statue, the nature of the temptation is directly relevant to Hawthorne himself. For Miriam tempts Kenyon to become an actor/creator of her story by listening to it sympathetically. Having just seen how sympathy and creation conjoined in his making of the Cleopatra, in effect she asks him to have a similar relation to her: " 'Oh, my friend,' cried she, with sudden passion, 'will you be my friend indeed? I am lonely, lonely, lonely! There is a secret in my heart that burns me!—that tortures me! . . . Ah, if I could but whisper it to only one human soul! Perhaps—perhaps, but Heaven only knows—you might understand me!' " (959). Kenyon hesitates, pulls back, and is, for the moment, safe. In the sculptor's reluctance to join with Miriam in the perpetration of a common story, however, Hawthorne is also defending himself.

His self-defense comes a bit late, since he does understand Miriam and presumably knows her secret. But what is happening in this scene could cause him to incur additional guilt. For it is the exact equivalent of what happens to the Cleopatra: *The Marble Faun* is growing (Miriam's words are doubly appropriate in that it is she herself who quickens here) "towards hot life beneath [Hawthorne's] hands." The mysterious Miriam is proposing to take charge of her mystery, to act out the implicit autonomy of the interiority it signals, to become a living (picture) being. By hearing her story, Kenyon would develop a matching autonomy: they would be living in relation to each other, and out of the relation they would generate events and actions, in fact their own story, a story of individualists constructing history. Miriam tempts Kenyon to knowledge—and Hawthorne to Realism. The qualities and capacities Donatello develops as a result of his fall are precisely those of individualists and novelistic characters: an extensive interiority, an irreducible complexity even to the point of contradiction, a henceforth inalienable ability to choose his path in life, and the determination to do so—existential autonomy. As Kenyon points out, it is difficult to regret all this.

One is reminded at this point of Thoreau's cry in the "Higher Laws" chapter of *Walden:* "Nature is hard to be overcome, but she must be overcome" (498). For so apparently is and must be art. Not art as a transcendent idea, once the dross of life has been filtered from it, but art as it is practiced in the byways of cities and the dark corners of studios: like the nature to which Thoreau aspires when he has overcome its grosser temptations, the art to which Hawthorne struggles to dedicate *The Marble Faun* instead is abstract. It is an art that does not "artfully arrange" and rearrange its own scenes but mirrors the abiding truth, the art of the copyist Hilda, whose activity fulfills and unfolds but never changes. In its literary form, it is the art of allegory. Thus in his last novel Hawthorne returned to a form he had abandoned with his first. There are elements of allegory in *The Scarlet Letter*, to be sure, but the symbolic complexity of the letter itself expresses an ambition to pursue meaning deep into its origins in the complications of living experience. I noted earlier that when Hester Prynne comes to counsel would-be rebels against rebellion the letter that signified her own rebellion flattens into an allegorical cipher. In *The Marble Faun* Hawthorne worked to reduce the plot as well as the characters to much the same status as the "A" on Hester's tombstone.

I have said that he "reduced" Miriam, Donatello, and their story, but he would surely have said that he was attempting to contain them, to prevent them from usurping his moral tale. The problem, as we have seen, is that the tale of the individual's ideal oneness with art and nature (and therefore of each of those with the other), makes the characters' depth and their ability to generate a plot precisely what needs to be contained. If they are to be kept in line, as it were, they must be reduced to lines. In *The Marble Faun* this necessity emerges with particular force because Hawthorne is writing *about* sketching and the tendency of character outlines to thicken. Thus the struggle within the work between novelistic and allegorical tendencies is fully explicit, and the allegory Hawthorne opposes to the novelistic thrust of the Miriam and Donatello story may be read directly as an allegory about the perils of writing novels. From the critical mass at the hot center of scenes like Miriam's temptation of Kenyon or Kenyon's temptation by art, Hawthorne pulls back to what is explicitly a sideline, from which, devoutly inspired by Hilda, he observes a morality play in which both self-making and the making of selves and worlds lead to disaster. And mocking the expectations of the play's deluded puppets that an open future offers the hope of qualified punishments and relative fates, the allegory's foregone conclusion ensures that the defeat of vice will be as absolute as the triumph of virtue. In establishing that symmetry, Hawthorne calls on a powerful resource in the discovery myth, one he had reversed by bringing Hilda and Kenyon from the New World to the Old. When he abjures their quest, that design will reassert itself and carry them, propelled as if by a natural force, all the way back to the right place.

But the cost of the voyage is nonetheless steep. To choose Hilda, both Kenyon and Hawthorne must not only condemn Miriam but relinquish her. And with the abortive ending of the scene in which Miriam praises the Cleopatra and tries to entice Kenyon further into living his creativity, the wonderful statue disappears from the novel. The next time Kenyon has to do with statues is at the very end of the book, when during a walk he comes upon the pieces of what the narrator speculates may have been the prototype for the Venus of the Tribune. Picking up the scattered fragments and assembling them, Kenyon becomes essentially like Hilda, a copyist. The broken statue has lain unknown for centuries, and Kenyon, now obstetrician rather than father, discovers it. What he discovers, let me emphasize, is an already complete entity—an America. In contrast, the Cleopatra he showed Miriam was not yet cast; it was still made of clay and mutable; it awaited his making. To reveal the Venus, he wipes away the clay that history has deposited on it; then "the beautiful Idea at once asserted its immortality, and converted that heap of forlorn fragments into a whole, as perfect to the mind . . . as when the new marble gleamed with snowy lustre" (1206). It is the idea itself, not Kenyon's assembly of them, that converts the fragments into a statue. On its own, the immortal idea fully transcends its historical burial. The statue's meaning for the beholder is directly and identically an idea, which Kenyon neither mediates nor interprets but only uncovers.

The idea speaks through Kenyon unchecked, with original energy. But what it tells is neither nature nor America but an ancient civilization to which Kenyon can have only the most passive relation. The substitution of this civilization for the America of a Walt Whitman exposes an aspect of this prophetic stance that is not apparent when prophet and prophecy are contemporaries. It is a profoundly conservative stance that preserves what already exists and defends it against innovation. In the context of *The Marble Faun*, this conservatism is peculiarly radical, indeed destructive. For in reassembling the Venus, Kenyon denies more than his own Cleopatra; ultimately he negates all of Hawthorne's *Marble Faun* as well. As we will see, its possibilities as a "living picture" in the lives of Miriam and Donatello are denied along with its philosophical life. Hilda's hushing of moral speculation reverberates through the closing pages in which Kenyon finds the ancient statue. In fact, when he finds it, he is really looking for Hilda (who, in a rather contrived twist of the plot, has been kidnapped by Miriam's insidious pursuers). Hawthorne's hero speaks for an anxious author when he exclaims, "What a discovery is here! . . . I seek for Hilda, and find a marble woman! Is the omen good or ill?" (1206).

Kenyon's immediate question is whether finding the statue means he will find Hilda also. But on another level he has already found her, having turned to her decisively at an earlier critical moment in which he might instead have opted for Miriam, or for Miriam's way. The story presents him with this choice in the course of a long episode that intervenes a little awkwardly just as the plot seems to be getting under way. Right after the murder, when Donatello has run away to Tuscany leaving a desperate Miriam behind, summer arrives and, as is the custom, everyone in Rome prepares to leave for the countryside. The story wanders onto a long side track during which we lose sight of Hilda and Miriam while Kenyon travels to visit Donatello at his ancestral estate, Monte Beni.

The ancestral mansion is dominated by a tower, a square, massive "old pile of stone-work" whose time-worn stones, covered over by "immemorial" lichens and mosses, remind us that Donatello is of an ancient lineage. This tower becomes the focus of our reconsideration of the unhappy young Donatello, whom until now we have seen only in relation to either transcendent art, as he resembled the Praxiteles statue, or timeless nature, as he also modeled a faun. For instead the tower represents history. "What a fine old tower!" Kenyon exclaims when he first sees it, "Its tall front is like a page of black-letter, taken from the history of the Italian republics" (1032). From earlier even than this, the tower has organized the meaning of family and communal life in its Tuscan valley. The tower is a version of the houses of Balzac's village of Saumur, with the history of Donatello's family inscribed upon it, and Donatello, as its sole remaining occupant, is not a transcendent creation of either art or nature, but a lonely and very mortal survivor. He too is constituted by history, and in climbing his tower he heightens his connection to the world on which it stands.

Donatello's is not the first tower featured in *The Marble Faun*. Earlier Hilda is seen to inhabit a tower in the middle of the city, atop which is a shrine to the Virgin, which the Protestant girl tends in homage to its image of chaste womanhood. Hawthorne makes much of this tower and of the small room at the very top, luminous with Hilda's spirit, where she lives companioned only by a flock of snowy doves. Hilda's aerie is the image of her transcendence of earthly contamination: her dress is whiter than the birds' plumage, and she soars higher than they. "Sometimes," she tells Miriam, "I feel half-inclined to attempt a flight from the top of my tower, in the faith that I should float upward" (896). When Miriam once visits her, Hawthorne describes the climb as so high that "the city bustle, which is heard even in Rome, the rumble of wheels over the uncomfortable paving-stones, the hard harsh cries, re-echoing in the high and narrow streets, grew faint and died away; as the turmoil of the world will always die, if we set our faces to climb heaven-ward" (895).

These alternative towers, Donatello's representing the way history towers over mortal man and Hilda's the way the transcendent spirit can soar above the mundane, become focal images whose allegorical play now takes over the plot, and we recall, perhaps after a moment's confusion brought on by having been recently absorbed in the intense drama of Miriam and Donatello, that our major concern is the fate of the Americans, Hilda and Kenyon.

Like a New World Gawain traveling abroad to test and develop his American piety, Kenyon, ignorant of the crime his friend has committed, rides into the European wilderness to find Donatello in his faraway castle. Arriving before a great iron gate, he sees the antique tower and behind it a large country house, which is more modern, or at least looks so, for its "coat of stucco and yellow-wash, which is a sort of renovation very much in vogue with the Italians" (1031). The narrator offers this last item of information in a neutral tone whose omniscience, unlike Balzac's, connotes detachment rather than ubiquity. But its realism announces the central issue to be settled by Kenyon's visit: whether reality creates its own meanings or only dramatizes abiding truths. Indeed, this question justifies the pause in the story, since the answer, by defining the meaning of the crime just perpetrated, will motivate the rest of the novel. If reality creates its own meanings, the rest of the book will have to explore the new reality the crime has generated; if it only dramatizes existing truths, Hawthorne needs only to draw a long-existing moral.

In another sense this visit to the historical, immanent, realistic tower represents another of Kenyon's temptations, like the temptation of Miriam's story and that of the profoundly historical Cleopatra. The temptation is specifically to see Donatello's tower as Donatello sees it (as Kenyon's earlier temptations were to hear Miriam's story in her terms, and to make the Cleopatra live again as she once had) and that way to multiply authority and authors. (By the very process of appropriating the real world to his fictional one, Balzac relativizes meaning, precisely what Hawthorne seeks to avoid doing.) Understood in Donatello's secular terms, his tower negates Hilda's. This becomes inescapably clear one day when Donatello takes Kenyon all the way to the top.

The conflict begins at once, when Kenyon asks Donatello to "show" him the tower and receives the ungracious answer "it is plainly enough to be seen" (1061). The philosophical difference represented by these two formulations is a major one: Kenyon sees the tower as something to be shown, that is, as a repository of meanings awaiting explication, and Donatello considers it something to be seen, a thing in itself, which anyone may interpret. Kenyon still does not know the fatal cause of Donatello's despondency, and this is one reason for their different attitudes on the tour. But they disagree more profoundly. To the notion that the tower may be seen without being shown, Kenyon answers that though the "exterior" of the edifice is certainly "visible far and wide," his interest lies rather in its interior, and in the "traditions" that must "cling to the walls within, quite as plentifully as the gray and yellow lichens cluster on its face, without"; to which move from the historical to the exegetical, Donatello replies "no doubt . . . but I know little of such things . . ." (1061). Upon Donatello's reluctant "Come then . . . it has a weary staircase and dismal chambers, and it is very lonesome at the summit." Kenyon composes a variation on Hilda's theme. The tower is "Like a man's life, when he has climbed to eminence, or, let us rather say, with its difficult steps, and the dark prison-cells you speak of, your tower resembles the spiritual experience of many a sinful soul, which, nevertheless, may struggle upward into the pure air and light of Heaven, at last!" (1062).

"Donatello sighed again." And well he might. Not just because the allegory runs painfully counter to his own experience,

166

in which he has ascended to a peak of hellish remorse, but because of the allegorizing itself. When the two reach the top and emerge onto an open-air balcony to view the countryside, Kenyon exclaims, "How it strengthens the poor human spirit in its reliance on His Providence, to ascend but this little way above the common level, and so attain a somewhat wider glimpse of His dealings with mankind! He doeth all things right!" Donatello responds, "You discern something that is hidden from me . . . I see sunshine on one spot, and cloud in another, and no reason for it in either case. The sun on you; the cloud on me! What comfort can I draw from this?" (1066). Kenyon takes this inability to "catch the analogies which so cheered his friend" as a sign of Donatello's less developed mind. "The simple Donatello" has never thought to ask what things mean. When the American notices a plant miraculously growing on the stony balcony, Donatello asks "if the shrub teaches you any good lesson," for "if the wide valley has a great meaning, the plant ought to have at least a little one; and it has been growing on our tower long enough to have learned how to speak it" (239). Kenyon's reply is prompt: "Oh, certainly! . . . the shrub has its moral, or it would have perished long ago." The all-pervasive meaningfulness of the universe is just as eternally focused on the individual perceiver. "No doubt," Kenyon assures his forlorn friend, "it is for your use and edification, since you have had it before your eyes, all your lifetime and now are moved to ask what may be its lesson" (240). But this is too much benevolence for the unhappy Count of Monte Beni: "It teaches me nothing," he says gloomily, "but here was a worm that would have killed it; an ugly creature, which I will fling over the battlements" (1066–67).

This pointedly symbolic act reenacts the murder of the monk and repeats its rationale: failing to see any transcendent order in the shrub, Donatello has (once again) confronted a conflictual universe to his own purpose. When Kenyon in his turn flings a pebble from the parapet, the contrast between the Italian's relation to meaning and the American's continues to unfold. For unlike Donatello, who, in killing Miriam's persecutor, assaulted the hated thing itself, Kenyon throws down a surrogate with the express intention of disengaging himself from the reality it represents.

Thus, apologizing "for helping Time to crumble away your ancestral walls," he explains, "I am one of those persons who have a natural tendency to climb heights, and to stand on the verge of them, measuring the depth below. If I were to do just as I like, at this moment, I should fling myself down after that bit of lime . . . Have you never felt this strange impulse of an evil spirit at your back, shoving you toward a precipice?" (1068). The pebble represents Kenyon by replacing him, and its fall explicitly bespeaks his own successful resistance to falling. Beyond that, throwing down the pebble connotes Kenyon's general stance toward experience and material reality. By substituting a surrogate ritual for an impulse to act, he aborts the history he might otherwise have generated and instead reaffirms a timeless original piety.

For his part, Donatello would dearly love to be persuaded that he has but to look up to be free of the corpse he has hurled below. Only he cannot rid himself of memory. He has thought of entering a monastery, he tells Kenyon, the "horrible idea" of it expressing the inescapability of his crime. Kenyon is shocked that his friend would sink so, under any burden. "A monk—I judge from their sensual physiognomies . . . —is inevitably a beast! Their souls, if they have any to begin with, perish out of them, before their sluggish, swinish existence is half-done. Better, a million times, to stand star-gazing on these airy battlements, than to smother your new germ of a higher life in a monkish cell" (1074). Beyond a proper Protestant horror of the whore of Babylon, Kenyon speaks out of another characteristic American conviction: "If, for any cause, I were bent upon sacrificing every earthly hope as a peace-offering towards Heaven,—I would make the wide world my cell, and good deeds to mankind my prayer," (1074) he vows, incapable, in his optimism, of imagining "any cause" that could finally preclude the working out of a benevolent destiny. History is ephemeral, even the history of one's individual life. The universal design is good and always prevails.

In the context of Donatello's torment, such faith in a benevolent universe may seem shallow, perhaps even irresponsible. Is there no evil that matters finally, fatally? This is a question often asked of Emerson, but not so sharply as we might ask it here of Kenyon. For while Kenyon, in his ignorance of the exact nature

168

of Donatello's crime, might be as abstractly innocent as Emerson, we (Hawthorne and his story) are not innocent; we know that what is at issue is murder. Because this principle of transcendent goodness is being presented in a *story*, the evil it transcends has to be represented as well; indeed not only represented but focused on, the evil being quite simply the heart of the story. So even while Kenyon asserts transcending goodness, we are vicariously experiencing a reality that belies him. His abstraction cannot withstand our concrete knowledge, nor his teleology the history of *The Marble Faun* or of Donatello.

In fact, when the moment finally comes for Kenyon to articulate this teleology directly, words fail him. To Donatello's doubt about deriving comfort from a landscape in which there is "sunshine on one spot, and cloud in another," the answer must lie in the great transcendent oneness beyond such disparities; but Kenyon is somehow not able to say this:

> I cannot preach . . . with a page of heaven and a page of earth spread wide open before us! Only begin to read it, and you will find it interpreting itself without the aid of words. It is a great mistake to try to put our best thoughts into human language. When we ascend into the higher regions of emotion and spiritual enjoyment, they are only expressible by such grand hieroglyphics as these around us. (1066)

(Note that in the notion of a landscape that interprets itself, Kenyon projects exactly the distinction I suggested between the ways he and Donatello view the tower: Kenyon asks Donatello to "show" him the tower because he assumes about it, as about the page of heaven and earth spread before him, that its meanings are inherent, and that its owner can best explicate them.) The philosophical rationale of Kenyon's demurral is familiar from my earlier discussion of Emerson: "words" are either inadequate or blasphemous, and the ultimate, that is, the transcendent, form of language is an all-resonating silence. The new issue here is the context in which this idea is being expressed, as a speech delivered by a fictional character, and the way the idea reduces him to silence, not only ultimately but here and now.

For what can Kenyon say? If he gives the Emersonian answer,

that those who find themselves beclouded need to look harder for the sun, not only will he appear lacking in compassion, but more seriously he will deny the possible validity of Donatello's plaint, thus reducing his drama to a dramatization. To pronounce the Emersonian truth here is to bring the story as such to an end, while an answer sympathetic to Donatello, questioning the justice of the world's uneven illumination, damns Kenyon and Donatello both. This is one of those moments in stories when a character falls mute because there is nothing he or she can do or say. Though the scene continues, this is its climax. In evading it, Hawthorne tacitly acknowledges the radical nature of a conflict that can be resolved only at the cost of one of its sides. No degree of symbolic complexity could accommodate what is not, after all, ambiguity but outright contradiction.

In sending Kenyon to climb the old, earthbound (pagan-Catholic) tower, Hawthorne may have hoped it might be assumed into the new ideal (Protestant) world. Kenyon's voyage to the Old World would thus have succeeded in gathering European history and culture as materials for building the New World. The sculptor of Cleopatra who is also the suitor of Hilda is Hawthorne's best hope for such a resolution. But it is just as well that Kenyon's vision from the battlements strikes him dumb, for when he speaks, he is hugely tempted, in the act of reading the divine writ, to write his own. The comfort he offers Donatello, the possibility of redemption through good deeds, holds dire perils. For it implies the more immediate possibility that individuals, having broken the law, can repair it; that after destroying the order of things, they can then reconstruct it—and in that case that the creation of a new order gives positive value to breaking the law.

But the tower episode closes on the denial of any such value, which were it to emerge would yet not be communicable. An art born of trespass, a little like the prophecies of Cassandra, is forbidden its audience. As night falls, the two men atop the old tower hear a voice far below "singing a low, sad strain." It is Miriam, who has also come to Monte Beni. Her song makes both men weep, as if Hawthorne were making a last effort to reconcile their understandings of their common story: "it brought the tears into the sculptor's eyes, with remembrances and forebodings of whatever sorrow he had felt or apprehended; it made Donatello sob, as chiming in with the anguish that he found unutterable, and giving it the expression which he vaguely sought." But finally neither the Italian nor the American can accept the song's compromise:

> when the emotion was at its profoundest depth, the voice rose out of it, yet so gradually that a gloom seemed to pervade it, far upward from the abyss, and not entirely to fall away as it ascended into a higher and purer region. At last the auditors could have fancied that the melody, with its rich sweetness all there, and much of its sorrow gone, was floating around the very summit of the tower. (1075–76)

For his part Donatello is too bound by history, too wholly contained by it, as his coming incarceration will prove, to imagine even this degree of transcendence. "I dare not receive it," he tells Kenyon, "the anguish of which it spoke, abides with me: the hope dies away, with the breath that brought it hither. It is not good for me to hear that voice." To the sculptor, in contrast, the song is a siren call to an art fed by guilty knowledge (or, at any rate, by the guilt *of* knowledge). Instead of a reconciliation, then, Miriam's song evokes the hopeless opposition of Kenyon and Donatello, and beyond them, of America and Europe and their conceptions of art. Indeed, as the two towers embody these dichotomies, they represent mutually exclusive choices. Earlier, looking up (and away from the unseen Miriam at the foot of the tower), Kenyon had felt a timely "pull at his heart-strings," as if "all the way between these battlements and Hilda's dove-cote, had stretched an exquisitely sensitive cord" (1070). Before he returns to Hilda he will wander the Tuscan valley in Donatello's company, but the American's fate, or rather his career, is now decided. He has decided it by choosing the transcendent clarity of Hilda's tower over the ambiguities of Donatello's. Seeking Hilda, he has found the Marble Woman.

But almost immediately after the two Americans are reunited, Hilda disappears taken hostage by mysterious agents pursuing

Miriam, and Kenyon has to go on a further quest, this time for her. Recall that Hilda observed the murder of the sinister monk and, unable in her purity to harbor even the knowledge of evil, sought to cleanse herself by confessing to a priest; and that in the manner of the corrupt Catholic clergy, the priest relayed this confession to others who saw in Miriam's complicity a way to blackmail her into returning to them. Now these insidious forces have Hilda in their clutches and apparently will let her go only in exchange for Miriam. The choice Kenyon faced on the tower between Miriam's song and the pull of Hilda at his heartstrings is now organizing the story as a whole. From here on, the two young women never appear together, their mutual exclusion emerging as not only moral but existential. It becomes clear that they not only think and act differently, they *are* different: each one's way of being does not merely naysay but negates the other's.

In other words, they are made differently. Around Miriam, Hawthorne constructs an absurdly elaborate familial frame. At the beginning of the story, before the circumstances of the murder bring some elucidation of her mystery, he even ascribes to her several families. Roman speculations have it that she is "the daughter and heiress of a great Jewish banker," or possibly "a German princess," alternatively "the offspring of a Southern American planter . . . [with] one burning drop of African blood in her veins," if not "the lady of an English nobleman." This excess of social origin enmeshes Miriam in a historical net even Stephen Daedalus would find hard to break. The allusions to Jewish and African blood are more charged than we might immediately recognize: a New England Protestant author is likely to have been suspicious of Jews, and in 1859 Africans in America were slaves. Hawthorne, who was characteristically moderate on the subject of abolition, hardly meant by either association to enhance Miriam's spiritual stature. Rather the possibility of a banking or a slave-owning father fixes her in the physical realm of money and sex: "plucked up out of a mystery," she "had its roots still clinging to her" (870–871). The "misty substance" of the cloud in which Miriam moves is of an entirely different composition from the lucid bright air, "the ethereal and imaginative sustenance" (898) on which Hilda weightlessly floats.

What distinguishes the origins of the two heroines is not that one is a "daughter of the Puritans" and the other possibly of heathens or worse. Rather, it is that Miriam embodies family and history while Hilda has really no origin but the universal one. They seem to inhabit the same fictive world, but in fact they are incommensurate. Indeed, when Hawthorne once brings them together they cannot really meet. This incident has struck most critics as an artistic lapse, but this lapse bespeaks a fundamental disjuncture in the conception of the novel as a whole. After the murder, the despairing Miriam turns to Hilda for a sisterly sympathy that might at least comfort even though it cannot absolve. Hilda's rejection of the appeal translates her cool abstraction into a cold lack of feeling. Miriam's protest, "As an angel, you are not amiss; but as a human creature, and a woman among earthly men and women, you need a sin to soften you!" (1025), seems endorsed by the author himself. But Hilda's defense is also unanswerable. To Miriam's plea that a friend who has sinned needs friendship more than ever, Hilda responds:

> If I were one of God's angels, with a nature incapable of stain, and garments that never could be spotted, I would keep ever at your side, and try to lead you upward. But I am a poor, lonely girl, whom God has set here in an evil world, and given her only a white robe, and bid her wear it back to Him, as white as when she put it on. Your powerful magnetism would be too much for me. The pure, white atmosphere, in which I try to discern what things are good and true, would be discolored. And, therefore, Miriam, before it is too late, I mean to put faith in this awful heart-quake, which warns me henceforth to avoid you. (1025)

Hilda here penetrates to the heart of the contradiction that constitutes any individual, at once the perfect enactor of God's will and its greatest potential challenger. To use her definitive image for it, the problem she faces is how to retain a pure white vision (limpidly reflecting God's eternal truth) while distinguishing among the graded hues of human action. If she finds this impossible and, choosing to see her white God, bars color entirely from her atmosphere (her white is the opposite of Moby-Dick's, and instead of encompassing all colors, excludes them), what alternative does she have?

More to the point, what alternative does Hawthorne have? Like the moment on the tower when Kenyon is inexplicably unable to explain his creed to Donatello, the confrontation of Hilda and Miriam is more than an impasse inside the story, it is unwriteable *as* a story. Hilda's emotional failure in the scene is tantamount to a failure to live her fictive life: but if she were to do anything at all, listen, hear, understand, commiserate, or even condemn, she would become complicitous. Just listening would implicate her not in Miriam's sin but, as fatally, in the capacity to commit such sins, the concomitant of the capacity to understand their being committed by others. The moral issue for Hilda as for Hawthorne, as for any would-be good American, is the relation of the individual self and the global spirit. Their identity is the crucial axiom that must not be questioned, as Hilda would implicitly question it if she were to sympathize with Miriam despite her transgression. For the point of the relation is not first of all its moral or pragmatic value but the fact itself of their identity. That, to repeat, would be denied the moment Hilda even listened to Miriam's story of an alternative relation. Identity, sameness, oneness is all. Or, in Hilda's words, what God wants of her is not that she weave herself a white robe, however well it follows his pattern, but that she wear the one he gave her and return it to him in its *original* purity.

As moral philosophy, then, Hilda's reasoning works perfectly well. Nor does it seem to me problematical in her own character, whose severity, as Kenyon will later point out, is one of its charms. If she seems overrigorous in her response to Miriam, this is the only instance in which she develops an edge, hardens her ethereal femininity into a definite shape: it is pleasant to find something that the little copyist will not copy. The problem is that her refusal to listen to Miriam's story effectively stops not only Miriam but the development of the novel's story, at least in that direction. Indeed, Hilda's determination not to alter her divinely deeded robe would require her to reject any story, even one with a pious ending. *It amounts to a rejection of story as such.* And in fact, with Hilda's explicit repudiation of Miriam, *The Marble Faun* becomes more and more *self*-denying. Once the murder has been committed, the rest

174

of the novel recounts a series of denials by which the two sinners, instead of (like Julien Sorel in *The Red and the Black*, for instance) continuing the process their action has set in motion to *its* conclusion, incur a stopping of process. Not just the transformation of possibility, but its closure.

One such closure occurs, appropriately, during Kenyon's return to Rome and to Hilda after his visit to Monte Beni. Miriam, whose song failed to bring either Donatello or Kenyon to any new level of action or understanding, still hopes something can be made of the terrible new conditions she has helped to create. She prevails on Kenyon to arrange a meeting between her and Donatello, if it is only to ponder their guilt and its atonement. But her vivacity and the renewed color in her cheek when Kenyon agrees bespeak a greater ambition: "You see my weakness," she has just pleaded to Kenyon. "What I need, now, is an opportunity to show my strength" (1088).

Her ambition is grand indeed. She means to sacrifice herself wholly to the education of Donatello; she wants only "to instruct, to elevate, to enrich his mind" (1087). The irony in this of course is that she has already instructed and elevated him—by inciting him to murder. Penitent about having burdened him with guilt, she also rejoices in his transformation. "Is he not beautiful?" (1214), she asks Kenyon, exactly as she might glory in a figure in her painting; and in the guise of expiation, she plans how she will make him still more beautiful. Even in repentance, Miriam remains blasphemous, nor can one imagine her otherwise. As Hilda cannot contemplate blasphemy because she is defined by her identity with God, Miriam, who is defined in the opposite way by Rousseauian difference, is inherently, existentially recusant, and would cease to exist if she abandoned the competition with God by which she creates her art, her lover—and herself.

So Hilda is right after all, there is no way she could comfort Miriam without abetting her. When Miriam complains of Hilda's harshness, Kenyon justifies it: "The white, shining purity of Hilda's nature is a thing apart; and she is bound, by the undefiled material of which God moulded her, to keep that severity" (1091). Nonetheless he agrees to arrange Miriam's reunion with Donatello. The three are to meet in Perugia before the statue of Pope

Julius, at high noon: Hawthorne plans this scene so dramatically, not to say so melodramatically, that one expects . . . at any rate, one expects *something* to happen.

On the appointed day, at the appointed hour, Kenyon and Donatello are joined in their contemplation of the bronze statue by a pale but beautiful Miriam, who quickly ascertains that, though Donatello ran away from her after the killing, he still loves her. Reunited, the sad lovers gaze at one another, oppressed by their fate and each wondering whether their guilt ought not to preclude the comfort of love. In their perplexity, they welcome Kenyon's offer to "interpret or suggest some ideas which you might not so readily convey to each other." He begins therefore by pronouncing the bond between them, "a true one [that] never—except by Heaven's own act—should be rent asunder." The lovers join hands. "But," Kenyon continues,

> take heed . . . Take heed; for you love one another, and yet your bond is twined with such black threads, that you must never look upon it as identical with the ties that unite other loving souls. It is for mutual support; it is for one another's final good; it is for effort, for sacrifice, but not for earthly happiness! If such be your motive, believe me, friends, it were better to relinquish each other's hands at this sad moment. There would be no holy sanction on your wedded life.

The ceremony continues in its proper form. The couple answers, each in turn: " 'None,' said Donatello, shuddering, 'We know it well.' 'None,' repeated Miriam, also shuddering." The sculptor takes up the ritual:

> Not, for earthly bliss, therefore . . . but for mutual elevation, and encouragement towards a severe and painful life, you take each other's hands. And if, out of toil, sacrifice, prayer, penitence, and earnest effort towards right things, there comes at length, a sombre and thoughtful happiness, taste it, and thank Heaven! So that you live not for it—so that it be a wayside flower, springing along a path that leads to higher ends—it will be Heaven's gracious gift, and a token that it recognizes your union here below.

Kenyon is silent then, and Miriam and Donatello stand together, "the beautiful man, the beautiful woman, united forever" (1120– 21). The bronze Pope towering above them holds out his arms in benediction.

On one level all this is obvious enough, a marriage celebrated in sorrow rather than in joy, vows of lifelong fidelity in regret and repentance, a union for atonement and renunciation. But beginning with the silence that befalls the two sinners and requires Kenyon's intervention, something else is going on here, or rather something is stopping here. Kenyon's cry "take heed" responds to the lovers' too quick approbation of his first pronouncement that their bond is legitimate and not to be broken: " 'Ah; he has spoken the truth!,' cried Donatello, grasping Miriam's hand. 'The very truth, dear friend,' cried Miriam" (1120). Before their joyful acquiescence and eagerly joined hands, Kenyon becomes "anxious not to violate the integrity of his own conscience" (1120), and delivers the interdiction that grimly parallels the expected conjugal benediction. In a scene charged with erotic energy (we should remember the suggestiveness of Miriam's first euphoric declaration that she and Donatello were cemented together by their crime), Kenyon prohibits them an "earthly happiness" whose nature Miriam confirms when she echoes Donatello's "None." "Shuddering" she explains, "United (miserably entangled with me, rather) by a bond of guilt, our union might be for eternity, indeed, and most intimate; but through all that endless duration, I should be conscious of his horrour!" (1121).

On another level, then, the union of the two Europeans is not merely a shadow-marriage but an antimarriage condemning them to a nonlife together. Indeed, Hawthorne imagines their life only once more in the story and then as pure fantasy. On their last day of freedom, before they begin serving their life sentences (and thereby free Hilda to return and marry Kenyon), they frolic in the park: "To-day, Donatello was the sylvan Faun; to-day, Miriam was his fit companion, a Nymph of grove or fountain; to-morrow—a remorseful Man and Woman, linked by a marriage-bond of crime— they would set forth towards an inevitable goal" (1215). Those are the alternatives for them: creatures out of a long-vanished

177

mythology or doomed beings wedded only in their mutual lack of possibility.

The pseudomarriage of Miriam and Donatello inverts the marriage plot that commonly closes novels with the opening of history. But this lack of a future is apparently not due to their catastrophic crime, as the same lack marks the perfectly virtuous union of Hilda and Kenyon. Presumably, the two Americans marry in the full expectation of "earthly happiness." But Kenyon's proposal projects this joyful prospect just as terminally. He begins "Forgive me, Hilda!" and continues pleadingly, "so lonely as I live and work, I have neither pole-star above, nor light of cottage-windows here below, to bring me home. Were you my guide, my counsellor, my inmost friend, with that white wisdom which clothes you as a celestial garment, all would go well. O Hilda, guide me home!" (1236). So she does, and so they go home, to a Jeffersonian horizon, an infinity of identical days.

Hawthorne clearly intended to juxtapose the two marriages, but I would like to stress their mutual reflectiveness and to suggest that together they describe marriage as the social representation of man's natural identity with the world (woman being the means to realize that identity rather than in herself an alternative agent). Thus in contrast to the sad marriage of Eugénie Grandet, which soon ends in widowhood and is on the way to being replaced when the novel concludes, neither of the marriages that close *The Marble Faun* can be imagined having an independent aftermath. "Enshrined and worshipped as a household Saint, in the light of her husband's fireside" (1237), Hilda only unfolds the already implicit meaning of Kenyon's marriage. Unhappily, Miriam also unfolds the meaning of Donatello's antimarriage; the point is that neither the positive nor the negative representation of marriage is productive. They do not generate stories, indeed both are meant to bring stories to an end: Donatello and Miriam's marriage seals their story into a definitive recantation, and Kenyon and Hilda's into an affirmation as definitive, as encompassingly complete and thereby terminal.

Rather than the marriages that end novels, those of *The Marble Faun* recall the ever-after marriages at the close of fairy tales. The eternal happiness these project is entirely abstract—it has to be in order to be eternal. "They lived happily ever after" promises that nothing will ever happen again: not that something will continue, but that nothing will change. After such endings nothing further can be imagined. On the contrary, even the happy union of Elizabeth and Darcy at the end of *Pride and Prejudice* invites our further fabrications along lines set out by the several imperfect versions of marriage with which Austen qualifies and relativizes that of the Darcys.

Morality-play style, *The Marble Faun* represents two forms of one absolute, its fulfillment and its denial. Hilda and Kenyon witness the bad way and choose the good. In opposition to the earthbound love of Miriam and Donatello, the love of a blasphemer and a pagan, that of Hilda and Kenyon is altogether hallowed. Hilda is so pure, so purely spirit, that Kenyon cannot declare his passion, and even in proposing marriage speaks only of a spiritual bond. Hawthorne seems loath even to imagine, in the brief projection of their sanctified hearth, the sweet babe that usually inhabits such visions. But recalling that the antimarriage of Miriam and Donatello is celebrated by a sculptor and blessed by a statue will bring us back to the main point: that the lesson Hilda and Kenyon learn in Rome is primarily about art. In rejecting Miriam and Donatello, they reject not only a way of life but, more urgently, a way of art.

As the living image of an ancient statue whose subject—a faun—paradoxically connotes the timelessness and craftlessness of nature, Donatello embodies the transforming and potentially usurping dialectic of art. The original creator of the Marble Faun, the sculptor Praxiteles, interpreted not nature but a myth. The statue that inspired Hawthorne's fiction was already (in Miriam's words) "at odds with nature"; and not, as Emerson wished, in correspondence with it. *The Marble Faun* removes art still further from nature by portraying in Donatello a fictional character who incarnates a statue, which itself interprets a myth. At this third remove, art has usurped nature entirely. Herself the creature of such artistic transgression, Miriam in her turn makes Donatello into her version of Frankenstein's monster: a man made capable of dealing death by the way he was dealt life—through an act of blasphemous creation. She thus perpetuates blasphemy into a fourth generation of human creations. Her promise to continue the development of Donatello makes it clear that the process is in fact self-perpetuating and will continue endlessly, infernal creation spawning infernal creation. The injunction against Miriam's and Donatello's future acts of any kind represents the only way to end this process. Henceforth they must not do anything so as not to create anything. Then possibly God will send them "a somber and thoughtful happiness" like "a wayside flower"—*nature's* creation not only unaided but almost unseen by man.

While Miriam's innovating art is thus utterly condemned, Hilda's copying achieves an actual apotheosis. After offering one or two mundane suggestions about where the celestial girl might have passed the time of her kidnapping, Hawthorne suggests that instead of asking exactly where,

> it is better, perhaps, to fancy that she had been snatched away to a Land of Picture; that she had been straying with Claude in the golden light which he used to shed over his landscapes, but which he could never have beheld with his waking eyes, till he awoke in the better clime. We will imagine that, for the sake of the true simplicity with which she loved them, Hilda had been permitted, for a season, to converse with the great, departed Masters of the pencil, and behold the diviner works which they have painted in heavenly colors. (1230–1231)

Earlier, on earth, Hilda had been occupied with copying the portrait of Beatrice Cenci by Guido. Hawthorne implies parallels between Miriam's mysterious past and the story of Beatrice, the innocent daughter of a degenerate family who, it is said, when her virtue was threatened by her own father, participated in his killing, committing patricide to save herself from incest. Miriam shows intense interest in the painting and especially in Hilda's opinion as to whether Beatrice should be accounted innocent or guilty. In their discussion of the painting (905–906), Hilda is at first entirely sympathetic to its tragic model: "She is a fallen angel, fallen, and yet sinless." To Miriam's query as to why then Beatrice seems so very sad, Hilda answers, "Sorrow so black as hers oppresses her very nearly as sin would." Only at Miriam's further prompting, "Then . . . do you think that there was no sin in the deed for which she suffered?" does Hilda draw back. She had forgotten the story, she tells Miriam, "and was thinking of her only as the picture seems to reveal her character." But now she remembers that "it was terrible guilt, an inexpiable crime, and [Beatrice] feels it to be so. Therefore it is that the forlorn creature so longs to elude our eyes, and forever vanish away into nothingness! Her doom is just!" "O Hilda," Miriam protests, "Your innocence is like a sharp steel sword."

The image is apt, for Hilda's mode of innocence (the mode of obedience rather than of free choice) severs the good from the bad absolutely, denying any relation between them but that of opposition. The inextricable weave of sin and virtue that the legend of Beatrice epitomizes, and which is the common fabric of both art and history, Hilda will have none of. But if she would not entitle any book of hers *Sartor Resartus*, it is because she understands very well that in all the retailorings of individual creation, it is precisely the *tailor* who is remaking *himself*. Earlier in the story, just before Miriam comes to seek her help and is rejected, Hilda sits alone and saddened near her easel, on which the Beatrice copy still rests. "Now, opposite the easel hung a looking-glass, in which Beatrice's face and Hilda's were both reflected . . . Hilda happened to throw her eyes on the glass, and took in both these images at one unpremeditated glance. She fancied—nor was it without horror—that Beatrice's expression, seen aside and vanishing in a moment, had been depicted in her own face, likewise . . ." (1022). In this three-way relation, of a face and its reflection both in a mirror and in art, Hawthorne has projected the danger in any reflection, even the most truthful one. The reflections here are all three truthful and even unmediated. For Hilda has not created the Beatrice portrait but only copied it. Still, as she explains, this required letting the picture sink into her heart. The capacity of the heart to understand is also the capacity to change, to remake the maker's creation. As compared to the absolute stasis of the union of transparent eyeball and transparent universe, the problem with reflection is that it is implicitly productive. The very correspondence on which the power to reflect depends—the likeness of one's face to the one in the mirror or in the portrait, or the encompassing likeness of man to nature—contains the power also either to change the other or to become more like it. My double in the mirror is in my power, though sometimes I am in its power when it reveals aspects of me I had not yet seen. And if I see myself reflected in all nature, I can either transform the world or be globally transformed myself.

That the power implicit in art is the power of the self to reflect upon itself is what Hilda realizes in that terrible moment when she seems to glimpse the guilt of Beatrice in her own reflected and reflective glance. " 'Am I, too, stained with guilt?' thought the poor girl, hiding her face in her hands." "Not so, thank Heaven!" (1022), answers Hawthorne, but he is hard put to explain how she has escaped. By sending Miriam away unheard, therefore unreflected, she has saved herself from any ultimate sin. Before she understood how dangerous it might be, however, she permitted herself, in the name of art, a certain latitude of contemplation, of which the miraculously well understood copy of Guido's painting, one might say the extraordinarily *knowing* copy, is the tangible expression.

I would speculate that this moment in the novel is freshly problematical for Hawthorne as well, who has written his way to a realization he did not have earlier. The logic of Hilda and of the danger to which she is opposed has revealed itself to be more stringent than he initially imagined it. And to maintain it and Hilda's perfect virtue, he finds it necessary retroactively to narrow Hilda's range of understanding. If she could let the face of Beatrice sink into her heart it was because in fact Beatrice, contrary to legend, was innocent. Hilda's flitting resemblance to the picture has suggested "a theory which may account for its unutterable grief and mysterious shadow of guilt, without detracting from the purity which we love to attribute to that ill-fated girl" (1022). The theory itself is not very ingenious (Beatrice suffers from the knowledge of her father's sin but is herself blameless), but Hawthorne's interpolation of it here is significant in marking his movement to a more restrictive view of art whereby the very depiction of sin is sinful. This movement has a logic, too. Hilda does not again ponder the inextricable paradoxes of the Guido Beatrice. In fact she does not again ponder. The alternative to the possibly sinful portrait in the Roman gallery is a woman's face shown Hilda by the painter Perugino when she visits heaven. It is a face "so divine, . . . that a gush of happy tears blinded the maiden's eyes, before she had time to look" (1230). Her tear-blinded eyes see as Emerson saw through his transparent eyeball. The copyist who depicted without creating has transcended to seeing without looking. There is nothing less an artist can do.

Miriam's art comes to its end in hell, then, and Hilda's in heaven. In both the character of Miriam and the conception of art she projects, Hawthorne pursued the terms of novelistic fiction to their usurping and blaspheming extremity. In Hilda he represents as extreme an alternative in both her mode of characterization and her definition of art. By the end of *The Marble Faun* these extremes have come to dominate both the action and the tone. One is tempted, after finishing the book, to summarize it in the most schematic and allegorical terms, and so it has been frequently presented in the critical tradition. But for all its final Hilda-like absolutism, *The Marble Faun* does not rest easy in allegory. At certain moments it strains mightily in another direction altogether. In the exchange of Miriam and Kenyon over the Cleopatra, for instance, Hawthorne has created possibilities that have little to do with the illustration of morals and everything with the development of individual character. Had Kenyon not drawn back, the next events would be neither sins nor good deeds but revealing relations and evolutions, events and actions perhaps, but not allegorical dramatizations. Similarly, our regret when Hilda sends Miriam away is for the interplay between the two that would have otherwise ensued, interplay that again would have taken us not toward resolution but in fact away from it, toward qualification and contradiction. As for the third major refusal, the refusal of a future to Miriam and Donatello, it closes down what one can imagine could have been an entire novel of its own.

This last denial seems particularly drastic: God, after all, according to Milton, actually commanded the fallen Adam and Eve to go forth and generate their own story. Once they left the Garden they never looked at a morality play again. But of course Hawthorne's Adam and Eve have returned to the Garden: the allegory of Miriam and Donatello is played for the edification of Hilda and Kenyon, and Hawthorne's judgment of the Europeans implies an

American ethic. This ethic, however, plunges him into the depths of the quandary I defined in Chapter 4. Born of the American reconciliation between man and nature, that dilemma offers on the one hand, as Emerson promised it would, infinite possibilities. But in *The Marble Faun* the voice of ideal goodness cries "Hush!" to the very suggestion that an enlightened man may "ultimately rise to a far loftier paradise" than the one from which he fell into the Old World. "You have shocked me beyond words!" Hilda tells Kenyon, who at once forswears all further such talk.

More drastically, so does Hawthorne. The story has an apparently happy ending in the return of Hilda and Kenyon to America. But the tone of the last sentences is unmistakably one of abdication. On the eve of her departure Hilda receives a gift from Miriam, a bracelet with seven gems to which the irrepressible inventor of stories had once assigned seven "wondrous tales." As the bracelet passes into Hilda's possession, its potential meaning is commensurately changed: "happy as Hilda was, the bracelet brought the tears into her eyes, as being, in its entire circle, the symbol of as sad a mystery as any that Miriam had attached to the separate gems. For, what was Miriam's life to be? and where was Donatello? But Hilda had a hopeful soul, and saw sun-light on the mountain-tops" (1238). This is how *The Marble Faun* ends.[1] The "sun-light on the mountain-tops" is totally ephemeral and unrealizable in any further developments. The questions that precede this nonresolution are likewise only rhetorical. The fictions Miriam invented have been absorbed and dispersed in the "entire circle" of Hilda's perfect truth. Much as *The Scarlet Letter* ended with a ciphered code, this novel ends in a negation of the terms that made it possible. It is as if Hawthorne had shocked *himself* beyond words.

6 ✳ The Rebirth of Tragedy

*B*rother-sister incest, through which a man may reproduce himself in union with the female version of his own body, has a strict individualist logic: it incarnates the self-made man. And he could do worse, for insofar as incest retains a communal dimension, its potential for creating monsters is less dangerous to society than the ultimate individualist apotheosis of autoeroticism. The perils of the first transgression and its likely progress to the second are the themes of Melville's novel *Pierre*.

From the make-believe incest of Pierre and his mother in the opening scenes, the story moves to the real trespass of Pierre and his sister, which is concealed by their feigned marriage, to Pierre's withdrawal from even such antinomian relations into entire self-absorption. In a parallel way, he begins as a writer of popular verse about make-believe sentimentalities, and goes on to aspire to a book that would reveal the world's deepest duplicity. But in the throes of his ultimate self-involvement, he can no longer write, but only envisions inwardly an autobiography that concludes with the tragic recognition that he is at once arch-victim and arch-destroyer. Pierre is the stone upon which the church of his civilization has been built, and the stone that, self-hurled at the altar, has toppled it forever.

Melville's problem is Pierre's problem, that is, to stop short of the ultimate rebellion, while he can still write (act) his alienation. Wholly alienated, as Pierre becomes at the end of the novel, the writer can no longer produce his words; they fall back with him into the silence of true monologue. Except that the transcendent state here would be total withdrawal, this is the same problem that inspired Emerson's abiding in dualities when unity was at hand: one can only work, even to enact the unity, in the context of duality. *The Marble Faun*, however, demonstrated that in this interim state (apart from America even if only to learn to represent it better) one could be tempted to reconsider the unity—or worse, as Kenyon came perilously close to doing, to try one's hand at creating a new one. *Pierre*, which sets out to parody the conventional wisdom, goes further and defines writing precisely as the work of creating new unities; whereupon two things combine to destroy both hero and book. The first is that the fictive society rises against the would-be revolutionary and kills him. The second is that, reflecting on his hero's unlimited ambition to remake the world, Melville damns him for a satanic fool, and along with him damns the ambition represented by his story—and kills both. But it is kill or be killed: the world Pierre wants to remake is a living thing, incarnate in real land and real bodies, indeed finally incarnate in *him*. If Hawthorne finally rejects creation when he understands it as blasphemous, Melville acquiesces to blasphemy and discovers it is suicide.

In the beginning, however, everything seems supremely sanctified. Pierre Glendinning is young, handsome, and accomplished, the only scion of a wealthy landowning family soon to accede to the extensive estate of Saddle Meadows. He is also about to marry his perfect consort, the lovely, virtuous, blue-eyed Lucy; everything seems set for an ascension into total bliss. But one evening Pierre meets Isabel, a mysterious young woman who has recently arrived in the village attached to the estate. She tells him that she is the illegitimate child of his father and a vanished Frenchwoman. Pierre's father has been dead for some years, but his wife, Mary Glendinning, keeps his image constantly present as a noble model for her son to emulate. The family's pride depends on this image of patriarchal perfection, and its identity depends on its pride: it is Pierre's filial duty to preserve that pride from public dishonor.

Yet things must be set right, and precisely because he is heir to his father's ideality, Pierre has to fulfill it. To save his father's world as his father bequeathed it to him, he has to reconstruct it. He devises a plan for an interior rebuilding that will leave the facade intact: by pretending to marry Isabel, he will endow her with her familial rights and properties; by presenting her as his wife he will conceal the radical family flaw by which they share a father.

Of course the plan fails, though in one way, when the sham marriage is consummated in incest, it succeeds too well. The eloping couple travel to New York City, where Pierre, now disinherited by his mother, tries vainly to support them by his writing. After a time, they are joined by the angelic Lucy. Though she thinks that Pierre has really abandoned her and married Isabel, she has come to him sensing that somehow he still needs her. She is his only remaining friend, for his mother has died of a broken heart, and the cousin to whom she deeded Saddle Meadows opportunistically denies all relation to the outcast. The feud ends with Pierre's killing this cousin and being imprisoned for the murder. Then he too dies, along with both Isabel and Lucy, in a black dungeon beneath the Tombs prison in lower Manhattan. The Glendinning family dies with him. Pierre has completely laid waste the world he meant to preserve.

The ultimate hopelessness of his enterprise and its inherent contradiction are both evident to Pierre from the start. "Thy two grand resolutions," he taunts himself,

> —the public acknowledgment of Isabel, and the charitable withholding of her existence from thy own mother,—these are impossible adjuncts. —Likewise, thy so magnanimous purpose to screen thy father's honorable memory from reproach, and thy other intention, the open vindication of thy fraternalness to Isabel,—these also are impossible adjuncts. And the having individually entertained four such resolves, without perceiving that once brought together, they all mutually expire; this, this ineffable folly, Pierre, brands thee in the forehead for an unaccountable infatuate!   (202–203)

Pierre's plight is an exact instance of the situation in which Emerson's necessary actor set to work. Confronting "unmarriageable facts," Pierre too assumes it is his special task to reconcile them, and to knit the "separate strands" of his family into "a perfect cord." *Pierre* is explicitly a parody of popular sentimental fiction. But that the cord, tying together unmarriageable facts, weds a brother and sister, suggests that Melville's most scathing wit aimed at a more elevated literature; later in the novel, the odious Plotinus Plinlimmon satirizes Emerson.

Pierre's predicament also has a direct historical reference. His own generation, both in fiction and in history, faced the "impossible adjuncts" of keeping the patriarchal order intact while yet recreating the world in their own image. Though extravagantly developed, Melville's plot belongs to a familiar category of stories that might be called the American matter of the patriarch—stories that represent father-son relations as embodiments of the national character and experience. The personal interaction through which a boy becomes a man[1] was a natural theme for an emerging society intent on differentiating itself from its parent culture, and on doing so in particular through its progressive, expansive individualism. The individualist saga recounts, in place of prior tales of innately characterized beings assuming (or failing to assume) public roles, the private but universal process by which the child is made and makes himself a unique and continually evolving man. In this process, the chief actors are the members of the immediate family, and the action traces the son's preparation to replace his father. This is exactly where *Pierre* begins.

Right after the protagonist has been introduced—literally in a naming ritual conducted with Lucy, whose own obviously significant name points to the likely but still hidden meaning of Pierre's—he is described as "the only son of an affluent, and haughty widow," who is in her turn identified first by her remarkable youthfulness: "In mature age, the rose still miraculously clung to her cheek; litheness had not yet completely uncoiled itself from her waist, nor smoothness unscrolled itself from her brow, nor diamondness departed from her eyes"(8). These attractions, the narrator boasts, might win Mrs. Glendinning a host of suitors, "little less young than her own son Pierre," except that she discourages them all, finding "a reverential and devoted son . . . lover enough." Besides,

Pierre when namelessly annoyed, and sometimes even jealously transported by the too ardent admiration of the handsome youths, who now and then, caught in unintended snares, seemed to entertain some insane hopes of wedding this unattainable being; Pierre had more than once, with a playful malice, openly sworn, that the man—gray-beard, or beardless—who should dare to propose marriage to his mother, that man would by some peremptory unrevealed agency immediately disappear from the earth. (9)

Half a century before Freud analyzed the homicidal impulses of affectionate sons, Melville clearly understood in similar terms the "romantic filial love" (9) that has made Pierre "strangely docile . . . to the maternal tuitions" (22).[2] I speculated earlier that the currency of Freudian theories in America might reflect an American disposition to see individualism rooted in the natural body rather than in historical incorporation. Pursuing that notion, one could see Melville's portrait of a pious but patricidal son as a culmination of Freud's Oedipus thesis, as this outlines the familial middle-class ideology. While Emerson completed the evolution of individualism's public ideology, Melville drew a more problematical conclusion about its private ideology. Or rather, by seeing that the public and the private might diverge, he rendered problematical Emerson's view of a self so encompassing that it had no private dimension but was simply all-being. In his ideal state, the Emersonian man was "nothing" and saw "all." Melville's Pierre falls, in the end, into the opposite condition, when he sees nothing because he has made himself everything. The assertion of this possibility is significant, for it implies a dialectic of man and nature that Emersonian complementarity cannot resolve. Emerson discovered the American soul, but Melville found that this soul had a psyche, one whose discontents could destroy civilization outright.

Pierre and his mother, then, play at being lovers (among other ways, by calling each other "brother" and "sister"), although Pierre is already betrothed to the ideally sympathetic and beautiful Lucy. In fact, the prospect of this marriage pleases Mrs. Glendinning greatly, for, she reflects, this

little wife, that is to be, will not estrange him from me
. . . seldom yet have I known such blue eyes as hers, that
were not docile, and would not follow a bold black one, as
two meek blue-ribboned ewes follow their martial leader.
How glad am I that Pierre loves her so, and not some
dark-eyed haughtiness, with whom I could never live in
peace. (26–27)

When the dark Isabel appears, Mary Glendinning's premature self-congratulation seems ironically prophetic.

Actually, it is difficult to say that Isabel "appears," so shadowy
is she. As her luxuriant black hair hides her features, her equally
abundant words seem to obscure more than they reveal. Her some-times incoherent tale, of a lonely childhood divided among remote
houses where she was addressed only to be denied information
about herself and the circumstances of her birth, invokes not so
much a character as an outline, a space that the plot will never fill
in. Even her sexual appeal is, in a sense, negative, the projection
of the prohibited, of that which cannot be associated with either
Lucy or Pierre's mother. Looking at Lucy hovering translucent in
a sunny doorway, Pierre worries fondly that "one husbandly em-brace would break her airy zone, and she exhale upward to that
heaven whence she hath hither come, condensed to mortal sight"
(72). In the same way, the powerful implied sexuality of Pierre's
relationship to his mother measures its exceptional spirituality. In
the narrator's rhapsody, their tenderness has

that nameless and infinitely delicate aroma . . . which, in
every refined and honorable attachment, is cotemporary with
the courtship, and precedes the final banns and the rite; but
which, like the *bouquet* of the costliest German wines, too
often evaporates upon pouring love out to drink, in the
disenchanting glasses of the matrimonial days and nights;
this highest and airiest thing in the whole compass of the
experience of our mortal life; this heavenly evanescence—
still further etherealized in the filial breast—was for Mary
Glendinning . . . miraculously revived in the courteous lover-like adoration of Pierre. (22)

In this paradise of miraculous revivals and reincarnations of
perfect fathers through perfect sons, Isabel's illegitimate status in

itself signifies an alien carnal temptation. But as the image of "litheness . . . not yet completely uncoiled" from about Mary Glendinning's waist alerts us, Isabel is not the origin of that temptation. In the crossings and recrossings of thresholds that punctuate the beginning of the story, the liminal Pierre has been stumbling on a more pervasive subliminal temptation—and when he falls, Isabel is companion more than cause. In the charged atmosphere of Saddle Meadows, incest is in suspension, and Isabel is first the catalyst that causes it to precipitate, then a surrogate for its enactment. The real drama of this fall from a second Eden is between Pierre and his godlike (though perhaps ungodly) parents.

If this conflation of the Oedipal story with the fall seems odd, this oddness is just the point. In part, *Pierre* is about an exceptional American development in the definition of filiopiety, both familial and political, which lends generational succession the potential for blasphemy. This is the more remarkable, first, in that the modern family, which in the eighteenth century replaced restraint with nurture as the primary parental function, seemed to have removed the ground for blasphemy along with absolute patriarchal authority; and second, because this conception of the family was especially successful in America, where in the formative colonial period, as Jay Fliegelman has shown, it was taken to describe not only a familial ideal but a broad political one.[3] To the American colonists, prototypically self-made men, the model of the nurturing family, stressing education over obedience in the interest of individual competence and individualist autonomy, seemed to describe not only their own necessities but those of the New World. Usefully, this model cast the colonial situation as childhood and England as a parent bound to foster growth and self-reliance. A little later, the accusation that the king was a patriarchal tyrant argued that rebellion was justified and even that it testified to the rebels' maturity. Fliegelman has found "a call for filial autonomy" to be "the quintessential motif of the American Revolution" (*Prodigals and Pilgrims*, 3).

The Revolution projected its leaders as "Founding Fathers." These were explicitly fathers in the new mold, who constituted a social family that valued growth over stability, self-reliance over conformity, acquisition over heritage, independence over filiopiety. Yet, new generational problems arose that seemed exacerbated by the new model's very triumph. The first post-Revolution generation has been widely analyzed as being immobilized by a sense of inadequacy growing out of its reverence for its predecessors. Pierre too seems an unequal successor. His mother, teasingly upbraiding him for being a "milk-sop," continues: "Never rave, Pierre; and never rant. Your father never did either; nor is it written of Socrates; and both were very wise men" (25). The founders of America were equal, and more, to any comparison. Benjamin Franklin, who at other times was renowned for his sense of humor, transcribed what he said had been one of the precepts through which he had achieved success in this new world: "Be humble: Imitate Jesus and Socrates." Precisely by representing in his enlightened fatherhood its culminating social achievement, Pierre's loving liberal father has thus become the definitive embodiment of Western civilization. He is the literal embodiment of America, being the third Pierre Glendinning, after the hero's great-grandfather, who won the family lands from the Indians, and his grandfather, General Pierre Glendinning, who won them again from the English. All three of these founding fathers are dead at the beginning of the novel, but their physical passing has only concentrated their ideal presence, so that Pierre's own father is an exponential ancestor, looking down on his heir with infinite benevolence, and with definite expectations.

Moreover, in the image of that perfect and whole reproduction of each generation of Pierre Glendinnings by the next, their world is also perfect and whole. Family and world are thus one, as the single name Saddle Meadows attests by naming both the Glendinning lands and the local village. That Pierre's mother is named Mary points to an ultimate identity: the Glendinnings are one with heaven itself. Melville's allusion to the holy family is ironic, but it is also appropriate, for Pierre, the only descendant and thus the preserver, if not savior, of his race, is not meant to succeed his father but to reincarnate him. He is to *be* his father. This, to be sure, not in abnegation, as the son of an old patriarch might have surrendered himself to his father's purpose, but in self-fulfillment: "in the ruddiness, and flushfulness, and vaingloriousness of his youthful soul, he fondly hoped to have a monopoly of glory in capping the fame-column, whose tall shaft had been erected by his noble sires" (12). Pierre will realize himself by culminating his father; his ambition is to fulfill Pierre Glendinning, a task to which, since he also is Pierre Glendinning, he is perfectly suited. Such total correspondence of education to occasion is the ideal achievement of the nurturing family, demonstrating its wholly adequate preparation of its child. But the problem with it is apparent: how is Pierre to become as fully independent as his father became, and as his father prepared him to become, if the ideal expression of Pierre's independence is identical with his father's? Will he not, then, in the moment of becoming wholly himself, disappear; by becoming the fourth avatar of that ideal being "Pierre Glendinning," will he not cease to be himself? (How is an American to build his own America when he *is* America?) It is a peculiar dilemma, peculiar, that is, to Pierre's privilege; for elsewhere than in idyllic Saddle Meadows, sons may readily aspire to surpass unideal fathers who earlier surpassed theirs. Whether sons surpass fathers or not, the imperfection of both guarantees the possibility at least of change—thus of the sons' having their own discrete futures. If Pierre—like the first generation of American sons, whom Daniel Webster addressed as "children" standing "among the sepulchres of our fathers," and to whom Emerson complained that "our age is retrospective," that "we [only] build the sepulchres of the fathers"—is transfixed by the past, it is in part because the past, in Saddle Meadows and in America, is also the future.

Mary Glendinning's remarkable youthfulness is an ominous token of this negation of time. Mother and son appear of the same generation: "as the mother seemed to have long stood still in her beauty, heedless of the passing years; so Pierre seemed to meet her half-way, and by a splendid precocity of form and feature, almost advanced himself to that mature stand-point in Time, where his pedestaled mother so long had stood" (9). This rapprochement reverses the process whereby time accomplishes the separation of sons and parents. In the Freudian account, patricide remains a fantasy whose purpose is achieved by the father's aging—in other words, by history. In eternal and timeless Saddle Meadows, however, time is unreal; it has no effect, neither aging Mrs. Glendinning nor keeping her son visibly younger than she.

The success of the Revolution has essentially realized the patricidal fantasy, and the result is unexpectedly ironic. Thus: the
Freudian son's desire to take his father's place with his mother
connotes a transitory identification that in fact facilitates the son's
subsequent departure from both parents: the possibility of becoming not his father but like his father, a father himself because
distinct from his father. It is crucial that the "killing" of the father
remain metaphorical; were the father literally killed, as was the
father of Oedipus, the son would be stuck in a transitional moment. He would become, as Oedipus did in actually marrying his
mother, the old rather than the new father. The worst harm in
this, furthermore, would not be to the son, but to the son's son,
and to the subsequent social order. For how would the son's son
become himself? By actually possessing his mother, the patricidal
father co-opts succession; he and his son have the same mother,
and thus the son can only reproduce his father's self-making,
which transforms him into his father. History proceeds by unfolding, but the returning pattern of incest instead rewinds society
in a narrowing spiral whose center and ultimate goal, both, is the
patricidal patriarch.

The founding fathers, Pierre's and America's, might be seen
as patricidal patriarchs in this mold—revolutionaries who thus
actually "killed" their fathers and made the culminating progressive revolution. In so doing, they ensured but also co-opted the
progress of their sons. The plot of *Pierre*, which develops from
mobility to stasis and from lucidity to opaqueness, traces an incestuous regression that begins in a Pierre Glendinning whose
triumphal establishment of an all-beneficent family and estate implicitly encompasses the deeds of all future Pierre Glendinnings.
The spiral culminates not with him but with his son, only because
the son has usurped the father's place. His succession does not
bring about a different world, but only destroys the world he has
usurped.

Pierre suggests that, for the American Oedipus, succession is
either usurpation or assumption. The first is impermissible, under
penalty of recurrent primordial chaos. Therefore Pierre must assume his father's world, and with it, his father's identity. Intent
on being himself *originally* in the way for which his father(s) pro-

vided both the example and the benevolent nurture, Pierre rejects such identification, and thus the name of Pierre Glendinning. But in the absence of an alternative, since the success of the revolution that generated individual(ist) names has made all names identical in their equal perfection, his only identity is negative—not–Pierre Glendinning—and he descends into an oblivion as complete as the transcendence he abjures. The lasting resonance of the term "antinomian" in American thinking, long past its Puritan relevance, may have to do with this continuing dilemma, which might also have prompted Jefferson's meditation on each generation's need to water the tree of the Revolution with blood, as an attempt to transform what could be a paralyzing standoff into creative paradox. For Pierre, however, it is a fatal contradiction—trying to make his own revolution, he discovers that precisely the permanence of his father's Revolution prevents him.

The transcendent Revolution's equally absolute opposite term, in Pierre's fatal contradiction, would have been less apparent to Jefferson (before Emerson drew its personal implication), but conceptually it emerged with the "discovery" itself. *Pierre* shows it arising with the founding of Saddle Meadows, long before Isabel arrived there. If her bizarre story is immediately persuasive to Pierre, this is because it confirms certain intimations of his own, vague images of a feminine face much like his own; the narrator notes that Pierre has always yearned for a sister. Her absence, the "one hiatus . . . discoverable by him" in his perfect life, deprives him not of a companion actress but of the tangible representation of an aspect of himself, the manifestation of something implicit in him that he can realize only through her. The "hiatus" interrupts a process of self-realization. He wants in a sister "some one I might love and protect, and fight for, if need be. It must be a glorious thing to engage in a mortal quarrel on a sweet sister's behalf!" (11–12). This somewhat heavy-handed irony need not distract us from the precise articulation of Pierre's motive: he wants a sister in order to act as a brother. In fact, her advent triggers a fury of mortally quarrelsome activity which propels the siblings out of Saddle Meadows and into a story whose remarkably few events trace Pierre's withdrawal from all companionship and finally even from Isabel. He has then totally replaced "Pierre Glendinning" with himself, who, by an inevitable logic, is the anti–"Pierre Glendinning"—as Christ's alter-ego is the anti-Christ.

Early in the novel, the narrator issues a warning: "*Nemo contra Deum nisi Deus ipse*," Let no one go against God who is not himself God. But Pierre will in the end answer that one shows oneself divine precisely by challenging the gods. The two parts of the contradiction are here: a world whose order is God-given but that contains, as the implementer of this order, a man who is himself a god—for such Pierre has always been told he was, made in the image of his "dear, perfect father" in heaven. So as absolute as the world of his father is, his own would-be re-creation is equally absolute: he does not want just one plot on the revolutionary estate, he wants (can only conceive of wanting) all of it. This is the other effect of having a revolutionary-patricidal father: that his son acquires in him a model for patricide, for ridding himself of the past and of all dependence, for an independence perhaps even more complete than that of his father, who, in making the culminating revolution, engaged history if only as the stuff of his remaking. In fact, the illicit impulse that bequeathed Pierre an illegitimate sister is also the ancestor of his extravagant ambition. It is hinted that Isabel's mother was a refugee from the French Terror, which for most Americans connoted a murderous madness unleashed by excessive radical ambition, the French Revolution's all-destroying alter-ego. At the margins of the madness, Pierre's father was nonetheless drawn some way into its anarchic whirlpool. But he recovered himself and, living in the period of the institutionalization of the American Revolution, was able to express his ambition to transform the world in the making of productive institutions, that is, of institutions that would reproduce him. In a word, he married.

With those institutions established and representing the independent self's ideal context, however, his son's self-sufficiency can be expressed only solipsistically: Pierre's imperial self is its own only object. In this sense, *only* incest can satisfy him, as exogamy would disperse him and what he seeks is concentration. The acting out of the fantasy of killing has inverted its effect, so that now it precludes separation. Instead of separating from his father, Pierre seeks to absorb him. The story's movement from implicit sublimated incest with his mother to real incest with his sister marks the only two possibilities open to such a son. Both, in the image of the ideal self's ultimate self-sufficiency, are narcissistic; as his mother's "lover," Pierre was submerged in her image: "in the clear-cut lineaments and noble air of the son, [she] saw her own graces strangely translated into the opposite sex" (9). In this form, incest represents Pierre's absorption into Saddle Meadows, never to issue into a marriage (world) of his own. Since Mrs. Glendinning represents both physical and spiritual perfection in a timeless world, another woman could only represent declension, from transcendence to a prior and imperfect history. (Completely subject to her prospective mother-in-law's will and personality, Lucy does not really represent another woman, but she loses Pierre because she does not represent the "one" either.)[4]

Against his mother's pull to transcendent unity, Pierre counterposes the relation with a real sister who is essentially his own complementary female principle; and through the physical reality of this principle, he incarnates himself. Then, however, if he is to equal his father, he must achieve an all-encompassing wholeness, which even incest compromises. Therefore he withdraws from Isabel into a climactic masturbatory trance in which waking and sleeping, language and silence, self and world, all implode into a catastrophic recoil that fuses birth and death. So in the end, Pierre's family romance has turned out to be a murder-suicide. Everyone is dead, and the ancestral "fame-column" Pierre was to have capped has been cut down at the base. There are no male descendants of the Glendinning line. The original Oedipus did his family less harm.

Because it overthrew the reigning authority instead of succeeding to it, and then established a new form of authority based on (or successfully claiming to be based on) popular representation, the Revolution could appear as a culmination of the very history of authority. In turn, this achieved end preempted future succession. As in another context it was said of the French Revolution that it ate its children, we might say of the American that it swallowed its ancestors and therefore its descendants. For by presenting itself as the fulfillment of the past, it left its children no future but the fulfillment of the founding vision. In the familiar refrain, Americans would have "no sense of history," precisely because they had already done with history at the beginning.

To go against this ultimate world was perhaps conceivable for an ultimate individual; but insofar as each one embodied all Creation, such rebellion would be cataclysmic. So that, because the culmination of history left no way for future generations to define themselves through the difference they made, to be an American was everything and nothing. ("I am nothing," Emerson said. "I see all.") Certainly it was everything and nothing to be Pierre Glendinning, who was not only empowered but destined to enact his world's ideal consummation, and who by the same endowment was forbidden, if he would avoid blasphemy, to change anything. The events of *Pierre* are nonevents; what happens in the plot is that things don't happen, until the ending finally negates everything. Indeed nothing new can happen, for Pierre has no means, no identity even, with which to act. He can *only* say "No! in thunder."

That there exists an encompassing identity between the elder Pierre Glendinning and his world, and that this one fused universe is the ground of his son's enterprise, is apparent from the start, when the discovery of the injustice done Isabel exfoliates into a social pattern. As a stain can bring out the distinct threads and knots in a fabric that before appeared evenly woven, Isabel's arrival reveals that Saddle Meadows society is disparate and unequal. The first meetings between legitimate heir and outcast sister take place in a shabby rented farmhouse (rented from the Glendinnings), where Isabel is a servant. Approaching its low door, Pierre hangs back briefly. "Infallibly," the narrator explains, "he knows that his own voluntary steps are taking him from the brilliant chandeliers of the mansion of Saddle Meadows, to join company with the wretched rush-lights of poverty and woe" (133). Pierre's choice of poverty, however, is less momentous than the prior development of his perception that the world is divided; that, as ways of lighting the houses of Saddle Meadows, chandeliers and rush-lights form neither continuum nor correspondence, but are opposed.

198

Opposition, in a world he had taken as all harmonious complementarity, is the crucial message Pierre receives from Isabel's illegitimacy. Her status as a natural and yet not legitimate Glendinning means that the law denies her natural identity; and the very possibility of such a contradiction between nature and society calls Pierre's entire philosophy into doubt. Fondly, he had thought that the absence of a sister was the only "hiatus" in his perfect life. Her advent has opened a chasm at his feet, into which he plunges, not to hell but to a place under his world, to walk among the concealed arguments that motivate its basic, axiomatic assumptions. But these arguments, and even their existence, are the world's forbidden knowledge. Returning with his news that the nature of Saddle Meadows society is political, Pierre will be banished from both mansion and meadows.

Like his ancestors in the original paradise, he is forewarned. The morning after Pierre learns of Isabel's existence, there is staged, at his own breakfast table, a small morality play that makes it absolutely clear Saddle Meadows will not tolerate the impugning of its axiomatic assumptions or any questioning of its integrity in either sense. The subject, thus also announcing the resonance of Isabel's story, is an adulterous affair. The fallen woman is Delly, daughter of the farmers for whom Isabel is a servant; they have hired Isabel, in fact, in the disarray of their terrible shame. Now the minister of Saddle Meadows has come to consult Mrs. Glendinning, "Lady" of the estate and his patron. Mrs. Glendinning is perfectly clear about what is to be done: she wants the sinners removed from "any ground of mine": "as I loathe the man, I loathe the woman, and never desire to behold the child." The Reverend Falsgrave (this is indeed a morality play) mildly invokes the beauties of Christian charity, but when Pierre's mother suggests that the minister's one shortcoming is "that the benevolence of his heart, too much warps in him the holy rigor of our Church's doctrines" (122), he owns the possibility and is silent. Pierre then presses him to say whether Christ himself has not given the example for forgiveness, and he protests that it is a widespread error to think that ministers "know more of the moral obligations of humanity than other people," and that at any rate,

It is not every question, however direct . . . which can be conscientiously answered with a yes or no. Millions of circumstances modify all moral questions; so that though conscience may possibly dictate freely in any known special case; yet, by one universal maxim, to embrace all moral contingencies,—this is not only impossible, but the attempt, to me, seems foolish. (123–124)

The Reverend Falsgrave is presented as the *beau ideal* of unprincipled opportunism. "Heaven had given him his fine, silver-keyed person for a flute to play on in this world; and he was nearly the perfect master of it" (119). Melville thus accuses his acrobatic adaptability and the saccharine mellifluity of his delivery of the desired pronouncements rather than any positive evil. Falsgrave later tells Pierre that Delly "is to depart the neighborhood," and Pierre demands, *"How* is she to depart? *Who* is to take her? Art *thou* to take her? *Where* is she to go? *Who* has food for her? *What* is to keep her from the pollution to which such as she are everyday driven to contribute, by the detestableness and heartlessness of the world?"(194). The minister's response—"I choose to have no answer" for these "incidental questions"—represents irresponsibility, denial, disengagement, a refusal to align himself and to act—but still not any active evil. In *Pierre*, what differentiates the successful bad from the defeated good is action: Falsgrave's immorality is more of an amorality, an accommodation to injustice rather than its actual perpetration. Indeed, Mrs. Glendinning's more aggressive stance itself amounts to a more aggressive denial, not punishment but exile, with no concern for the aftermath.

In an unequal world, the powerful refuse to help the helpless: Pierre's initial complaint about his society is of an ideological piece with his original enthusiasm; he seeks not a new social order but the fulfillment of the old. His final disillusionment will be the more complete. If Pierre is a radical critic of his society, his is a pure radicalism referring entirely within, a reflexive radicalism that can only end by tearing up its own roots. Indeed, the eccentricity of Pierre's scheme arises in large part from the reflexiveness of his goal. Without any hope of changing the social order as such, he wants it to include Isabel; he is not attempting to amend it, but to transpose her inside—to re-fuse nature and society as seamlessly as ever he had thought them one. So, answering himself the questions the Reverend Falsgrave had refused to answer, *he* takes responsibility for Delly Ulver, and thus begins the gathering of the pieces of his shattered world, to be welded once more, since the world is heartless, in the furnace of *his* heart. In short, having found his world deceitful, he sets out to keep its promises.

This is the crucial way in which *Pierre* may be seen as returning to the issues of *Moby-Dick*, but this time confronting them in full. For if both Ahab and Pierre portray the danger of an unlimited individualism, only the latter reflects directly on the individualist society as well. The destructiveness of Ahab's goal and the hate that inspire him, in themselves, not only justify his defeat but seem even to explain it. He represents only the perversion of self-reliance, which, however likely, is certainly not inevitable. Pierre, in contrast, an Ahab on his first voyage, is an ideal young man trying to fulfill his society's ideals. If his goal turns out to be selfish, this is the saddest irony of all, since he has instead meant wholly to abandon himself and is puzzled only about how to do so on behalf of both his sister and his mother.

Ahab fails in colossal loneliness, but Pierre's failure implicates the world. For how could he have succeeded? He might easily have survived; he knows exactly how: "Had I been heartless now, disowned, and spurningly portioned off the girl at Saddle Meadows, then had I been happy through a long life on earth, and perchance through a long eternity in heaven! Now, 'tis merely hell in both worlds" (418). But he couldn't be "heartless" because he is an ideal father's ideal son; and "heart," that is, an instinctive virtue in the Latin sense, meaning manhood and the world's compilation of its loftiest values, is the primary characteristic of ideal sons. At one fraught moment in the Reverend Falsgrave episode, Pierre asks his mother how a legitimate child should treat an illegitimate child, and she tells him "Ask the world, Pierre . . . and ask your own heart." His response, "My own heart? I will, Madam" (123), is perfectly sincere. In sum, having seen injustice, Pierre is bound to correct it, and by the identical principles that prohibit his tampering with the perfect order of Saddle Meadows. This amounts to the highest filiopiety enjoining the deepest impiety; even Antigone had more leeway.

Nonetheless, as an account of the feasibility of reform in America, this seems unreasonably fatalistic. After all, reforms have been accomplished. The remarkable consistency in the self-presentation of American dissenters, from both the right and the left, is based precisely, however, on their universal denial of Pierre's dilemma: they argue on the one hand that a self-reliant activism is the essence of the American way, and on the other that the changes they propose neither expose nor reject the past but in fact implement it. Typically, it is claimed that the measures advocated are already implicit in the founding idea and/or the Constitution, and that therefore (this from the left) the effect will be to complete the Revolution, or (from the right) to return to it. This fundamentalism adds a significant dimension to the more common pattern of associating change with old verities. In this case, the old ways not only are cited as the basis for a new historical construction, but are said already to contain the new. So that, unlike Pierre, who leaves his paternal estate, unhappy American sons historically have answered the challenge to "love it or leave it" with the transcendent claim that they *are* it.

This argument was just being forged, dramatically and explicitly, in Pierre's time, by the antislavery movement, whose ability to associate the regional crisis with its cause would be the key to success. From as early as the 1820s, slavery emerged as the most important issue that would test the new nation, even to threatening its survival. Finally, as Eric Sundquist has put it, the antislavery cause "supplanted Manifest Destiny in the 1850s [when *Pierre* was written] as the spiritual content of American citizenship" ("Slavery, Revolution, and the American Renaissance," 9). Confronting their flawed Revolution, its heirs at first evinced a baffled and immobilized reverence that was surely the model for Pierre's decision never to reveal his father's lapse. But only in the very early stages of their campaign were the opponents of slavery thus trapped between acquiescence and rebellion. For while Webster argued that slavery should be tolerated in order to preserve the Union, by 1833 Lydia Maria Child was already berating the South for both its slavery and its secessionism. The ambivalences and ambiguities of the antislavery movement, as, for example, they are encoded in *Uncle Tom's Cabin*, are in part simply racist. But another part of their inspiration may be illuminated by Pierre's inability to go against his father even to succor his sister; and certainly the progress toward abolition was hastened by the strengthening of its association with the Union. Without rehearsing this now well-known process, we need only note its culmination in a civil war to preserve the founding fathers' new nation, in emancipation presented not as an end in itself but as an instrument of the preservation of that nation, and in a president whose dominant persona was (and is) as savior of the Union. Now, as Lincoln was seen to be finishing the incomplete Revolution, why could not Pierre, in his own words, have made a more perfect justice the capstone of his father's fame-column?

The fact that the plot of the novel makes it exceedingly difficult to imagine how he might have done this is not an objection to the question but, in fact, the answer. For the perfect coherence of Saddle Meadows necessarily implies hierarchy, which is in turn based on legitimacy, as the wholeness of the estate depends on its entire passage to a single male heir. Its division with an illegitimate heiress can hardly represent the completion of the Glendinning world building—unless the division becomes moot through Isabel's abnegation. Following that line, Pierre's scheme can be read as a mad parody of reform by implementation. Marrying his sister in order to endow her with her just property and rights, without altering the structure of Saddle Meadows, amounts precisely to continuing the patriarchal order and fulfilling it faithfully down to its most grievous flaws. Incest is revealed to be not an unfortunate by-product of Pierre's loyalty to his father, but one of its cardinal points. In the judgment that it is out of the question to reveal Isabel's origins to the world and Mary Glendinning, Melville is at one with his hero; any more moderate plan is inconceivable not only because of Pierre's character but because of the author's plot. When Pierre concludes that there would be no point "in stubbornly flying in the marble face of the Past, and striving to reverse the decree which had pronounced that Isabel could never perfectly inherit all the privileges of a legitimate child of her father" (206), Melville does not disagree. To be sure, this marble-faced past reflects Pierre's own stoniness; but then one could say the reverse as well, for Pierre, let us recall once more, is the ideal representative of the past. And if in the present he creates *in his turn* an absolute realm, he *thus*, as he would not through reform, follows his father.

Reform—change that does not altogether cancel the past—needs time: it has to be accomplished in a future that is distinct from the past. In other words, the proponents of reform need to assume historical process. As the very embodiment of a timeless mythology, Pierre cannot imagine reform, but it emerges in Melville's novel as a fatally missing term. For, like Hawthorne, Melville was continually rediscovering the categories of history in the act of inventing his novelistic fictions; and finding that, on one level as his artifacts and on another as imaginary beings, his characters were defeated in the end by a foreclosing closure that worked much as did Hilda's final "Hush."

In Saddle Meadows, this closure is embodied in, or rather is, the arrest of time. Mary Glendinning's amazing youthfulness is one sign that, in Saddle Meadows, everything seems to have stopped with the beginning of the story. In fact, the first paragraph tells us just this:

> There are some strange summer mornings in the country, when he who is but a sojourner from the city shall early walk forth into the fields, and be wonder-smitten with the trance-like aspect of the green and golden world. Not a flower stirs; the trees forget to wave; the grass itself seems to have ceased to grow; and all Nature, as if suddenly conscious of her own profound mystery, and feeling no refuge from it but silence, sinks into this wonderful and indescribable repose.

An odd beginning that comes to an immediate rest, this description of a stilled and silenced landscape might have been constructed as an antithesis to "Once upon a time." For if that opening commands our focused attention on the particular story to follow, Melville's proffered generalities ("some strange summer mornings") lead nowhere in particular. The wandering "sojourner from the city" never reappears in the novel, and the opening scene, instead of fields and flowers, depicts Pierre walking down a village street toward Lucy's cottage. This is the subject of the second paragraph, but the third again returns to "the verdant trance" inhabited only by "brindled kine, dreamily wandering to their pastures, followed, not driven, by ruddy-cheeked, white-footed boys." Pierre's and the plot's first movement forward is thus bracketed by a timeless silence described in a conventionally poetic style that makes it still more resistant to the business at hand, the business of getting the story under way. The mental voice catches on the hyphens—"wonder-smitten," "trance-like," and, even in the second active paragraph, the Glendinnings' "high-gabled" mansion, the "elm-arched" street, Pierre's "half-unconscious" steps; and finally the "ruddy-cheeked, white-footed boys'" who bring it all to a standstill. We contemplate a repose called "indescribable"; and we find no reason to read on.

Book I is entitled "Pierre Just Emerging from His Teens." His first act of emergence is leaving the paternal house on his way to visit Lucy, but the world into which he emerges is absolutely still, so that going to Lucy represents staying home. The present in *Pierre* is an arrested and eternal moment; the marble-faced past is irreversible; moreover, it is because the past is irreversible that the present is arrested. Although Pierre himself does not draw the conclusion this implies, the novel does. For in contrast to the outlandish scheme of pretending to marry Isabel, it is the more striking that revealing her identity, thus exposing but also redeeming the past, seems out of the question. It is out of the question not because the sin she embodies is itself so unforgivable that it can never be admitted, but because a sin that might only qualify a historical identity would altogether destroy one that is transcendent. What is at stake is not after all the elder Pierre Glendinning's honor, but his ideality. The past might be reversed, but only if it were relativized into history, and then time, the dimension of the past, would continue extending into the present and become the stage of change. To put this more simply, if Pierre were able to expose the past injustice he could then redress it, and the fact that he cannot either expose or redress it, is not due to the nature of the injustice but to the nature of its context. What renders the "impossible adjuncts" impossible is their *identity* of opposition. And in fact, if he destroys the Glendinning family in trying to save it, he does preserve its transcendent image: betrayed, as the world sees it, by his unworthy son, the elder Pierre Glendinning will remain forever the "perfect father" his wife pronounced him. But a finite mortal Pierre Glendinning would have had a son who *could* preserve his honor (in part) and still (partly) redress his errors. Not that Melville actually articulates this historical option, but after the others have been exploded, this unarticulated one is almost tangible by its absence; it is there as what Pierre Macherey has termed the "not-said" (*Pour une théorie de la production littéraire*, 60–61).

Timelessness is thus the curse of Saddle Meadows, as in those fairytales of arrests of time that plunge castles and kingdoms into eternities of sleep, from which a redemptive hero on *one* day awakens them. But Pierre cannot be that hero for being himself accursed: he too is eternally asleep, in identity with his kingdom (so that all he can do is to realize the sleep in death). Indeed, this identity of prince and kingdom is another form of timelessness: in the arrested world of Saddle Meadows, in which past is also present and future, Emerson's complementary dualism has collapsed into ambiguity. In an ambiguity, a single term can have two apparently conflicting meanings. Unless one meaning is jettisoned, no resolution is possible, because there is only one term and therefore no ground for mediation. An ambiguity, in other words, is a problematical identity.

The book's title expounds on this: *Pierre; or The Ambiguities* at once names Pierre himself as the central ambiguity. He is himself, and also a corporate person (father, grandfather, and great-grandfather) with one name. The problem is that each meaning is wholly antagonistic to the other, and seeks to absorb the other whole. The best or most viable result is a standoff, as at the beginning of the story when the two meanings of Pierre, the emerging individual and the corporate heir, both float quiescently in their mutual unselfconsciousness. But any act (thus including the start of the story), coming from either aspect of his ambiguous self, evokes the ambiguity: is Pierre acting as Pierre or as "Pierre"? Being incapable of resolution, ambiguity is exacerbated by action, until it explodes, or rather implodes. In almost his last words, Pierre banishes both Lucy and Isabel: "Away! —Good Angel and Bad Angel both! [which is which is ambiguous]—For Pierre is neuter now" (418). Thus in a world that has already resolved its last dialectic into identity and transcended the historical time that is the dimension of dialectical transformation, action can only be destructive.

To survive and let others live, one must be still: this is the argument of the repellent Plotinus Plinlimmon, whom Pierre encounters in New York. (The neo-Platonist Plotinus was poorly regarded in the nineteenth century, which saw his difficult elliptical style as reflecting illogical or idiosyncratic reasoning.) In Plinlimmon's "blue, bright, but still quiescent eye . . . the gay immortal youth Apollo seemed enshrined; while on that ivory-throned brow, old Saturn cross-legged sat." Thus eternally youthful, Plinlimmon also encompasses old age: he has absorbed time, is himself both history *and* its transcendence, in himself both founding father and son, as Pierre will never be with *his* father. This then is the ultimate positive fulfillment of the relationship of ideal father and ideal son:

> The whole countenance of this man, the whole air and look of this man, expressed a cheerful content. Cheerful is the adjective, for it was the contrary of gloom; content—perhaps acquiescence—is the substantive, for it was not Happiness or Delight. But while the personal look and air of this man were thus winning, there was still something latently visible in him which repelled. That something may best be characterized as non-Benevolence. Non-Benevolence seems the best word, for it was neither Malice nor Ill-will; but something passive.

Plinlimmon is a philosopher, though he is never known

> to write with his hands (he would not even write a letter); he never was known to open a book. There were no books in his chamber. Nevertheless, some day or other he must have read books, but that time seemed gone now; as for the sleazy works that went under his name, they were nothing more than his verbal things, taken down at random, and bunglingly methodized by his young disciples. (338–339)

The meeting throws Pierre into great agitation, for Plinlimmon is the author of a pamphlet that Pierre found in the coach that carried him away from Saddle Meadows, and whose theme has been growing more resonant ever since. The doctrine of this essay is simple and to the point. It begins by noting that virtue is seldom rewarded, that the corrupt thrive, that the weak suffer at the hands of the powerful—that the world is not just. Justice, however, is perfectly imaginable, and its principles in fact are well established as the ethical teachings of religion. Should not a moral man, then, devote his life to bringing these teachings into practice? Not at all, for a deeper investigation of the state of the world reveals that justice and truth were never meant to exist on earth; they would be personally impractical and socially destructive:

> A virtuous expediency . . . seems the highest desirable or attainable earthly excellence for the mass of men, and is the only earthly excellence that their Creator intended for them. When they go to Heaven, it will be quite another thing. There, they can freely turn the left cheek, because there the right cheek will never be smitten. There they can freely give all to the poor, for *there* there will no poor to give to. (251)

When a man fails to understand the difference between the terrestrial and the heavenly ethic, he may tend to useless self-sacrifice, and then, in his disillusionment, to misanthropy and even atheism. But none of these is justified. A proper understanding will reveal that, precisely by their apparent contradictions, God's truth and man's truth are in fact "made to correspond": man's most earnest study, rather than to change the world in the direction of heaven, should be to see how "this world's seeming incompatibility with God, absolutely results from its meridianal correspondence with him" (250).

In a sense, Plinlimmon only goes a step beyond those who seek to improve things in the implicit way I described as interpretive implementation; he is wholly consistent and trusts the world's basically benevolent destiny to implement itself. He draws the conclusion that the reformers keep in abeyance long enough to permit their act of interpretation—and he declines to act at all. Pierre imagines Plinlimmon to be saying "Vain! vain! vain! . . . Fool! fool! fool! . . . Quit! quit! quit! . . ." and finally *"Ass! ass! ass!"* (341–342). Now, Pierre has certainly acted in vain, he has been a vain fool and an ass, but the advice to quit is in no way Melville's. In an ambiguous cast of characters, Plinlimmon is unambiguously evil—he has resolved the problem of ambiguity, effectively by declaring it not a problem but an advantage. What this requires, quite explicitly in Melville's exposition, is an endorsement of the deprivation of some: if ambiguity is an advantage, the advantage is to Plinlimmon. His doctrine was prefigured in that of the Reverend Falsgrave. The opportunistic moral orthodoxy of the church and the amorality of transcendentalism have arrived together at a criminally uncaring irresponsibility. By contrast, Pierre's terrible error is nonetheless noble.

Moreover, Plinlimmon's doctrine is not only evil but also, from Melville's perspective, finally self-destructive. Recall here my discussion in Chapter 5 of the dependence of fiction precisely on action. In fact the pamphlet Pierre finds is incomplete, torn off with the "most untidy termination" at the words "Moreover: if . . ." (252). And when later, his every effort stymied, Pierre remembers the pamphlet and wants to consult it for clues to his failure, he cannot find it. It later turns out that he had it all the time, in the hem of his coat, where it had fallen through a hole in his pocket. But in Pierre's first clutching it unconsciously in the coach and later misplacing it, Melville represents it as an alternative text, the text he excluded in writing his novel. He excluded it both formally and ideologically: formally by the decision to write the story of Pierre's fatal crusade, and ideologically by the assertion that inspires the novel and constitutes its initial act of faith—that if it is vain and foolish, it is finally also a better thing to engage the world, even on behalf of a mistaken vision of justice. The only problem is that the attempt is doomed.

Change is impossible, but the ambitious hero cannot accept the way things are: this is the formula for tragedy. In fact, after its reluctant opening, *Pierre* almost at once telegraphs a tragic end. The narration is punctuated by warnings, such as the muttering, when Pierre yearns for a sister, that "he did not then know, that if there be any thing a man might well pray against, that thing is the responsive gratification of some of the devoutest prayers of his youth" (12). These warnings only make explicit the sense of foreboding that pervades the book, from the continual "presentiments" of the characters as from the overwrought irony of the writing itself, which seems unusually defensive. "This history goes forward and goes backward, as occasion calls," the narrator notes sarcastically. "Nimble center, circumference elastic you must have" (67). And the fact that the hero of *Pierre* is himself a writer tends to blur the boundaries between his unhappily unfolding story and Melville's romance as such. In fact, Pierre's writing and Melville's writing about Pierre do evolve together, from initial exaggerated conventionality to final incommunicability.

Just as Melville starts out with a rosy tale of innocent young love, Pierre begins by writing such exquisite verses and sensitive essays as "The Tropical Summer: a Sonnet," "The Weather: a Thought," "Life: an Impromptu," "Beauty: an Acrostic," and "The Pippin: a Paragraph" (289). With these, he quickly rises to an eminence that warrants an offer from Wonder and Wen Publishers to bring out his "Complete Works" in an illustrated edition suitably bound for libraries. Heir-apparent to Saddle Meadows and intended of the incomparable Lucy, Pierre is at this time also the great hope of American letters. No wonder that when he decides to leave Saddle Meadows he is confident that he will be able to support himself by writing.

But at this point both he and his author abandon fashionable idylls. Now that Isabel has opened his eyes to the existence of sin and suffering, Pierre sets out to write a "great, deep book" that will not only earn him his living but also tell improving truths. Melville's account of the production of this book is one of the most painful ever written of the work of writing. Unable to afford fuel in a bitter cold winter, Pierre sits in his garret wrapped in blankets like a frozen corpse in his shroud, trying to force his congealed imagination to create fiery life. An absurd caricature of the author, with fingers too stiff to form words, he is at once a pathetic saint of true art and the self-blinded butt of Melville's despairing fury. Pierre's new publishers, Steel, Flint and Asbestos, having contracted for a popular novel, are outraged by his "blasphemous rhapsody, filched from the vile Atheists, Lucian and Voltaire" (413–414). When he sends them the manuscript, they write to inform him that they have instructed their lawyers to retrieve at once the advance he has swindled from them.

It has often been suggested that Pierre's "great, deep book" is *Moby-Dick*. But even that story of mad blasphemy, *as a story*, is not as desperate as either Pierre's book or *Pierre*. For when Ahab goes to his death, made mute at the last moment by the "lifeline" around his throat, the story is not silenced but continues through Ishmael. Moreover, Ishmael's interpretation of it, as a doomed assault that nature has repulsed with one swipe of the whale's tail and one overwhelming ocean wave, secures it permanently inside the realm of acceptable and therefore communicable meaning. In other words, the division of actor and narrator in *Moby-Dick* preserves the book from its all-destructive protagonist. But Pierre is inescapably the actor of his own tale—Pierre is *Pierre*.

The two works reveal a similar contrast at the level of language and literary mode, with the language of *Moby-Dick* permitting a meaningful closure while that of *Pierre* precludes it. Thus, the symbolism of *Moby-Dick* enables it to penetrate the surface of life in Jacksonian America, but it also provides an alternative ground, a separate imaginative realm apart from the world it interprets. It should be noted that Ishmael survives as myth-maker/interpreter, literally on the level of myth—*vide* the epilogue's suddenly calmed seas, its "hawks with sheathed beaks," its cruising "Rachel." Ishmael's explanation of Ahab and the pursuit of the white whale has its own linguistic viability. Not so the language of *Pierre*, which, being, in itself and its ideological implications, directly what the novel seeks to confute, disintegrates as the story progresses, finally leaving Melville with neither characters nor words, silenced at the same time and in the same way as Pierre, by having been fully confrontational without an alternative. The tragedy of *Pierre* is total, beyond any that was possible in *Moby-Dick*; it is a tragedy not only in but *of* the work.

Indeed, the tragedy is so complete it can be seen as tautological. From the start, on the eve of Pierre's departure from Saddle Meadows to embark on a new self-reliant life, Melville warns that his plight precludes even the temporary hope of ordinary tragedy. At this structurally hopeful moment, Pierre finds himself looking down at two books fallen open on his desk, *Hamlet* and the *Inferno*.

In the latter, the first thing he reads is the inscription over the gate of hell:

> Through me you pass into the city of Woe;
> Through me you pass into eternal pain;
> Through me, among the people lost for aye.
> . . . . .
> All hope abandon, ye who enter here. (199)

Melville interprets the *Divine Comedy* as a poem of doom:

> The man Dante Alighieri received unforgivable affronts and insults from the world; and the poet Dante Alighieri bequeathed his immortal curse to it, in the sublime malediction of the Inferno. The fiery tongue whose political forkings lost him the solacements of this world, found its malicious counterpart in that muse of fire, which would forever bar the vast bulk of mankind from all solacement in the worlds to come. (200)

Again, Melville is associating himself with Pierre's despair. This account of the *Inferno* is not the character's but the omniscient narrator's, as is also the report of Pierre's recognition of his fate in "the hopeless gloom of [Hamlet's] interior meaning"; together, these prophetic texts prove (still in the narrator's words) that "the intensest light of reason and revelation combined, can not shed such blazonings upon the deeper truths in man, as will sometimes proceed from his own profoundest gloom" (200–201).

Falling midway in the book and immediately before Pierre's fatal decision to leave Saddle Meadows in pretended elopement with Isabel (the next chapter is entitled "The Unprecedented Final Resolution of Pierre"), this meditation on Shakespeare and Dante appears weightily explanatory. A reader feels on firm ground in these strikingly parallel stories—until she realizes that actually neither is really parallel to that of Pierre (and that Pierre's situation is far worse). Even as an isolated text, the *Inferno* is more unlike Pierre's story than like it. For the Dante whom Virgil guides through that gate has reached the middle of the journey of his life and become discouraged about its prospects and the benefits of virtue. Moreover, he enters hell as a supplicant observer, not to challenge its eternally punishing order. Pierre is "just emerging from his teens" with every hope of a bright future, and about to sacrifice everything for one heroic good deed that will make final retribution for past sins.

The comparison to Hamlet's situation is only closer in that the two are more directly opposed. From Shakespeare's play, Pierre and the narrator cite what seem at first the obvious lines:

> The time is out of joint; —Oh cursed spite,
> That ever I was born to set it right! (198)

But neither the way the time is out of joint in Saddle Meadows, nor the way Pierre means to set it right, is that of *Hamlet*. Where Hamlet's father was the innocent victim of conjugal treachery and has appealed to his son to avenge him (thus also removing any doubt about the treachery itself), Pierre's father has sinned and, were he asked, would want his son to help conceal his sin. Pierre's task is not to vindicate honor, as Hamlet is called to do, but to hide dishonor.

If *Hamlet* and the *Inferno*, invoked as exemplary myths to illuminate Pierre's crossing of his Rubicon, are not illuminating, the more elaborate mythology through which Melville wants to explain the catastrophic conclusion of the journey is also at first sight appropriate and on reflection not. Almost at the end of the book, when Pierre has become entirely discouraged even about writing, so that his eyes will not look down on the page but "[roll] away from him in their own orbits," he falls one day into a trance and has a "remarkable dream vision." He sees himself in a familiar mountainous landscape not far from his ancestral home, trying to climb its highest peak and failing. In this vision Pierre acquires his third mythical avatar, after Hamlet and Dante. For the retreat from the impassable mountain takes him past another landmark of his youth, a boulder strangely resembling the figure of a man, and more specifically a statue of which the original is at Versailles, the statue of Enceladus the Giant, as the sculptor Marsy imagined him vainly assaulting Olympus. The climax of the trance comes with Pierre's recognition that "on the Titan's armless trunk, his own duplicate face and features magnifiedly gleamed upon him with prophetic discomfiture and woe" (402).

213

This is how Pierre, and also the narrator, explains the association: Enceladus's Titanic father, the son of Heaven and of Earth, married his mother, thus making Enceladus "both the son and grandson of an incest." This inheritance, which banned Enceladus from heaven as the perversion of its original design, also inspired him to seek his birthright:

> For it is according to eternal fitness, that the precipitated Titan should still seek to regain his paternal birthright even by fierce escalade. Wherefore whoso storms the sky gives best proof he came from thither! But whatso crawls contended in the moat before that crystal fort, shows it was born within that slime, and there forever will abide. (402–403)

Thus, recognizing himself in Enceladus, Pierre sees to the bottom of his plight and wakes, the narrator tells us, "from that ideal horror to all his actual grief" (402). But the "ideal horror" does not really match the "actual grief."

In most accounts, the Greek myth differs somewhat from Melville's version, identifying Enceladus not as a Titan but as a Giant sprung from the blood of the castration of Uranus (Heaven) by his Titan son, Cronus, who then reigned until he was overthrown himself by his son Zeus. The rebellion of the Giants occurred later, against the victorious Zeus and his Olympian Gods, and it was then that the forces of Earth were definitively conquered by the gods of Heaven and imprisoned under volcanoes that their raging materiality would fuel forever.

These two wars—the war of the Olympians against the Titans and the subsequent rebellion of the Giants—have often been associated and confused as they are by Melville. By a Titanic Enceladus, Melville means to represent an inevitably defeated, and therefore tragic, mortal ambition. But as a representation of Pierre this is problematical. For while the myth of the birth of Enceladus, paradoxically from the unmanning of his father, might resonate in Pierre's life, there is a larger dissonance between them in the fact that Enceladus is twice excluded from a succession, first Titanic, then Olympian, and is never the heir. The crucial omission in this last representation of Pierre, as a repulsed assaulter of the sky, is his prior voluntary departure from Olympian Saddle Meadows. Instead of Enceladus, that hapless brute enraged by the denial of a higher station he could never rightly inhabit, it is rather a fallen Apollo that Pierre evokes—or, to turn to a nearer mythology, a fallen Angel, such as the one who fell from the right hand of the Father.

Indeed, as if still searching for an adequate mythology, Melville last of all invokes Satan. In terms reminiscent of Ahab's last speech, Pierre, finding his hopes of global redemption travestied by the hell in which he is living his last moments and the eternal hell he expects shortly to enter, hurls out a last challenge: if it be hell here and forever, "Well, be it hell. I will mold a trumpet of the flames, and, with my breath of flame, breathe back my defiance" (418). Only moments before, taking up two pistols with which to kill his perfidious cousin, who has inherited Saddle Meadows and now denies him, and Lucy's brother, who should have been his brother too but has instead joined in his persecution— thus preparing to bring down the remnants of the rightful, once righteous order—Pierre mutters to himself, "Ha! what wondrous tools Prometheus used, who knows? but more wondrous these, that in an instant, can unmake the top most three-score-years-and-ten of all Prometheus' makings" (416). Transforming the fire of redemption into flames of eternal death, Pierre moves toward a death which seems to bring his story at last to a final and familiar signification.

But has it? Again, as with the earlier associations, that with Ahab or Satan is less clear on a second look. Crucially unlike either Ahab or Satan, Pierre has intended his rebellion to serve others. He has reason to call himself "the fool of Truth, the fool of Virtue, the fool of Fate" (415). The two men he kills have in fact injured him. Melville commits himself to that as he does not to Moby-Dick's purported prior assault on Ahab; when Pierre cries out that he will "send 'em back their lie, and plant it scorching in their brains!" (416), he has cause.

This time, then, the difference between mythical model and character is that the character is *less* guilty. Earlier Pierre was more guilty than Hamlet—Hamlet only did his father's bidding, while Pierre essentially defies his. He is also a greater sinner than Dante, and the New York Inferno is at least in part Pierre's own construction. Nor did he have the implicit justification of outcast Enceladus, the "armless giant who, despairing of any other mode of wreaking his immitigable hate, turned his vast trunk into a battering-ram, and hurled his own arched-out ribs again and yet again against the invulnerable steep" (402). All Pierre's defeated rage is manifest in the "impotent Titan" but none of Pierre's power, which is considerable enough to have brought his entire world down in ruins. But though more blamable than Hamlet, Dante, and Enceladus, Pierre is still no Satan. Pierre meant to redeem the world he destroys: rather than Satan, he might better be seen as a failed Christ. In short, missing from all the exempla by which Pierre seeks to explain and understand himself is the crux of his identity: the godlike sufficiency and benevolence of America's Pierre Glendinnings. Entirely potent and responsible, wholly well-meaning and as totally destructive, a Pierre Glendinning is not a tragic hero in either the classical or the Christian sense. The Glendinning flaw is his perfection.

If Pierre is thus *sui generis*, why does Melville invoke all those precedents for him? In part, they seem to measure Pierre's self-delusion. But beyond the character's crisis of identity, I would suggest, they represent an authorial crisis in character identification. The inadequacy of Pierre's mythological associations reveals a deep formal and linguistic inadequacy: the story Melville was telling in *Pierre* had no formal precedent.

Novels depict characters in historical settings that they neither initiate nor bring to a permanent end, but on which they always have an effect. This effect, which is also always reciprocal, is the story, whose outcome, sad or happy, is a stage in the unending construction of the future, and can thus be imagined being reversed later. In universal settings, since these are by definition immutable or at any rate beyond human agency, the story is not about process but about discrete events, and its ending is *either* comic or tragic: the protagonist either adjusts to the universe or dies. The American "romance" is a novel in a universal setting. In my discussion of *The Marble Faun* I focused on the contradiction in this and read the ending as what might be called Hawthorne's decision to live. Kenyon and Hilda return home and marry. This return recasts the transforming trespasses of Donatello and Miriam into a continued cautionary allegory. *The Marble Faun* is finally comic. In contrast, the very cast of characters in *Pierre* tends to preclude a comic ending, if only because it would mean not only Pierre's but Melville's abject surrrender. Kenyon has a surrogate in Donatello, as Ishmael has in Ahab. But in *Pierre*, by what one senses as an act of desperate integrity, Melville allows himself no out: he has only one hero choosing between light and darkness, the good angel and the bad, total compliance and total violation. At one point, Pierre is overwhelmed by doubts and berates himself as a "poor and feeble one," a "blind grub" incapable of high deeds. On one level, this discouragement only implies his delusions of grandeur; more deeply, it also reflects the dangerously unmediated dichotomy of Melville's plot. One cannot imagine Pierre returning to Saddle Meadows; what it would entail, to "Beg humble pardon of thy mother, and hereafter be a more obedient and good boy to her" (203), is no more a possibility than it would be for Hamlet to embrace his uncle and be a good boy to him.

But the compounding of tragedy in *Pierre* multiplies the difficulty Hawthorne encountered in *The Marble Faun*, of reconciling characters empowered to create themselves and the world with a world that was already made. Since the tragic hero maintains his cosmic challenge to the end, an omnipotent hero confronting an absolute world means the end of both. In fact, Pierre does destroy everything. His tragedy, moreover, produces no catharsis, has no purgative effect, implies no later resumption of even a diminished order. It is literally, as Isabel says, *all* over in the end, and we know him not: that is, not even his story is left, the tragedy itself has been destroyed. Not just a hero but the all-representative American man in a universal Gaza, he has pulled down the pillars of the universe.

This story, not that of one man's war with the universe but that of the universal man's assumption of his cosmos, cannot be told, or at any rate cannot be concluded: triumphant, this man is unimaginably transcendent and contains multitudes, including the multitudes of words whose separate meanings he dissolves in his oneness; his defeat, on the other hand, means mutual extinction of man *and* multitudes, like the crew of the Pequod and like Pierre's entire family along with Pierre. Triumph is not at issue here, since, implying apotheosis, it would be the stuff of fantasy, and would evade the limits of realistic fiction. Melville's theme is defeat, and mortality, or, in his words, "the perils and the miseries thou callest down on thee [son of man], when, even in a virtuous cause, thou steppest aside from those arbitrary lines of conduct, by which the common world, however base and dastardly, surrounds thee for thy worldly good" (209).

This may be fiction's most common subject, but it contains a special problem for Melville (and for American writers generally) in the special character of these otherwise traditional opponents. For Melville's crusading "son of man" (the allusion underlines the reference of Pierre's name to Peter, the rock upon which the church rests, as well as to the Rock of Ages and to Moses' rock) is a godly figure meaning to build a world absolutely true to his nature. But because the world he has inherited is already ideal, the confrontation of ideal world and ideal hero is apocalyptic, a final apocalypse of which even the record disappears. There were no models for such an event—hence the inadequacy of those Melville cites—and in particular there were no models for the fully self-empowered individual, the transcendent ultimate Romantic, who is at once Melville's inspiration and his terror.

To put it another way, Pierre has created his "impossible adjuncts" by taking on *both* the positions reserved in classical tragedy as the separate functions of society-world and self-hero. It is as if Hamlet sought to preserve his mother's good name while avenging his father, or Oedipus tried to be a good son to Jocasta. These conservative functions are elsewhere, as in *Hamlet* and *Oedipus Rex*, those of the established authority. But Pierre, conflating American and America, assumes them along with those of the rebellious individual. The ensuing tragedy is thus internal to both the world and the hero, and therefore destructive of both. Its form, *Romantic* tragedy (the ideal, culminating literary form of the culminated ideology of liberal individualism), is a logical concept without a conceivable literary realization, a limit toward which an author writes, but which he reaches in silence. It is the ultimate silence. Pierre's existentially absurd story is the Romantic assertion of the power to create authentically through language, turned suicidally on itself.

The vision in which Pierre sees himself as Enceladus represents the tragic limits of the American romance graphically, and familiarly, through a landscape that at first seems welcoming but then reveals itself to be impassable. I began to survey this landscape earlier as the site of Pierre's discovery of Enceladus, which in fact culminates and articulates his route. At the beginning of the dream, Pierre sees himself standing on the piazza of his mansion, looking toward "the Mount of the Titans, a singular height standing quite detached in a wide solitude not far from the grand range of dark blue hills encircling his ancestral manor." Originally, this mountain had been named the Delectable Mountain, after the peak in *Pilgrim's Progress* from which the Promised Land can at last be seen; then, "a high-aspiring, but most moody, disappointed bard" had renamed it in the image of his less successful journey. At first, however, it seems rather to merit a more hopeful title, as from the house it presents "A long and beautiful, but not entirely inaccessible-looking purple precipice, some two thousand feet in air, and on each hand sideways sloping down to lofty terraces of pastures." The prospect remains optimistic even on a nearer approach: "the precipice did not belie its purple promise from the manorial piazza—that sweet imposing purple promise, which seemed fully to vindicate the Bunyanish old title originally bestowed." But then,

> coming still more nigh, long and frequent rents among the mass of leaves revealed horrible glimpses of dark-dripping rocks, and mysterious mouths of wolfish caves. Struck by this most unanticipated view, the tourist now quickened his impulsive steps to verify the change by coming into direct contact with so chameleon a height. As he would now speed on, the lower ground, which from the manor-house piazza seemed all a grassy level, suddenly merged into a very long and weary acclivity, slowly rising up to the precipice's base.

Unable to believe how different the terrain is from what he had been led to expect, the "tourist" still hopes to conquer the mountain.

> Quitting those recumbent rocks, you still ascended toward the hanging forest, and piercing within its lowermost fringe, then suddenly you stood transfixed, as a marching soldier

confounded at the sight of an impregnable redoubt, where he had fancied it a practicable vault to his courageous thews. Cunningly masked hitherto, by the green tapestry of the interlacing leaves, a terrific towering palisade of dark mossy massiness confronted you; and, trickling with unevaporable moisture, distilled upon you from its beetling brow slow thunder-showers of water-drops, chill as the last dews of death. Now you stood and shivered in that twilight, though it were high noon and burning August down the meads. All round and round, the grim scarred rocks rallied and re-rallied themselves; shot up, protruded, stretched, swelled, and eagerly reached forth, on every side bristlingly radiating with a hideous repellingness. Tossed, and piled, and indiscriminate among these, like bridging rifts of logs up-jammed in alluvial-rushing streams of far Arkansas: or, like great masts and yards of overwhelmed fleets hurled high and dashed amain, all splintering together, on hovering ridges of the Atlantic sea,—you saw the melancholy trophies which the North Wind, championing the unquenchable quarrel of the Winter, had wrested from the forests, and dismembered them on their own chosen battle-ground, in barbarous disdain. 'Mid this spectacle of wide and wanton spoil, insular noises of falling rocks would boomingly explode upon the silence and fright all the echoes, which ran shrieking in and out among the caves, as wailing women and children in some assaulted town.

Stark desolation; ruin, merciless and ceaseless; chills and gloom,—all here lived a hidden life, curtained by that cunning purpleness, which, from the piazza of the manor-house, so beautifully invested the mountain once called Delectable, but now styled Titanic.   (397–399)

This complete barring of the way comes as a horrible surprise. The language of the passage reflects shock and even panic as the path comes to an end suggestive of death and damnation. As the sojourner stands bewildered and unable to proceed, the very geography of the scene expresses an appalling disorientation. The rocks toss about "round and round" in every direction and none; they "reach forth" with "hideous repellingness," entrapping as they exclude. The elements war without issue, hurl themselves at each other without purpose but "wide and wanton spoil." The ocean, for Whitman an image of America's peacefully infinite latitude, here represents the ultimate fragility of all order, as the chaos commonly evoked by storms at sea is worsened by the added confusion of earth with the air and water. But this chaos is particularly terrifying because of the malevolence that is its only structuring principle. Nature in Pierre's nightmare is cunning, deceptive, evil, the mountain pitted with "wolfish caves," an underworld paradoxically secured on an unscalable peak. The Mount of the Titans does not merely rebuff all hopes and efforts; it mocks them in a derisive reversal of our most fundamental expectations.

Its very fertility is a cruel parody. The beautiful fields at the mountain's base are "thickly sown with a small white amaranthine flower, which, being irreconcilably distasteful to the cattle, and wholly rejected by them, and yet, continually multiplying on every hand, did by no means contribute to the agricultural value of those elevated lands." The disheartened farmers are helpless before the overwhelming vitality that blights their lives.

> The small white flower, it is our bane! The aspiring amaranth, every year it climbs and adds new terraces to its sway! The immortal amaranth, it will not die, but last year's flowers survive to this! The terraced pastures grow glittering white, and in warm June still show like banks of snow:—fit token of the sterileness the amaranth begets! (397–398)

Nature's capacity for eternal rebirth has here become an everlasting doom, and where men cannot climb, the amaranth still ascends to add its hostile strength to the mountain's impregnability. The landscape's horizontal axis, which made all the world seem attainable from the manor's veranda, has become insurmountably vertical.

This pivoting of the axis of the landscape describes Pierre's own withdrawal into a vertically self-contained selfhood, and it is thus while recoiling from the mountain that he comes upon the Enceladus boulder. Both as natural outcropping and as sub-Olympian incarnation of the material earth, the "American Enceladus" returns Pierre, heretofore a more spiritual, metaphorical sort of "rock," to his identity with the land. In this identification, it seems he has simply failed to ascend—to transcend. But again, we need to look twice. For Pierre's identification with the earth-boundedness of Enceladus is as ambiguous—that is, as ironic and self-contradictory—as all his identifications: it does represent the limits he has failed to go beyond, but inextricably also his still global extent. If he has not ascended, he has descended like Dante into hell, to the deepest bottom from which all directions are up. In his dungeon-grave, the turnkey says, he "might hear a rabbit burrow on the world's t'other side" (420): this is a mockery of transcendence, but also its catastrophic negative fulfillment. Ironically, Pierre's absolute negation may claim still greater power than Emerson's ultimate harmony. "Utter darkness" can illuminate better than light, Melville suggests; in the dark a benighted man "cat-like . . . distinctly sees all objects through a medium which is mere blindness to common vision." "Wherefore have Gloom and Grief been celebrated of old as the selectest chamberlains to knowledge? Wherefore is it, that not to know Gloom and Grief is not to know aught that an heroic man should learn?" (201). The universal self dissolves in identity with the universe; but it becomes supremely and uniquely itself as *the* rebel-destroyer. In the end, Pierre's defeat is also a perverse triumph, as always in tragedy, but as much greater than the triumph of the classic hero as Pierre's tragedy is greater. In its cataclysmic global reach, his tragedy might be called transcendent, although this amounts to a contradiction in terms. But by the end of his story, Pierre himself, in the terms of his ambiguity, has become altogether, unviably contradictory. Pronouncing on his death—"All's o'er, and ye know him not!" (420)—Isabel reverses Emerson's supreme declaration. "I am nothing; I see all" (*Nature*, 10). Pierre has tried to be everything and has finally realized that he saw nothing. With his all-consuming death, we are blinded as well.

The pivoting of the axis of Pierre's landscape is an explicit event occurring over the course of the story. When he leaves the agrarian abundance of his wide natal meadows, Pierre passes through "an almost unplowed and uninhabited region," to arrive finally in the "lower old-fashioned part of [New York City], in a narrow street . . . filled . . . with immense lofty warehouses of foreign importers" (309). There, near the decrepit tower of the Church of the

Apostles, he finds his new place in a "new building [which] very much exceeded the body of the church in height. It was some seven stories; a fearful pile of Titanic bricks, lifting its tiled roof almost to a level with the top of the sacred tower" (310). From this building, the window of his narrow room looks out on "desolate hanging wildernesses of tiles, slate, shingles and tin" (316). He sinks deeper and deeper into penury and isolation, until the end of his backward and inward journey comes one sundown in "the pent twilight of the contracted yard," where he stands "solitary in a low dungeon of the city prison. The cumbersome stone ceiling almost rested on his brow; so that the long tiers of massive cell-galleries above seemed partly piled on him" (418). The now vertical landscape has reared up, the way Ahab described the "wall" of universal necessity "shoved" near to him. When Pierre strikes through, *everything* crashes down, and he is not drowned, with connotations of communion, but annihilatingly buried, himself turned to stone, under the stony rubble.

In retrospect, the horizontal availability of the landscape was always qualified. Even when Pierre rode over his lands so harmoniously that "his very horizon was to him as a memorial ring" (13), this ring, which proved the wide expanse of Saddle Meadows, also enclosed it. Jefferson's horizon lay at an infinite linear distance; and the Blue Ridge peak, part of an extended range that pointed toward the horizon, was a readily accessible high point from which to look farther out. Pierre's mountains stretch reflexively around the plains of Saddle Meadows, so that when he and Lucy, early in the story, go riding, their outward transit ends in the hills, from which the prospect is not so unidirectional as Jefferson's. The beauty of the view comes indeed from its duality: "corn-crested uplands, and herd's grass lowlands,"

> and long-stretching swales of vividest green, betokening where the greenest bounty of this earth seeks its winding channels; as ever, the most heavenly bounteousness most seeks the lowly places; making green and glad many a humble mortal's breast, and leaving to his own lonely aridness, many a hill-top prince's state. (45)

Although Lucy and Pierre are looking outward, the landscape they survey is already organized vertically, by contrasting elevations.

Lucy's plea the next moment would make no sense in the context of Jefferson's entire exaltation: "Up, my Pierre; let us go up, and fly these hills, whence, I fear, too wide a prospect meets us. Fly we to the plain. See, thy steeds neigh for thee—they call thee—see, the clouds fly down toward the plain—lo, these hills now seem all desolate to me, and the vale all verdure." And, speeding "fast for the plain . . . they find peace, and love, and joy again" (48).

Its upending is thus not altogether a transformation of this landscape. "The grand range of dark blue hills encircling [Pierre's] ancestral manor" (397) never offered the visionary freedom of Jefferson's "catch of smooth blue horizon." The "memorial ring" that was earth's "love-token" to Pierre has closed in and strangled him.

Having finished recounting this fatality, Melville then dedicated *Pierre* "To Greylock's Most Excellent Majesty."

> In old times authors were proud of the privilege of dedicating their works to Majesty. A right noble custom, which we of Berkshire must revive. For whether we will or no, Majesty is all around us here in Berkshire, sitting as in a grand Congress of Vienna of majestical hill-tops, and eternally challenging our homage.
>
> But since the majestic mountain, Greylock—my own more immediate sovereign lord and king—hath now, for innumerable ages, been the one grand dedicatee of the earliest rays of all the Berkshire mornings, I know not how his Imperial Purple Majesty (royal-born: Porphyrogenitus) will receive the dedication of my own poor solitary ray.
>
> Nevertheless, forasmuch as I, dwelling with my loyal neighbors, the Maples and the Beeches, in the amphitheater over which his central majesty presides, have received his most bounteous and unstinted fertilizations, it is but meet, that I here devoutly kneel, and render up my gratitude, whether, thereto, The Most Excellent Purple Majesty of Greylock benignantly incline his hoary crown or no.

This real-life model for the encircled landscape of Saddle Meadows wholly reverses Jefferson's Blue Ridge passage. Melville stands, then kneels in the well of an amphitheater at the foot of the mountain, looking up to a colossus that entirely blocks his line of sight. He sees no horizon, for there is none; the mountain, as the receptor of the earliest rays of all the Berkshire mornings, interposes an antihorizon. The writer's personal vision, described as "my own poor solitary ray," contrasts unhappily with Jefferson's visionary eye, which was expandingly projected as an impersonal "your" eye, until finally it became "the" eye and, in its universal persona, composed itself on a universal horizon.

Moreover, the natural civilization of the Berkshires has here become political. Mt. Greylock is not generically dubbed regal, but cast specifically as a participant in the reactionary Congress of Vienna that sought to return emerging modern Europe to protofeudalism. Nature no longer seems to decree liberal democracy. All this is bitter wit: spurned by his human audience, Melville is seeking a gentler patron in the granite peak. But to represent the ruin of his ambition, he mocks the country's—which in the American way he had identified as his own—in a metaphor that essentially turns the ideology of the incarnation on itself. The natural continent's client-artist, he is grateful to be inspired as the maples and the beeches are fertilized. Melville hopes only that his work will please his geographical lord and fulfill the *lord's* ideal. For Melville, it all seems to have ended with Columbus.

The despair implied in the apostrophe to Mt. Greylock is rather extravagant, as absolute as Pierre's, which was, in turn, the mirror image of Pierre's initial optimism and of his vision of a special Saddle Meadows destiny. Similarly, Hawthorne seems excessively alarmed in *The Marble Faun* by Kenyon's vivid Cleopatra and overly stringent in countering it with Hilda's copies. At the other extreme, the vision of human possibility in Emerson's *Nature* is no more likely. But rather than the likely, I have been concerned in this book with the limits of the imaginable. To be sure, most Americans, and undoubtedly Melville, Hawthorne, and Emerson themselves, actually lived and wrote not on the horizon but in that middle landscape where, as Emerson once put it, "we dress our garden, eat our dinners, discuss the household with our wives" ("Experience," 492). Although he went on to say that "these things make no impression, are forgotten next week," remembering them now, upon emerging from the overwrought world of *Pierre*, provides a welcome respite.

Once we have descended, however, from the hyperbolic heights upon which much of this discussion has balanced, and are standing with Emerson in the back garden rather than out in nature, something becomes visible that was invisible from above: the terrain is much more varied than it is projected by most of the texts and authors treated here, and America is not the monochrome, unisex, and one-class society implied by the term "American." Of course, Emerson readily admits "that the world I converse with in the city and in the farms, is not the world I *think.*" But cautioning us to be "very suspicious" of the apparent reality of daily commerce, he asserts that the world of his thought is in fact more real. Thus he recommends leaving behind gardens, dinners, households, and wives, and returning to "solitude" where a man has "a sanity and revelations, which in his passage into new worlds he will carry with him" (491).

But recently gardeners, cooks, housekeepers, and wives have been pointing out that Emerson did not pass alone into new worlds, nor alone build his own world. On an immediate level, such protests are leading to a fairer accounting of the world's work. But recognizing that Emerson had help also has a reflexive implication that enters into the basic conception of this essay. For once his idealism is seen to involve arrangements with the material, not idealism's external relations but its inner structure appears altogether different. When we recognize monologue as dialogue— with gardeners and wives—in that dialogue the authoritative voice itself emerges dual. It affirms but also denies, promises and refuses, projects and limits. Querying the ideological implications for action in the ideal concepts of America and American evokes such dualisms. Given the monism of the American incarnation, the emergence of dualism at once brings both concepts down to earth, and unearths them.

✳ *After the Culmination*

*A*ny account of the thinking of the past also interprets the present. The question that has been implicit throughout this book is how the founding belief in an American incarnation influences current thinking. The crucial characters in that myth were the individual and the land, both of which have by now been radically transformed. It is now commonplace to analyze the tale of America's discovery as propaganda. What has happened to the ideas and ideals, the ideology embodied in the tale?

This is a particularly difficult question because American ideology is a declared advocate of change. It counts progress among its cardinal principles and describes itself as, paradoxically, traditionally revolutionary. Moreover, this paradox itself has been extraordinarily productive of *both* progress and stability. Pierre, whose catastrophic failure I traced in Chapter 6, is after all an extremist. A character I did not discuss, Holgrave in Hawthorne's *The House of the Seven Gables,* also cited the Revolution to argue that a partial transfer of power to a new generation actually fulfilled the old design. Over the course of American history, reformers like Holgrave have drawn much of their strength from the common agreement that restorative reform is as deep in the American grain as radicalism is against it. Well into this century, trust-busters and union-builders alike invoked democratic ideals the more effectively because these ideas could be said to constitute not just the right way but the American way. And left-wing critics like Vernon Parrington and Granville Hicks, or later F. O. Matthiessen, were convinced that the American literature they championed bespoke democratic values consonant with the reforms they sought.[1] Besides calling themselves Progressives, Populists, grass-roots radicals, Marxist-Socialists, or Christian-Socialists, they would also have said they were Jeffersonians. Parrington, Hicks, and Matthiessen stressed different parts of the tradition but affirmed a common certainty that their hopes for the future of America required no radical departure from America's first principles.

Matthiessen's version of this argument was probably the most influential.[2] In *American Renaissance* he claimed to be primarily concerned with the writings of Emerson, Thoreau, Hawthorne, and Melville "as works of art, with evaluating their fusions of form and content" (vii). But (surely inspired by the intellectual currents circulating during the period of the New Deal) he said he could readily imagine writing other "notable" books on the same subject, and among these, one that "could concentrate on how discerning an interpretation our great authors gave of the economic and social forces of the time" when, in the ideals of transcendentalism, they voiced "fresh aspirations for the rise of the common man" (viii). He would have entitled this alter-book "The Age of Fourier," indicating its focus on contemporary radical movements, some of which "anticipated Marxism." For this book, he speculated, he would probably have used the same approach as Hicks, or he might have modeled himself on Newton Arvin's "detailed examination of Whitman's emergent socialism" (viii). Still, he went on, although *American Renaissance* was literary rather than political, even its aesthetic analysis revealed an inherent political ideal: "The one common denominator of my five writers, uniting even Hawthorne and Whitman, was their devotion to the possibilities of democracy" (ix). While valuing the literature for itself, Matthiessen, like Parrington and Hicks, read the writings of a previous century as the ideological blueprints of his own; and like his colleagues he had a stake in the coincidence. In 1933 Hicks had invoked a "great [cultural] tradition" to testify for social and economic reforms, and in 1941 Matthiessen's vision of a democratic renaissance was equally responsive to the contemporary need. The spirit of American democracy would be reborn to inspire armed resistance against tyranny, as almost two centuries before it had arisen in a war of liberation that declared America's permanent revolutionary ethos.

But after World War II came the Korean War, then the Cold War in the fifties, followed in the sixties by the war in Vietnam. From the perspective of these less inspiring battlefronts, retrospective complications began to emerge in the founding war. Historians rediscovered America not as the vacant continent even Perry Miller described, but as the site of a prior civilization the destruction of which was an important part of the creation of the new country. Edmund Morgan argued that slavery was no aberration in America but a condition for the establishment of white democracy.[3] Others investigated the tension between leadership and its constituency of artisans and yeomen.[4] Thus cross-examined, the founding vision has lost some of its mystique and, more important, much of its sufficiency.

This loss of sufficiency is the more important development for me because I am concerned less with changing interpretations of historical content than with subterranean transformations of categories. Earlier radical accounts often disputed the content of Revolutionary history, but seemed nonetheless to accept the notion of an ideal transcendent Revolution that had established a nation whose flaws would result from failures to fulfill the Revolutionary ideals.

Along with the idea of the Revolution, that of the Individual has also been largely unquestioned. The assumption has been remarkably enduring that each man is an independent entity, that total self-definition is his right, and that therefore he defines himself in a dichotomy with society, so that freedom is freedom from it and from others. This transcendent individual is the unchallengeable hero of Matthiessen's *American Renaissance*. But by a nice coincidence, in the same year that book was published another writer, Isaac Asimov, imagined how transcendence might *dis*empower. And he also got the idea from a Renaissance text.

"Nightfall," the short story that brought Asimov his first and most lasting success, was suggested by this sentence from the opening of *Nature:* "If the stars should appear one night in a thousand years, how would men believe and adore; and preserve for many generations the remembrance of the city of God?" John W. Campbell, the editor of the magazine *Astounding Science Fiction,* discovered Emerson's interest in the stars and passed the reference on to Asimov. The next morning Asimov began writing "Nightfall." Here is a brief summary of the story:

The planet Lagash is lighted by six suns, at least one of which is always visible, so that it is never night. A cyclical catastrophe shadows this sunny state of affairs: every 2050 years the inhabitants of Lagash inexplicably destroy their entire civilization in one night of fire and rampage. As the story opens, in the last year of the cycle, a group of astronomers think they have discovered why. From occult tales of a great Darkness made even more terrifying by the concurrent appearance in the black sky of millions of cold fires called Stars, they have deduced, what all experience would deny, that the heavens can be entirely devoid of suns.

The Book of Revelation explains that the Stars harvest the planet's matured souls and abandon their brute bodies to burn and pillage their world back to the stone age. Having discovered that the Darkness is only the natural result of an eclipse, the scientists hope this time to mitigate its catastrophic results. In a hideout equipped with torches, they have secreted a small group of enlightened citizens and a library. When the suns return, these survivors will emerge with their heritage of learning to rebuild civilization at the level it had already attained. Nonetheless, they await the eclipse fearfully, because they still have not penetrated the mystery of the Stars, which, according to Revelation, are the most terrifying aspect of the whole cataclysm.

The last sun sets and the deepening gloom triggers a strangling claustrophobia in even the most rational scientists. Busying themselves, however, with photographs and measurements, so that a scientific record may free future civilizations from the destructive terrors of an unmediated vision of nature, they hold on to reason—until, at total darkness, the Stars appear. The planet is located in the middle of a star cluster, and its skies are far more brilliant than Earth's. The Darkness is unimaginably bright. Blazing, unfathomable light inundates the planet and its inhabitants, who, perceiving themselves in all that immensity as infinitesimal shadows, struggle madly to retain some selfhood by producing their own light in the fires that destroy their civilization. The last sentence of the story is "The long night had come again."

This is obviously not what Emerson had in mind. For him, the transcendent beauty of the stars did not dwarf man but invited him to ascend. "One might think," he wrote in the same paragraph from which Asimov culled his motif, "the atmosphere was made transparent with this design, to give man, in the heavenly bodies, the perpetual presence of the sublime." Unlike Asimov's stars sucking soul from body, Emerson's would expand the soul, until all sense of the limits of one's mortal shell dissolved in spirit. Projected visually beyond his body, man contemplated a divine principle that was actually the image of his own transcendent divinity.

Asimov's Lagashians, with names such as Aton 77 and Theremon 762 identifying them not as avatars of the whole man but as parts of groups, fall back from the vision of the greater universe beyond, into selves that are fatally diminished by the contrast. Alone, they are claustrophobic, and experience the unknown not as an infinitely permeable medium for personal expansion, but as walls moving in to crush them. Infinity explodes or, more precisely, implodes them along with their limits.

The difference between Matthiessen's Emerson and Asimov's goes beyond these two authors' differing frames of reference in literature and physical science. Some of their divergence may be personal or political. "Nightfall" shows a deep anxiety about the war that in 1941 was raging in Europe; and in that context *American Renaissance* more optimistically mobilizes the Renaissance tradition as a powerful defender of liberal democracy. But there is another issue toward which Matthiessen and Asimov take opposite stands.

In this opposition, Matthiessen represents an abiding if embattled humanism that is not only a political creed but a cosmology organized around the principle of a human creativity that realizes itself in producing its world. It is on the basis of this humanism that he asserts not only the desirability but the rectitude and even the necessity of individual freedom and of a democratic society. (In his conception, socialism would fulfill the liberal ethic, by removing economic and political obstacles to individual self-realization.) The sublime—that is to say the world beyond, the realm of the transcendent, infinity—functions in this cosmology as a moral imperative, an objective correlative for the infinity of human aspiration.

In Asimov's story, on the contrary, the universal sublime negates the mundane. The suggestion of infinity contained in the Stars drains all meaning from the finite world—not because the finite world is less significant than the infinite but because infinity is meaningless, being incomprehensible to mortals. The emergence of the infinite, as represented in the Stars, actually reduces the range of the humanly meaningful and valuable. The discovery of an infinitely greater light than they have ever known blinds the Lagashians; and when through their science they thrust the awful sublime back, they extend the range of meaning. Their doomed attempt to save their civilization from being smothered by sublimity is a heroic defense of history against myth. As they and Asimov see it, the worst of the recurrent holocausts is that they leave each new civilization precisely in what Emerson would have found an ideal situation, standing on bare ground, with no retrospective vision, no sepulchres and no biographies, histories, or criticism.[5] By their inability to withstand the sight of the stars, Asimov finds them deprived not of the world beyond but of this one, not of timelessness but of history, not of the unlimited but of their own limits.

In short, Asimov's interpretation of Emerson in "Nightfall" is antitranscendent. Sight, for Emerson the vehicle of transcendence, provides knowledge for Asimov in the opposite way, by marking the physical limits beyond which neither reason nor the imagination can pass. His first thought about the Stars, which provided the basis of his plot, was that they were visible only in the dark. For Emerson, they epitomized a luminous heaven. Emerson's transparent eyeball is an image of spiritual fulfillment that reverses physical laws: a real transparent eyeball would be blind. Asimov's limited beings are subject to these laws and are indeed blinded, first by less light than their eyes need for seeing, and then by more than they can tolerate.

Where Matthiessen found a humanist touchstone in the vision

of a transcendent universe, Asimov saw an image of chaos. But if we recall when they were writing, their disagreement is less surprising: the liberal idea (ethnic, aesthetic, and politic) that inspired Western Europe and America in World War II both helped win the war and was exposed by it. Asimov foreshadowed that exposure, having perhaps divined that the revolution of scientific paradigms in the first three decades of this century implied a transformation of world-views. In cosmological terms, Matthiessen continued to assume a prior, essentially Newtonian universe. Asimov, younger and more attentive to scientific developments, elaborated Emerson's idea in a way that reversed Emerson as Einstein's physics reversed Newton's: by examining sight not as it connotes vision but as a problem in the conditions of seeing.

Matthiessen made his own modern adjustments. His emphasis on the language and form of the Renaissance writings insisted on a distinction the Renaissance writers themselves had barely made. For Emerson language was active simply and directly because the speaker had power over all the world; for Matthiessen language is discretely powerful, and literature does not create this world but, in Richard Poirier's memorable phrase, a world elsewhere.[6] But while this modernist rendering develops the Romantic concept and retains its crucial principle, Asimov's interpretation denies its essence.

To the concept that a whole man is capable of whole sight, "Nightfall" posits the contrary, the partiality (meaning both less than whole and interested) of all seeing. Unlike Emerson's stargazer, who sees by identifying with his object, Asimov's interacts in order to see, and therefore sees wholly neither himself nor his object, but instead sees their relation, which is itself relative to external necessities that no one transcends. Such an observer cannot generalize his perceptions into universal laws. He knows these laws only as they manifest themselves to him in response to his actions.

The most influential Western philosophers and scholars of the last two decades would have been entirely at home on Lagash. They do not believe in infinity and transcendence either—structuralists and poststructuralists, psychologists and ecologists begin alike with the premise of a limited self in a limited universe. This profound revision of the philosophical consensus has greatly complicated the task of interpreting earlier thought. Because of our changed assumptions, we have become unable any longer to read the classical literature and the nineteenth-century humanism of Emerson directly—or at any rate as directly as did Matthiessen. In this book, therefore, I have done the reverse. By taking eighteenth- and nineteenth-century axioms as my foremost issues— analyzing what they posit—I have focused on the disparity between then and now in an attempt to find a mediating language in the terms of disparity. Thus, in exploring the limits of American ideology, I have emphasized the notion of unlimited possibilities, valuing that notion just because it is alien.

This approach is essentially the opposite of the one that seeks a "usable past." Finding a usable past entails reclaiming the bits of history that are most like the present; this assumes universality and even implies the possibility of historical transcendence. I am proposing, on the contrary, that we concentrate on the parts of the past that differ most from the present, and that we probe their difference not in *their* terms but in ours. While this process may at first appear perverse, it is actually the friendlier approach in that it grants each previous era its own character. It also renounces the claim of many progressive historians that the present is ever better than the past and that we, having absorbed the essential value of all those who came before, are clearly, arithmetically, their betters.

My primary reason for recommending this stance, however, is not diffidence. As a general phenomenon, we know a thing more profoundly by its variance than by its likeness. Working the opposite way from empathy, analysis is aided by a separation that forces us to seek the other's different principles of coherence, which thus stand out *as* principles. Thus radical difference penetrates further into the structures of both the observed and the observer. As handles on objects of analysis, contradictions are more securely attached than agreements.

American thought is a subject that demonstrates this phenomenon with particular force. In this country, to stress connections to the past is so much to fulfill the injunctions of the past as to run a serious risk of merely paraphrasing what one means to analyze; of doing exegesis instead of deconstruction. The net of the great American tautology, first and best expressed in the concept of the discovery, is hard to evade. The premise coming so trippingly off the tongue that the essence of America is permanent and global makes it extremely difficult to interrupt oneself and recall that no national identity transcends time and social conflict.

But what first suggested this book to me was a sense that we are in a period of philosophical and ideological transition. The presidential rhetoric may still have it that "for two hundred years we have always lived in the future," but ordinary Americans no longer gaze toward an infinite horizon. Looking in one direction most would now recognize the borders of Mexico, and in the other those of Canada. Taking passage across the Pacific, we do not pass beyond but arrive at the borders of India. Horizon and border both name lines that organize the landscape, and the replacement in our mental geography of one line by the other expresses a larger change in American thinking. A horizon marks as far as the eye can transcend; it is a frontier and refers outward, implying expansion. A border is a boundary, thus also an outermost line, but one referring inward: it marks the limit of even the farthest sight.

"Horizon" and "frontier" are archetypal eighteenth- and nineteenth-century American words. The currency of "border" and "boundary" today is certainly not peculiar to America, but it poses a special problem for Americans. For the very being of America, as defined by the ideology of incarnation, is entwined with "horizon" and "frontier," and is therefore affronted by borders. As the culmination of history in nature, the concept of the American incarnation necessarily implies universality. In the New World that concept became virtually universal—an idea that found not only its time but its place. But its time, inevitably, is passing. Its place is developing other ideas, their emergence of itself demonstrating that no idea is either universal or incarnate. Thus the very core of the meaning of America is changing, and changing to allow the possibility of change. This connotes both hope and danger. The hope, unimaginable to Melville, is that it will become possible for bastard children to inherit their portion of the estate. The danger is that the affronted Glendinning fathers, who still claim that the borders of Saddle Meadows encompass the global horizon, will defend their continual incarnation to the end of the earth.

✳ Notes

Introduction. One Man, One World

1. A generation of students of American history and culture followed Perry Miller in taking the Puritan landing at Plymouth as the beginning of their stories. In the last few years Americanists have tended to begin at a new beginning with implications that revise our understanding throughout. The significance and indeed the definition of the "discovery" have come under scrutiny, along with accounts of successive landings and explorations, now taken as interpretations rather than reports of actual events. Wayne Franklin, for instance, in *Discoverers, Explorers, Settlers: The Diligent Writers of Early America*, traces the linguistic growth of the idea of America as the construction of a language and a narrative. The tendency toward a historical recasting of America's origins is evident in recent Puritan studies. Sacvan Bercovitch, in *Puritan Origins of the American Self*, examines the contingent making of national identity; in *American Jeremiad* he compares the American and English traditions of the jeremiad precisely to trace differing historical evolutions. There are also transatlantic revisions of the discovery concept, notably Tzvetan Todorov's *Conquest of America*; these, however, tend to be about Europe's view of America rather than America's of itself.

2. From a very different perspective, Sharon Cameron, in *The Corporeal Self: Allegories of the Body in Melville and Hawthorne*, deals with this same issue of the insistent corporeality of American thought. When she writes that the works she examines "posit a third term or entity which, neither body nor soul, neither one self nor another, knits the respective entities together" (1), she seems to me to be describing the same distinguishing phenomenon, the peculiar fusion of body and soul that could only be achieved in the fused matter and spirit of the American continent.

1. Starting with Columbus

1. In his essay "Jefferson's Prospect," Mitchell Breitweiser disagrees with two recent revisions of Merrill Peterson's standard reading of the *Notes*—those by Wayne Franklin (in *Discoverers, Explorers, Settlers*) and Robert Fer-

guson (in "Mysterious Obligation")—for deducing from the discovery of contradictions in the work that Jefferson was himself "disunified and incoherent" (16). Separating himself from both Peterson and his critics, Breitweiser then attempts to show that the *Notes* "is neither a homogenization of experience and theory through induction nor a polarized disjunction: it is an antithetical unity, a regulating discrepancy, a separation of powers" (16). I invoke this debate about coherence and disunity here because it is resonant of debates about the coherence of American thought generally and because the Jefferson passage suggests (confirming Breitweiser's view) that the problem may lie in the definition of coherence. "Antithetical unity" is a good way to describe the reconciliation achieved in the Blue Ridge landscape, a reconciliation already implicit from the beginning of the upheaval. Such coherence does not depend on reasoning but is implicit beyond process, in a transcending purpose.

2. Annette Kolodny has explored the role of gender in American writing in two works. In *The Lay of the Land: Metaphor as Experience and History in American Literature* (1975) she shows how American attitudes toward nature and the landscape were early organized by a male-female dichotomy such that the "virgin" continent was conventionally seen as the rightful object of male possession. Focusing on the psychology of this dichotomy, Kolodny attributes some of the destructiveness of the continental conquest to the violence this culture associates with sexual and gender relations. In *The Land Before Her: Fantasy and Experience of the American Frontiers* (1984), Kolodny continues this examination of the relation between gender and the settlement of America into an analysis of the strikingly different attitudes of westering women.

2. The Mammoth Land

1. Since my interest here is rather with the ideological paradigm as such than with its evolution, I have used eighteenth-century writings rather than earlier ones in order to have the fullest formulations with which to work.

2. Thad W. Tate documents this difference as part of his survey of colonial views of the South in "The Discovery and Development of the Southern Colonial Landscape."

3. Karen Ordhal Kupperman, in "The Puzzle of the American Climate in the Early Colonial Period," pulls together the extensive literature on this subject and traces the course of the climate argument to the middle of the seventeenth century. See also her "Fear of Hot Climates in the Anglo-American Colonial Experience" for a discussion of the anxiety produced by the unfamiliar environment and the search for an adaptive way of life.

4. This sense of harmony is the subject of Cecelia Tichi's *New World, New Earth*. Tichi shows that the settlers viewed their domestication of the wilderness not as its transformation, still less as its destruction, but as an "environmental reform" that fulfilled an already implicit potential.

5. See William Cronon, *Changes in the Land*, chs. 3 and 4, on the rationale for dispossession of the Indians. In *Changes in the Land* as a whole Cronon seeks to replace, as organizing principles of colonial history, the dichotomies of Indians versus Europeans and wilderness versus settlers with a model of interaction—an ecology. See also Cronon's Bibliographical Essay for a comprehensive review of the literature about the physical environment of the colonies and strategies for dealing with it.

6. Needless to say, the ideology I am describing is not that of actual peasants or even of many farmers but of those, largely from the middle class, who wrote directives to farmers: it is an official ideology whose hegemonic sway remains to be determined.

3. Necessary and Sufficient Acts

1. A familiar line of descent runs from Franklin's discovery that the divine commandments were promulgated to ensure not the glory of God but the good of man, to Emerson's conception of nature as a human "discipline" training us to live frugal and chaste, to William James's reaffirmation that in a benevolent universe, the good works. The optimism represented by this descent arises out of more than faith or conviction or the consciousness of plenitude; it is firmly grounded in a vision that, after European thought had extracted morality from nature and located it in history so that it was permanently mutable, reconnected morality with the natural universe itself. And since nature, according to modern natural law, was man's kingdom, his good (in both senses of the word) was its necessity.

2. It should be noted that twentieth-century Marxisms have often looked not to the Utopian end of contradiction but rather to its benign transformation. An early preeminent instance of this revision is Mao's notion of a category of contradictions that are "nonantagonistic"; emerging after the socialist abolition of class exploitation, this kind of contradiction remains dialectical without being destructive. See Mao Tse-tung (Mao Zedong), "On the Correct Handling of Contradictions among the People."

3. A parallel process, I believe, is described in B. L. Packer's *Emerson's Fall: A New Interpretation of the Major Essays*. Packer shows that the operation of the Fall in Emerson's thinking is analogous to that of Genesis in Puritan thought—as a "convenient mythus" (xi) around which explicatory theories and fables cluster to organize experience. She is not directly concerned with how this replacement of Genesis by the Fall affects the possibilities for action in the real world, but I would like to suggest as an extension of her analysis that it does so in the way I have described dualism working, both to permit and to engender action. As an achieved unity transcends action, so for Emerson to have focused directly on the perfection of Genesis—given his view that this perfection remains available to the transcendent observer—would imply only contemplative rest. Even if it turns out to be the result of partial

239

or misaligned vision, the appearance of a fallen world moves us: to seek the perfection of Genesis.

4. My emphasis on the enabling (energizing, activating) implications of Emersonian thinking (rather than on its injunctions to reflect) is by no means original. Richard Poirier in *A World Elsewhere* (1966) has read Emerson's assertion that the eye was the "best of artists" as expressing an ambition through sight to possess the world whole and to revise (re-envision) the fallen mundane into the perfect transcendent (50–51). Harold Bloom in *A Map of Mis-Reading* (1975) has invoked Nietzsche's admiration of Emerson as a contemporary recognition of Emerson's intention, by his questioning of authority, not to subvert it as such but to "re-center" the world around *his* authority (176). (Bloom has elaborated this view recently in the *New York Review of Books* in an essay entitled, much to my purpose, "Mr. America.") In two books published in 1981, Eric Cheyfitz and Carolyn Porter, albeit from widely divergent perspectives, both stress the powerful Emerson. Cheyfitz, in *The Trans-Parent*, dubs Emerson "a devout psychologist of power" and examines his projection of the principle of potency in a commanding masculine self that is continually engaged and challenged in the essays by a counterpointing identity Cheyfitz calls "our beautiful mother, Emerson." The issue, beyond the perception of a conflict of gender, is the establishment of a still more powerful and active Emerson (involving "a savage hermaphroditic figure . . . aligning itself with a growing feminine power") than was evident when he represented only "a dream of the *Father*" (167). Porter, in *Seeing and Being*, beginning the discussion of Emerson with what she takes as his defiance of authority in resigning from the Unitarian ministry, depicts an Emerson in active revolt against the "reification" that has reduced individual Americans to objects of their capitalist society. "Emerson's procedure in *Nature*," she writes, is actively embattled: it is "designed to overcome man's alienation in a world defined by its commodity structure" (116). While these four critics assign different goals to Emerson's ambition, they all locate power at the center of his thought.

4. Plain and Fancy Fictions

1. It is as part of Rousseau's attempt to differentiate himself, that we should read his description, as almost the first thing he tells us of his life, of his peculiar sexual attraction to corporal punishment: having been frequently spanked as a boy by a pretty maidservant, he has all his life yearned for such stimulation. I suggested earlier that the modern emphasis on sexuality as the core of personal identity might be related to a desire to establish a material base for individualism. Rousseau's boast—for it is effectively a boast—of sexual difference certainly seems to have that intention.

2. Such difference is not the same as eccentricity; eccentricity is exaggeration, which is a function of comparability rather than of uniqueness, while on the contrary the conformity that tends to prevail in individualist

democracies represents the claim to universality of each individual, expressed precisely in his lack of any peculiar identity. In slightly other terms Tocqueville observed this conjunction of individualism and conformity a century ago.

3. According to Hawthorne, this story was inspired by an anecdote about the painter Gilbert Stuart, recounted in William Dunlap's *A History of the Rise and Progress of the Arts of Design in the United States*, I, 221–222. Stuart was employed to paint the portrait of a General Phipps prior to the general's departure for imperial service in India. Upon seeing the portrait, the general's brother protested that it was unlike the original, but Stuart insisted "I see insanity in that face." Shortly afterward, the general became mad and committed suicide. "It is thus," Dunlap moralizes, "that the real portrait painter dives into the recesses of his sitters' minds, and displays strength or weakness upon the surface of his canvas. The mechanic makes a map of the man."

4. Both Barthes, who in *S/Z* repeatedly demonstrates the ways Balzac constructs the reality he describes, and Fredric Jameson, who in *The Political Unconscious* argues that "not Balzac's deeper sense of political and historical realities, but rather his incorrigible fantasy demands ultimately raise History itself over against him, as absent cause, as that on which desire must come to grief" (183), project an author for whom history is a means rather than an end.

5. Transgression and Transformation

1. I refer to the original ending. A year later, under pressure from readers to elucidate the mysteries he had left dark, Hawthorne added another conclusion—but it in fact explained little, and in any case the further explanations are not relevant to my point.

6. The Rebirth of Tragedy

1. This can*not* be generalized to describe the way a girl becomes a woman: to repeat an earlier stipulation, the ideology of modern individualism excludes women from such conflicts (and achievements) by making them the objects of conflict and achievement.

2. What follows is not a psychological analysis in the sense of Frederick Crews, *The Sins of the Fathers*. My interest in the psychological remains ideological, and this is about the relation of the private family to the political public. In that context, note that the relation between Isabel and Pierre remains ambiguous to the end. But if it is not actually incestuous, it *amounts* to incest, Melville's concern, as I understand it, being primarily political.

3. This conjunction of familial and political ideologies in the construction of individual identity during the colonial and early national periods is the subject as well of Eric Sundquist's *Home as Found* (1979). Sundquist finds in

241

works of Cooper, Thoreau, Hawthorne, and Melville a common central tension, at once personal and national, between "finding" (returning to) and "founding" a home. Sundquist's interpretive categories derive primarily from psychoanalytic theories, as his approach draws on the methodology of deconstruction. Michael Paul Rogin's exploration of the same theme of generational succession in *Subversive Genealogies* is more directly political. Rogin seeks the origin of what he sees as Melville's political radicalism in his alienation from the values of his Gansevoort relations, and by extension those of the contemporary family as such and the social world of Jacksonian America.

4. Mary Glendinning, who describes herself as a "martial ram" to Lucy's "ewe," is a kind of founding father in her own right. Herself the proud daughter of a general, she "swell[s] out" in contemplating on her mantelpiece the baton of General Glendinning, this "symbol of command." But her male force in no way undermines her womanhood. Rather it expresses her oneness with the heritage of Saddle Meadows that she is grooming her son to assume.

Epilogue. After the Culmination

1. See Alfred Kazin's summary of Parrington's critical stance in *On Native Grounds,* pp. 125–132; Hicks, *The Great Tradition,* Preface; Matthiessen, *American Renaissance,* Preface. The general attitude that the foundations of American thought not only could support dissent but actively implied it was perhaps summed up by an advertisement for the left-wing magazine *Mother Jones,* entitled "*Mother Jones* Is Exactly What Our Founders Had In Mind When They Wrote The First Amendment." The appeal to Thomas Jefferson in the first line of copy ("Do you suppose Thomas Jefferson believed that airbrushed centerfold nudes, CIA news plants or corporate-dominated media would protect the public from power-hungry politicians, arbitrary judges and venal business executives?") makes perfect American sense.

2. The ideological implications of *American Renaissance* have come under scrutiny in two recent essays which inform my discussion here. Jonathan Arac, in "F. O. Matthiessen: Authorizing an American Renaissance," and Donald E. Pease, in "*Moby-Dick* and the Cold War," both reconnect the canon Matthiessen constructed to the historical moment of its construction. Arac seeks this connection in an international context while Pease places Matthiessen in a national "scene of cultural persuasion" (113). Both seek through this historical re-placement to permit us to see the *Renaissance* canon as ideologically active in our time as well.

3. Morgan argues in *American Freedom, American Slavery* that the granting of broad democratic rights by the Constitution was predicated on the maintenance of a relatively homogeneous population, which in turn required preventing the development of a large working class. If indentured immigrants had been recruited to work the southern plantations, at the end of their indenture they would either have competed locally with their former

masters or drifted north into urban industrial centers and possibly outnumbered the middle classes there. Black slaves did the requisite work without posing any political threat. Hence, Morgan concludes, the extent of American freedom was directly proportional to the extent of slavery.

4. Eric Foner, in *Tom Paine and Revolutionary America*, and Jesse Lemisch, notably in "Jack Tar in the Streets," were early revisionists of the notion that the Revolution and the early national period were characterized by an essential political consensus. Sean Wilentz, in *Chants Democratic: New York City and the Rise of the American Working Class, 1788–1850*, as the reference of the subtitle to E. P. Thompson's *Rise of the English Working Class* indicates, seeks to show that American history has been characterized by social and class conflicts equivalent to those of European history.

5. *Nature* opens with the complaint "Our age is retrospective. It builds the sepulchres of the fathers. It writes biographies, histories, and criticism" (5).

6. In *A World Elsewhere* Poirier uncovers the historical ambition to create a new world at the heart of an American attitude to language; language, beginning with Emerson, is seen as building its own world. Indeed language alone may be able to build the New World. "American books are often written as if historical forces cannot possibly provide such an environment, as if history can give no life to 'freedom,' and as if only language can create the liberated place" (5).

* Works Cited

Arac, Jonathan. "F. O. Matthiessen: Authorizing an American Renaissance." In *The American Renaissance Reconsidered: Selected Papers from the English Institute 1982–83*, ed. Walter Benn Michaels and Donald E. Pease. Baltimore: Johns Hopkins University Press, 1985.

Asimov, Isaac. "Nightfall" (1941). In Asimov, *Nightfall and Other Stories*, pp. 9–43. New York: Fawcett Crest Books, 1969.

Atwood, Margaret. *Survival: A Thematic Guide to Canadian Literature*. Toronto: Anansi, 1972.

Balzac, Honoré de. *Eugénie Grandet*. Trans. Marion Ayton Crawford. Harmondsworth, Middlesex: Penguin Books, 1983.

Bartram, William. *Travels of William Bartram*. Ed. Mark Van Doren. New York: Dover, 1955.

Bercovitch, Sacvan. *Puritan Origins of the American Self*. New Haven: Yale University Press, 1975.

———*The American Jeremiad*. Madison: University of Wisconsin Press, 1979.

Bloom, Harold. *A Map of Misreading*. New York: Oxford University Press, 1975.

——— "Mr. America." *New York Review of Books*, November 22, 1984, 19–24.

Breitweiser, Mitchell. "Jefferson's Prospect." In *Prospects: An Annual Journal of American Cultural Studies* 10 (1985): 315–352.

Buffon, Georges-Louis Leclerc de. *Morceaux choisis*. Paris, 1911. (My translation.)

Cameron, Sharon. *The Corporeal Self: Allegories of the Body in Melville and Hawthorne*. Baltimore: Johns Hopkins University Press, 1981.

Carlyle, Thomas. *Sartor Resartus*. In *Sartor Resartus and On Heroes and Hero Worship*. London: Everyman's Library, 1967.

Carpenter, Frederic Ives. *Emerson Handbook*. New York: Hendricks House, 1953.

Cheyfitz, Eric. *The Trans-Parent: Sexual Politics in the Language of Emerson*. Baltimore: Johns Hopkins University Press, 1981.

Chinard, Gilbert. "The American Philosophical Society and the Early History of Forestry in America." *Proceedings of the American Philosophical Society* 89 (1945): 444–488.

245

——"Eighteenth-Century Theories on America as a Human Habitat." *Proceedings of the American Philosophical Society* 91 (1947): 27–57.

Crèvecoeur, J. Hector St. John de. *Letters from an American Farmer* (1782). Garden City, N.Y.: Dolphin Books, n.d.

Crews, Frederick. *The Sins of the Fathers: Hawthorne's Psychological Themes*. New York: Oxford University Press, 1966.

Cronon, William. *Changes in the Land: Indians, Colonists and the Ecology of New England*. New York: Hill and Wang, 1983.

Dunlap, William. *A History of the Rise and Progress of the Arts of Design in the United States* (1834). New ed. with additions by Frank W. Bayley and Charles E. Goodspeed. 3 vols. C. E. Goodspeed & Co., 1918.

Eliot, Jared. *Essays upon Field Husbandry in New England, and Other Papers (1748–1762)*.Ed. Harry J. Carman and Rexford G. Tugwell. New York: Columbia University Press, 1934.

Ellis, William. *The Modern Husbandman, or the Practice of Farming As It Is Now Carried On by the Most Accurate Farmers in Several Counties of England*. London: T. Osborne, 1742.

Emerson, Ralph Waldo. *Nature* (1836). "The American Scholar" (1837). "The Method of Nature" (1841). "Experience" (1843–44). All in *Emerson: Essays and Lectures*. New York: Library of America, 1983.

—— *The Correspondence of Emerson and Carlyle*. Ed. Joseph Slater. New York: Columbia University Press, 1964.

Ferguson, Robert. " 'Mysterious Obligation': Jefferson's *Notes on Virginia*." *American Literature* 53, no. 3 (1980): 381–406.

Fliegelman, Jay. *Prodigals and Pilgrims: The American Revolution Against Patriarchal Authority, 1750–1800*. Cambridge: Cambridge University Press, 1982.

Foner, Eric. *Tom Paine and Revolutionary America*. New York: Oxford University Press, 1976.

Franklin, Benjamin. Letter to Richard Jackson, May 5, 1753. In *The Writings of Benjamin Franklin*, ed. Henry Smyth, III, 133–141. New York: Macmillan, 1905.

Franklin, Wayne. *Discoverers, Explorers, Settlers: The Diligent Writers of Early America*. Chicago: University of Chicago Press, 1979.

Frye, Northrop. "Conclusion." In *The Literary History of Canada*, Carl F. Klinck, general ed. Toronto: University of Toronto Press, 1966.

—— *The Bush Garden: Essays on the Canadian Imagination*. Toronto: Anansi, 1971.

Harris, Kenneth Marc. *Carlyle and Emerson: Their Long Debate*. Cambridge, Mass.: Harvard University Press, 1978.

Hawthorne, Nathaniel. *The House of the Seven Gables* (1851). *The Marble Faun* (1860). *The Scarlet Letter* (1850). All in *Hawthorne: Novels*. New York: Library of America, 1983.

—— "The Prophetic Pictures" (1837). In *Hawthorne: Tales and Sketches*. New York: Library of America, 1982.

Hegel, G. W. F. "The Philosophy of History" (1822). In *The Philosophy of Hegel*, ed. Carl J. Friedrich. New York: Modern Library, 1953.

Hicks, Granville. *The Great Tradition: An Interpretation of American Literature since the Civil War* (1933). New York: Quadrangle, 1969.

James, William. *Pragmatism* (1907). In *Pragmatism and Four Essays from The Meaning of Truth*. Cleveland: Meridian, 1964.

Jameson, Fredric. *The Political Unconscious: Narrative as a Socially Symbolic Act*. Ithaca: Cornell University Press, 1981.

Jefferson, Thomas. *Notes on the State of Virginia* (1785). In *Jefferson: Writings*. New York: Library of America, 1984.

Jones, D. G. *Butterfly on Rock: A Study of Themes and Images in Canadian Literature*. Toronto: University of Toronto Press, 1970.

Kazin, Alfred. *On Native Grounds: A Study of American Prose Literature from 1890 to the Present* (1942). New York: Doubleday Anchor Books, 1956.

Klinck, Carl F., general ed. *The Literary History of Canada: Canadian Literature in English*. Toronto: University of Toronto Press, 1966.

Kline, Marcia B. *Beyond the Land Itself: Views of Nature in Canada and the United States*. Cambridge, Mass.: Harvard University Press, 1970.

Kolodny, Annette. *The Lay of the Land: Metaphor as Experience and History in American Literature*. Chapel Hill: University of North Carolina Press, 1975.

—— *The Land Before Her: Fantasy and Experience of the American Frontiers*. Chapel Hill: University of North Carolina Press, 1984.

Kupperman, Karen Ordahl. "The Puzzle of the American Climate in the Early Colonial Period." *The American Historical Review*. 87, no. 5 (Dec. 1982): 1262–1289.

—— "Fear of Hot Climates in the Anglo-American Colonial Experience." *William and Mary Quarterly* 41, no. 2 (1984): 213–240.

Lemisch, Jesse. "Jack Tar in the Streets: Merchant Seamen in the Politics of Revolutionary America." *William and Mary Quarterly* 25, no. 3 (July 1968): 371–407.

Lorain, John. *Nature and Reason Harmonized in the Practice of Husbandry*. Philadelphia: H. C. Carey and I. Lea, 1825.

Macherey, Pierre. *Pour une théorie de la production littéraire*. Paris: François Maspero, 1966.

Mao Tse-tung (Mao Zedong). "On the Correct Handling of Contradictions among the People" (1957). In *Selected Works*, V, 384–421. Peking: Peking Language Press, 1977.

Matthiessen, F. O. *American Renaissance: Art and Expression in the Age of Emerson and Whitman* (1941). New York: Oxford University Press, 1964.

Melville, Herman. *Pierre* (1852). In *Melville*. New York: Library of America, 1984.

Miller, Perry. *Errand into the Wilderness* (1956). New York: Harper Torchbooks, 1964.

—— *Nature's Nation*. Cambridge, Mass.: Harvard University Press, 1967.

Moodie, Susanna. *Roughing It in the Bush; or, Life in Canada* (1852). London: Nelson, 1932.

Morgan, Edmund S. *American Slavery, American Freedom: The Ordeal of Colonial Virginia*. New York: Norton, 1975.

Morse, Jedediah. *The American Universal Geography; or, A View of the Present State of all the Empires, Kingdoms, States and Republicks in the Known World and of the United States of America in Particular*. 2nd ed. In two parts. Boston: E. Lincoln, 1805.

O'Gorman, Edmundo. *The Invention of America: An Inquiry into the Historical Nature of the New World and the Meaning of Its History*. Bloomington: Indiana University Press, 1961.

Packer, B. L. *Emerson's Fall: A New Interpretation of the Major Essays*. New York: Continuum, 1982.

Parrington, V. L. *Main Currents in American Thought: An Interpretation of American Literature from the Beginnings to 1920*. New York: Harcourt, Brace, 1930.

Pease, Donald E. "*Moby-Dick* and the Cold War." In *The American Renaissance Reconsidered: Selected Papers from the English Institute, 1982–83*, ed. Walter Benn Michaels and Donald E. Pease. Baltimore: Johns Hopkins University Press, 1985.

Pierson, Sam. *The Present State of the Tillage in Ireland Considered, and some Methods Offered for its Improvement*. Dublin: printed for George Grierson, 1730.

Poirier, Richard. *A World Elsewhere: The Place of Style in American Literature*. New York: Oxford University Press, 1966.

Porter, Carolyn. *Seeing and Being: The Plight of the Participant Observer in Emerson, James, Adams, and Faulkner*. Middletown, Conn.: Wesleyan University Press, 1981.

Rogin, Michael Paul. "Nature as Politics and Nature as Romance in America." *Political Theory* 5, no. 1 (Feb. 1977): 5–30.

―― *Subversive Genealogies: The Politics and Art of Herman Melville*. New York: Knopf, 1983.

Rousseau, Jean-Jacques. *The Confessions* (1781). Trans. J. M. Cohen. London: Penguin Books, 1954.

―― *The Social Contract* (1762). Ed. Lester G. Crocker. New York: Washington Square Press, 1974.

Rye, George. *Considerations on Agriculture, Treating of the Several Methods Practiced in Different Parts of the Kingdom of Ireland, with Remarks Thereon*. Dublin: printed for George Grierson, 1730.

Sarmiento, Domingo F. *Life in the Argentine Republic in the Days of the Tyrants; or, Civilization and Barbarism* (1868). Trans. Mrs. Horace Mann. New York: Hafner Press, n.d.

Savage, Henry, Jr. *Discovering America, 1700–1875*. With an introduction by Henry Steele Commager and Richard B. Morris. New York: Harper and Row, 1979.

Slater, Joseph, ed. *The Correspondence of Emerson and Carlyle*. New York: Columbia University Press, 1964.

Slotkin, Richard. *Regeneration through Violence: The Mythology of the American Frontier, 1600–1860.* Middletown, Conn.: Wesleyan University Press, 1973.

Smith, Henry Nash. *Virgin Land: The American West as Symbol and Myth* (1950). New York: Vintage Books, 1961.

Spurrier, John. *The Practical Farmer: Being a New and Compendious System of Husbandry Adapted to the Different Soils and Climates of America, Containing the Mechanical, Chemical and Philosophical Elements of Agriculture with Many Other Useful and Interesting Subjects.* Wilmington, Del.: Brynberg and Andrews, 1793.

Stilgoe, John R. *Common Landscape of America, 1580–1845.* New Haven: Yale University Press, 1982.

Sundquist, Eric. *Home as Found: Authority and Genealogy in Nineteenth-Century American Literature.* Baltimore: Johns Hopkins University Press, 1979.

—— "Slavery, Revolution, and the American Renaissance." In *The American Renaissance Reconsidered: Selected Papers from the English Institute, 1982–83,* ed. Walter Benn Michaels and Donald E. Pease. Baltimore: Johns Hopkins University Press, 1985.

Tate, Thad W. "The Discovery and Development of the Southern Colonial Landscape: Six Commentators." *Proceedings of the American Antiquarian Society* 93, no. 2 (1983): 289–311.

Thomas, Keith. *Man and the Natural World: A History of the Modern Sensibility.* New York: Pantheon, 1983.

Thoreau, Henry David. *Walden* (1854). In *Henry David Thoreau.* New York: Library of America, 1985.

Tichi, Cecelia. *New World, New Earth: Environmental Reform in American Literature from the Puritans through Whitman.* New Haven: Yale University Press, 1979.

Tocqueville, Alexis de. *Democracy in America* (1835). The Henry Reeve text as revised by Francis Bowen now further corrected and edited with a historical essay, editorial notes, and bibliographies by Phillips Bradley. 2 vols. New York: Vintage Books, 1945.

Todorov, Tzvetan. *The Conquest of America: The Question of the Other.* Trans. Richard Howard. New York: Harper and Row, 1984.

Tull, Jethro. *The New Horse-houghing Husbandry; or, an Essay on the Principles of Tillage and Vegetation.* Dublin: Aaron Rames, 1731.

Volney, C. F. Chasseboeuf de. *A View of the Soil and Climate of the United States of America: with Supplementary Remarks Upon Florida; on the French Colonies, on the Mississippi and Ohio, and in Canada; and on the Aboriginal Tribes of America* (1803). Trans. Charles Brockden Brown. Philadelphia: J. Conrad, 1804.

Webster, Noah. *A Collection of Papers on the Subject of Bilious Fevers Prevalent in the United States For a Few Years Past.* Compiled by Noah Webster Junior. New York: Hopkins, Webb & Co., 1796.

—— "Dissertation on the Supposed Change of Temperature in Modern Winters." In *A Collection of Papers on Political, Literary and Moral Subjects.* New York: Webster and Clark, 1843.

Whicher, Stephen. *Freedom and Fate: An Inner Life of Ralph Waldo Emerson.* Philadelphia: University of Pennsylvania Press, 1953.

Wilentz, Sean. *Chants Democratic: New York City and the Rise of the American Working Class, 1788–1850.* New York: Oxford University Press, 1984.

Williams, William Carlos. *In the American Grain* (1925). New York: New Directions, 1956.

Wills, Garry. *Inventing America: Jefferson's Declaration of Independence.* Garden City, N.Y.: Doubleday, 1978.

* Index